COLONEL S. G. SHEPARD

COLONEL S. G. SHEPARD

Reta Moser
Alice Hughes Shepard Carver

iUniverse books may be ordered through booksellers or by contacting:

iUniverse
1663 Liberty Drive
Bloomington, IN 47403
www.iuniverse.com
1-800-Authors (1-800-288-4677)

Because of the dynamic nature of the Internet, any Web addresses or links
contained in this book may have changed since publication and may no longer be
valid. The views expressed in this work are solely those of the author and do not
necessarily reflect the views of the publisher, and the publisher hereby disclaims
any responsibility for them.

ISBN: 978-1-4502-1731-6 (sc)
ISBN: 978-1-4502-1733-0 (hc)
ISBN: 978-1-4502-1732-3 (ebook)

Library of Congress Control Number: 2010902655

Printed in the United States of America

iUniverse rev. date: 04/14/2010

Dedicated to Alice Hughes Shepard Carver and her daughter, Alice Carver Cramer, daughter and granddaughter of the colonel. To the Cramer family, the Carver family, the Shepard family, and to all the other offspring of Colonel Shepard.

And to all the military men and women who have served this country.

Contents

Acknowledgments

WITH MY GRATITUDE ...

This is my first and last history book. Oh, my goodness. What a research task. I didn't know that a history book required the help of so many conscientious citizens. I didn't know or hadn't even thought about it before. A lot of things I learned writing this book—this was only one.

From Lebanon, Gladeville, Mt. Juliet, and other places close to these, I particularly want to thank Wylene Pafford because she is a mental repository for historical facts and was so gracious in her giving. She was more or less my director during my trip to the colonel's area. She is the one who told me where the colonel lived. Wylene was also the instigator to get Glendon Lannom to donate the photo of the colonel and Mrs. Shepard. She led me to Mr. and Mrs. Fred Simms, Blanche Catron, Margie Spickard Lamb, John "Bev" Spickard, and the Catos on my visit to Lebanon. Each of these individuals in one way or another added to the depth of the book. These are just a few things attributable to Wylene.

Linda Grandstaff of the Wilson County Archives worked diligently to give me the written facts she had for Colonel Shepard and his family. She even suggested documents in some cases and other available sources.

John "Bev" Spickard spent the last weekend in April 2003 showing me documents of the Seventh Tennessee Infantry in the recorder's office. Bev also provided me with a list of names of the Seventh, Company G, and the Spickard genealogy. He showed me the house, which he was remodeling, that was built in 1815 and had always been owned by a Spickard. One knew the colonel had spent time in that house. Bev or

COLONEL S. G. SHEPARD

Wylene arranged for me to see and take pictures of the Shepard home that Colonel Shepard built.

Bev also took me to the Shepard cemetery that had been part of the colonel's property. This is where I believe the colonel's son Arthur and daughter Fanny are buried. He also took me to the Lebanon Cemetery to show me the graves of the colonel, Mattie, their daughter Agnes, and their son Sam.

And then there were Mr. and Mrs. Jack Cato, who are the guiding lights for the Sons of United Confederate Veterans. Their office is used for the meetings and is a repository for Civil War books. It looks like the only book missing on the bookshelf is the one about Colonel Shepard. Jack Cato sent me a copy of John A. Fite's memoirs and a few other articles. I mentioned in our phone conversation that I was missing a couple of the *Confederate Veteran* articles. When I got to their office, Mrs. Cato had books opened for me on a long table. Mr. Cato unfurled the Seventh Tennessee Infantry flag. I had never seen the Seventh Tennessee Infantry flag, other than the one depicted on the Gettysburg Tennessee Monument. This is a family venture for the two of them.

The one person I missed in town was Frank Burns, the Wilson County historian and Cumberland University (Lebanon, Tennessee) archivist. His history of Wilson County was very helpful to give me a feel of the county as well as some facts. His research on Colonel Shepard and General Hatton was most helpful. He thought Colonel Shepard had possibly attended law school at Cumberland between 1860 and 1861 but had no proof. According to Colonel Shepard's daughter, he did not attend.

Erick Montgomery was helpful with the Bradshaw, Robinson, and Shepard genealogies also.

Gilbert Campbell of the Tennessee Supreme Court Society gets special thanks for trying to help me find papers verifying the colonel's law license and to Sharon Ballinger and Elizabeth Simms who helped me with the same pursuit.

Regina Davis put a rush on all the pertinent National Archives microfilms in Washington, D.C. for me.

Thanks also goes to Dr. E. Woodson "Woody" Brewer, reference librarian at the Southern Baptist Theological Seminary, for the biographical sketches of Dr. William Owen Carver and Dr. John Watson Shepard, whose lives were such a part of that establishment.

Darlene F. Slater of the Virginia Baptist Historical Society of the University of Richmond sent me copies of the obituaries for Dr. John Watson Shepard, a son of the colonel, and Dr. James Carver, a grandson of the colonel. They both received degrees from the University of Richmond. The latter obituary led me to great-granddaughter Carol Whitehead in North Carolina and great-grandson Owen Carver in Colorado. Ms Whitehead is the one who led me to the colonel's granddaughter, Alice, in New Jersey.

My hat's off to archivists Chaddra A. Moore and Fran Schell of the State of Tennessee, Department of State, Tennessee State Library and Archives in Nashville. I cannot say enough about these two or the team of researchers there. They and Linda Grandstaff of the Wilson County Archives have just been indispensable with facts backed up with the paperwork. Debbie May and Wanda Meadows of the Nashville Public Library were also helpful.

A special thanks goes to Mike Malsbury, my brother, who formatted the book and did the illustrations. And to Krissi Geary-Boehm, a friend, a special thanks for her loving support and for checking it all.

To Scott Thun who provided the spark that initiated this book—thank you. It's been a trip!

To the Shepard-Carver family who handed me the manuscript, I, and everyone who reads this, should feel grateful—for without the family's cooperation, there would be no book this revealing.

My gratitude also goes to Colonel S. G. Shepard's granddaughter, Alice Carver Cramer, who gave me another insight into the Colonel—particularly what he looked like as well as the charisma he had. Her tapes are a treasure of more than just an insight to the Colonel.

And to his daughter Alice Hughes Shepard Carver—what can I say? You are so special. I have felt your helping hand. I was deeply touched by the love you felt for your father. I hope this book meets your expectations as a tribute to Colonel Shepard—a tribute to your father.

reta moser

Foreword

A century and a half after the beginning of the War Between the States, happy accidents still lead to the discovery of material dealing with the people and the events of that era. Such a discovery led Reta Moser to the story of Lieutenant Colonel Samuel George Shepard of Wilson County, Tennessee. An interest in Shepard led Moser to a few scattered facts but nothing that told the life story of a man who had played a significant part in local and state affairs and who found himself thrust into the cataclysm of war. At one of the crucial moments in that war, at Gettysburg, Shepard was thrust into a leadership position that he did not expect nor yet seek; but when duty called, Shepard responded. Subsequently, although Shepard lived a full and eventful life, he become obscured by the mists of time.

Then the happy accident occurred. Moser was handed a manuscript written by Alice Hughes Shepard Carver, a daughter of the colonel. This record of stories recounted in the family circle gave Shepard life. In this manuscript, the existence of a man who was both humble and extraordinary was brought vibrantly alive. The discovery of this manuscript allowed the author of the present work to complete what had seemed to be a frustrated attempt to delve into the past.

Academics will have some complaints about this book. The manuscript written by Alice Hughes Shepard contains conversations, the content of which cannot be verified by independent sources. Yet, Moser's careful research has verified the accuracy of names, dates, places, and events contained in the Shepard manuscript. It is also the case that the conversations ring true in language and tone to the period at which they are said to have occurred. In short, while some license was no doubt exercised by Alice Hughes Shepard, the story she wrote is true in its essence and in most of its details. Thus, it provides a good foundation for Moser's book.

Lieutenant Colonel Samuel G. Shepard served in the Seventh Tennessee Infantry Regiment in the Army of Northern Virginia. The Seventh Tennessee, along with the First Tennessee (also known as Turney's) and the Fourteenth Tennessee infantries, made up a unit commonly called the Tennessee Brigade. These men arrived in Virginia in 1861, and the survivors made their way back to Tennessee in the spring of 1865. They had not seen home or family for almost four years. This brigade was in the hottest corners of the most fiery battles ever fought by American soldiers. Their memories deserve the recognition this book provides.

An odd feeling fills me as I write these words for I am writing about a man my great-grandfather knew, although he would have known Sam Shepard at a distance. My ancestor was Private Andrew Jackson Bradley, First Tennessee Infantry Regiment. As the number of soldiers present for duty in the Tennessee Brigade shrank to a handful, the Private and the Colonel no doubt passed each other frequently.

As the Private would have done, so do I. Colonel, I salute you! And I salute Reta Moser for telling so ably the story of Lieutenant Colonel Samuel George Shepard and the men who fought with him.

Michael R. Bradley, PhD

Dr. Michael R. Bradley is the author of eight history books; a professor of history; member of the Southern Historical Association, American Association of University Professors, and the Society for Military History; and an ordained minister of the Presbyterian Church. He has been a fellow with the National Endowment for the Humanities and the National Science Foundation. He was the recipient of the Jefferson Davis Medal in Southern History. Presently, he is Commander of Tennessee Division of the Sons of Confederate Veterans.

Preface

With unfailing regularity, people always ask: Why Colonel Shepard? To make a long story short, I started with a name that ran into a curiosity that continued to grow with each uncovered fact. Then I had an uncompromising desire to share this man I had found with the world. I could not believe the part this man played in the Civil War, yet he had not received summary recognition of his part. No one, including his living family, knew his name was on a monument at the staging area for Pickett's Charge, Gettysburg. His words, his figures were on other monuments there. Was he not a missing page in our Civil War history?

This man lived courage, principles, family, and the power and love of his God. His is the story of one humble man's uncountable trials, tribulations, and accomplishments, all wrapped into one lifetime. What I found left me in total awe of what he had survived and accomplished and with a feeling of inadequacy on my part to paint this man in the light he should be portrayed. His obituary in the *Nashville Banner* said, " … his long life has been one of usefulness both to his country and his fellowman."[1]

The following are just some of his Civil War accomplishments:

- He was elected Captain of Company G—the Hurricane Rifles—of the Seventh Tennessee Infantry Regiment in 1861.

- He started signing as commander of the Seventh Tennessee Regiment in April 1862.

---

[1] "Col. Shepard Dead in Lebanon," *Nashville Banner*, June 7, 1917, 14.

COLONEL S. G. SHEPARD

- General Robert E. Lee sent him on a secret mission in 1862 that led him back to Tennessee for a short time.

- He had just become a Lieutenant Colonel when he led the Seventh Tennessee Infantry Regiment up Cemetery Ridge and over the stone wall fence at Gettysburg. He and his men got caught in "The Angle." When he retreated from Cemetery Ridge, he was—probably unbeknownst to himself—in charge of Archer's Brigade, more commonly known as the "Light Brigade," after the capture of Colonel B. D. Fry that day. Colonel Fry had succeeded General J. J. Archer in command after Archer had been captured on day one, July 1.[2]

- Captain J. H. Moore of Company B, Seventh Tennessee Infantry Regiment, and later the official Tennessee Civil War historian, wrote that Colonel Shepard was the only field officer in the division (General Henry Heth's Division) not to be wounded, killed, or captured at Gettysburg. "Lieut. Col. Shepherd [sic], the 'Old Reliable,' in the center, also did his full duty, and was the only field officer in the entire division that escaped unhurt from the battle."[3]

- Captain J. H. Moore also noted in the same article that Colonel Shepard was in charge of the complete division (Gen. Henry Heth's division) for several weeks after Gettysburg. "He, for some weeks afterwards, commanded the division."[3]

- Colonel Shepard's Official Report (OR), "Report of Lieut. Col. S. G. Shepard, Seventh Tennessee Infantry, of Operations of Archer's Brigade, June 3-August 1, 1863—The Gettysburg Campaign, 10 August 1863," is to this day one of the most

---

[2] Clement A. Evans, ed., *Confederate Military History*, vol. VIII, (Atlanta: Confederate Publishing Co., 1899), 200.

[3] Capt. J. H. Moore, "Heroism in the Battle of Gettysburg," *Confederate Veteran*, vol. 9, January 1901, 15–16.

definitive recorded renditions of Gettysburg.[4] This OR provides irrefutable proof that Heth's Division was lined with, not in support of, Pickett's division on the way up Cemetery Ridge. It also proves that Confederates other than Virginians and Carolinians crossed the stone wall.

- Colonel Shepard may have been the first to hear General Robert E. Lee say at the Gettysburg battleground, "The fault is all mine, but it will all be right in the end."[5] Captain Moore witnessed and recorded the event. Whether he was the first, last, or in between doesn't matter.

- The Colonel was apparently the Spanish-looking man ("the Spaniard") who was a hero at the Battle of the Wilderness, but he was never recognized as such until after the war.[6]

- The Colonel was in some twenty battles, according to his pension application[7]—six of the battles are listed as the ten costliest battles of the Civil War. The other four "costliest battles" were not fought by the Army of Northern Virginia.

- On April 9, 1865 at Appomattox, he was the final commander of what was left of the Seventh Tennessee Regiment—47 men. He was given a handwritten copy of the terms of peace, dated April 10, 1865, signed by J. Longstreet, Lieut.-General; John Gibbons, Maj. Gen. Vols; J. B. Gordon, Maj.-Gen.; Charles Griffin, Bvt. Maj. Gen. Vols; W. N. Pendleton, Brig.-Gen. and Chief Artillery; and W. Merrett, Bvt. Maj. Gen. It stated on his copy that it was "For Lieut.-Col. Shepard, Commanding Seventh Tennessee." (He

---

[4] Lt. Col. S. G. Shepard, OR 552, "Report of Lieut. Col. S. G. Shepard, Seventh Tennessee Infantry, of Operations of Archer's Brigade, June 3–August 1, 1863—The Gettysburg Campaign, 10 August 1863," *The War of the Rebellion: A Compilation of the Official Records of the Union and Confederate Armies*, ser. I, vol. XXVII, pt. II (Washington: Government Printing Office, 1889). See Appendix A for complete report.

[5] John Berrien Lindsley, *The Military Annals of Tennessee,* vol. I, (Nashville: J. M. Lindsley & Co., 1886), 251.

[6] "What Command Was It," *Confederate Veteran,* August 1895, 239.

[7] S. G. Shepard, Military Records, Civil War (1861–1865), Pension No. 14493.

would later read these surrender terms from the preserved paper at the Confederate Veterans Convention in Nashville, June 1897.)[8]

The Colonel left the war at Appomattox.

Before returning to Gladeville after the war, Shepard made a quick trip to what is now Washington, D.C. He arrived in full uniform the morning after President Abraham Lincoln was shot, before the assassin was caught—not the time and place for a Confederate officer to be and particularly in uniform.

Then he returned home to Gladeville. He married Martha Jane (Mattie) Major. He practiced law, ran a cotton gin, ran a farm, served as a school superintendent, built his house, and continued to be active in the Baptist church.

He and Martha Jane had six children.

In 1870, he was elected one of two men from Wilson County to assist in revising the constitution of the State of Tennessee, which was the 1870 Constitutional Convention of Tennessee. He was subsequently elected in 1871 to serve in the thirty-sixth general assembly, Tennessee House of Representatives, from 1871 to 1873.

After he was elected a state legislator, he was also ordained a Missionary Baptist minister in 1872 and served in churches in many of the local counties.[9] Alice, his granddaughter, says, "They were called preachers then ... not ministers."

His heart was in serving his God.

The Wilson County Camp of Confederated Veterans was named the S. G. Shepard Camp No. 941 of United Confederated Veterans in his honor in 1897. He was elected the first commander and served as chaplain until his death.[10]

---

[8] "About Capitulation at Appomattox," *Confederate Veteran*, vol. V, August 1897, 405.

[9] Robert McBride and Dan M. Robison, eds., *Biographical Directory of the Tennessee General Assembly*, Vol. II, 1861-1901 (Nashville: Tennessee State Library and Tennessee Historical Commission, 1979), 811–12.

[10] Thomas E. Partlow, comp. and ed., *Minutes United Confederate Veterans Camp #941, Wilson County, Tennessee, 1897-1928* (Baltimore: Gateway Press, 1975).

I troubled over how to bring this humble man to a reader. I had so little information. *Perhaps a magazine article*, I thought. I was piecing a few facts together here and there. The people in Tennessee who knew of him were as helpful as they could be. Most were thrilled at the idea of the colonel being put to paper and bent over backward to share their information with me.

There were no papers, no memoirs, no letters, only sporadic newspaper stories—none local—and no photo albums. There were biographical sketches in Goodspeed Publishing Company's *History of Tennessee* and the *Biographical Directory of the General Assembly*. There were mere paragraphs in history books that contained his name. More revealing articles turned up in the *Confederate Veteran* magazines. There were dates of appearances at Baptist churches.

It was as if the man lived an honorable, fruitful life based on historical facts. But all the written words and photos that told of the man between the facts were not available. It was as if there were only footprints verifying his existence.

Then I uncovered an obituary, which led to another obituary, which led me to a relative. Carol Carver Whitehead of North Carolina was the great-granddaughter of Colonel Shepard. She led me to the colonel's granddaughter, Alice Carver Cramer, who was living in an assisted-living home in New Jersey. Although only five years old when the colonel died, she had wonderful memories of him. Alice, the granddaughter, and I spent many an hour on the phone discussing the colonel and his family. She was the only living relative I found who knew him when he was alive. What a blessing!

And then the gift of his daughter's words was handed to me. Alice's mother, Alice Hughes Shepard Carver, the colonel's daughter, had written about him. Her family handed me the manuscript.

What a treasure her manuscript is. She tells us what this man who served with such distinction did before the war—what he did after the war—and what others, who served with him, said he did during the war. It is the rare opportunity to see "first hand" the man through the eyes of his daughter, who obviously knew at the time that her father was special. The additional bonus is giving the reader a first-hand glimpse of life in Tennessee during that period.

COLONEL S. G. SHEPARD

While she claims in her foreword that all events and facts attributed to the colonel are true, Alice's manuscript did not include any official papers or letters. Plus, it was written in the narrative style and implies fiction. These characteristics presented a problem: publishers are not interested in "fictionalized historical biographies." The daughter mentions in the manuscript that none of the family, including her, really knew the Civil War exploits of the colonel until twenty years after his death. Then, as near as can be determined, she spent the time going through his papers, history books, memoirs, and so on, to set the record down for posterity, which became her manuscript. Perhaps, she did it just for the family or for possible publication. No one knows for sure.

The colonel's daughter's story was filled with warmth and charm. She put life into the facts. I spent several years after receiving the manuscript verifying events and facts she attributed to her father regarding the war, his life, and his family. I decided to work around the manuscript. I filled in with facts I gathered that she perhaps didn't mention or know about for one reason or another. I also eliminated or summarized some of her story when I believed it was necessary. In addition, I included stories that Alice, the granddaughter, told me about her grandfather. I added information but tried not to change her manuscript. All facts are footnoted. I tried to set the record straight, if at all possible, when and if I thought she took literary license.

I found little straying from the truth throughout the complete manuscript, maybe a date here and there, but *none* concerning the colonel. I have tried to verify all names and footnoted where I could; those not verified were friends, neighbors, or a few who were given fictitious names. The letters were changed a little, and dialect was made more readable.

There is a Jake Magruder who is a big part of the story. I could not find a Jake Magruder in the national or Tennessee records to fit the role Alice gave him. Jake bunked with the colonel and wrote letters home explaining the accomplishments, the hardships, the movements, and the battles of the war the colonel encountered. The colonel wrote letters too, but they said nothing specific. Alice used Jake, apparently, as a fictional character to convey factual stories and events that really did occur in the colonel's life during the war. From what I know of the colonel now, I know he, with all his humility, would never have explained what he was living. Jake Magruder, as the *only* fictional character in the book, probably is a composite of many characters exposing factual stories and events. We'll never know, but the character gets the job done with finesse. If he did exist as Alice wrote, I humbly apologize.

I visited Lebanon and Gladeville, both in Tennessee. I went through the home he built, visited his towns, and visited many of the battlefields. In addition to inserting facts and footnotes to embellish the story, photos and pertinent articles were added. National Park Service figures were selected for battle casualties because they use the official records (OR) to tally the numbers. I have written the introductory pieces, the epilogue, and appendix D, which is titled "Private Sam." The introduction is a summary of part one of Alice's manuscript. It is about her father's family and life prior to the beginning of the Civil War.

Private Sam is the colonel's colorful grandfather who fought in the Revolutionary War and was one of the original twelve settlers in Wilson County, Tennessee. No story of the colonel could be complete without including his grandfather. It is assumed, although not mentioned by Alice, that the colonel's grandfather played a big part in his life during his formative years.

I researched a lot of facts, so I know a lot about dates and events.

But Alice breathed life, color, charm, and love into the dates and events in her story of the man whom we both, with great admiration, refer to as "the Colonel."

Hopefully, this will give him his rightful page in our Civil War history.

Introduction

A lice Hughes Shepard Carver's original manuscript was divided into three parts: before the war, during the war, and after the war. This introduction is mainly a summary of her part one. Most of the facts dealing with part one were not verifiable, and it dealt primarily with the pros and cons of the Civil War. It is not the purpose of this book to "pro-and-con" the Civil War; the purpose is to tell Colonel Shepard's story. There are so many learned scholars who have handled the Civil War with aplomb. I bow to them and thank them for their works.

Some of the quotes in part one that Alice attributes to Colonel Shepard will be stated in this introduction so that readers can get a better picture of the man who chose to fight for the South.

Before the war, Colonel Samuel George Shepard was called George. George was born in—or very near—Gladeville, Tennessee, January 28, 1830,[1] to John Shepard and Francis G. Graves. Gladeville is about twenty-five miles east of Nashville and twelve miles southwest from Lebanon, the Wilson County seat. He was Samuel George Shepard, but because his grandfather and namesake, Samuel, lived nearby and out of respect for this man who served in the Revolutionary War—and also to eliminate confusion—he was called George. Apparently, George was a family surname on his mother's side from way back. Colonel Shepard

---

[1] A note here to state that dates are only written to be challenged it seems. Colonel S. G. Shepard's tombstone and his pension papers state his birth as January 28, 1830. His death certificate states his birth year as 1829. This later date does not correspond with any of the censuses or other records. This confusion is indicative of dates prior to the recording of birth certificates and proper death certificates. In many cases, I have taken the liberty to accept the date best suited. In this case, there is no contest. His birthdate is January 28, 1830.

COLONEL S. G. SHEPARD

was George to his family and friends until the Civil War when his records started to reflect "Samuel G. Shepard," or more frequently, "S. G. Shepard." In fact, he was called "Georgie" until he put a stop to it when he was five years old. After the war, he was referred to with respect by friends and acquaintances as "the Colonel." Throughout these pages, he will be referred to by the name appropriate for the time and occasion, which would be either George or colonel.

Both parents were born in Virginia, John in 1785 and Francis in 1800[2] or 1805[3], and moved with their families to Tennessee. John and Francis were married on January 2, 1823 after obtaining their license on December 23, 1822.[4] John died in 1836 of cholera. They had seven children. See Figure 1 for descendents of George's grandparents and his parents.

According to George's daughter, John died of cholera after volunteering to help others in another town—what town is unknown. According to Wilson County historian Frank Burns, "Early in the summer of 1835, Lebanon was first visited by cholera. A number of residents and persons passing through the village were attacked."[5] Perhaps John went to Lebanon to help.

Alice wrote, "He had been gone nearly three weeks and had gone where lots and lots of folks had cholera. The doctors had asked for healthy people to come and help nurse the ill, and Grandpapa went."

Little is known of George's father other than that he was a teacher and a farmer. He was buried in Gladeville. When John died, he left Francis with seven children—Benjamin, known as "Brother" (12 or 13), Beverly, known as "Brother Bev" (around 10), Amanda, known as "Sis" (9), Octavia, known as "Tavia" (7), George, known in his very young

---

[2] Thomas E. Partlow, *Two Dozen Families of Wilson County, Tennessee*, (1976), page 172.

[3] V. K. Carpenter, trans., *Wilson County, Tennessee, Population Schedule of the United States Census of 1850*, (Huntsville, Arkansas: Century Enterprises, 1969), 3.

[4] Marriage License (Between John Shepherd [sic] and Francis G. Graves), Wilson County Archives.

[5] Frank Burns, ed., *The History of Wilson County, Tennessee: Its Land and Its Life, Second Edition,* (Lebanon, TN: History Associates for Wilson County, 1987), 171.

INTRODUCTION

years as "Georgie" (5), Sarah Jane, known as "Sallie" (3), and Francis John or Johns, known as "Fannie" or "Fannie John" (who was less than a year, if born yet).

Little is known or authenticated about the family after the death of John. The 1840 census[6] shows Grandfather Sam as having a boy between five and ten years old living with him. Perhaps this was George. According to the 1850 census,[7] Ben had already left for California to seek his fortune in the gold fields. Ben will later return, as seen in the book. The remaining children were still living at home in Gladeville with their mother, or at least they were counted as such in the 1850 census. A few letters Fannie John wrote in 1856 to her cousin Fannie Logan Graves[8] verify also that Ben had gone to the gold fields of California and had not returned. He had sent pictures and newspapers from California.

Brother Beverly was about to impart to New Orleans to work on the riverboats. Beverly claimed, according to the manuscript, that he could make five dollars per day and have free room, board, and clothes. He drowned working on the riverboats in New Orleans sometime between 1856 and 1860.

In the letters, Fannie John said, "Brother George has not come home yet but will in a few weeks." There is no mention of where he was; he was twenty-six.

It looks like between the 1850 census and when Fannie John wrote the letters in 1856, Amanda or "Sis" married and moved to Texas. She had three sons. She also will return, as seen later in the book.

Octavia or "Tavia" married and moved to Ohio, and there is no mention of her again.

Sallie married William Bradshaw (about 1853)[9] and lived nearby. (Alice referred to him as Williamson. Bradshaw genealogy states William.)

---

[6] *Federal Census of 1840*, Wilson County, Tennessee.

[7] V.K. Carpenter, trans., *Wilson County Tennessee Population Schedule of the United States Census of 1850*, (Huntsville, Arkansas: Century Enterprises, 1969), 3.

[8] Erick Montgomery (contributed by), "News From Across the River," 1856, 1859, provided by Wilson County Archives.

[9] Genealogy supplied by Erick Montgomery.

COLONEL S. G. SHEPARD

Fannie John went to school at Mount Juliet. She later became a teacher and lived at home or with relatives until she was married late in life to Jordan Robinson (1873).[10] She lived with her sister, Sallie, during the Civil War. She was George's closest member of the family. (The spelling for "Fannie" varies frequently with "Fanny." Alice spells it with a *y* in the manuscript, and all the legal documents found with her name use the *y*. But her letters use the *ie*.)

There are only a few things that are verifiable for George during these years. He was a teacher. His listing in the *Biographical Directory of the Tennessee General Assembly* states, "When of age went to Mississippi to teach school before beginning study of law."[11] He did teach school; whether it was in Mississippi or not is unknown. The directory claims he taught in Mississippi, and it was later picked up in his obituary.[12] Those are the only two places that mention where he taught. His daughter, Alice, in the manuscript claims he was the sole support of the family from the time he was seventeen, which would have been 1847. That fact is neither disputable nor verifiable. Someone had to support the family. The 1860 census[13] shows him living with A. J. Spickard and lists his profession as a teacher. He may have been a summer farmhand for the Spickards, or he may have lived there and taught school nearby at that time. (The census was taken in the summer.)

George's mother died in 1860. According to Alice in the manuscript, he obtained his certificate to practice law from Judge Gooch in Nashville the day his mother died. George had been studying law at home where he lived with his mother and Fanny. As near as can be determined, George was self-taught and probably was home-schooled when younger. I tried to track down a law certificate and was unsuccessful. Apparently in those days, many studied with a mentor and then were certified. Perhaps the

---

[10] Marriage License and Marriage Bond of Jordan T. Robinson and Fanny (sic) J. Shepherd (sic). The middle initial for Jordan Robinson is not distinguishable.

[11] Robert McBride and Dan M. Robison, eds., *Biographical Directory of the Tennessee General Assembly, vol. II, 1861–1901* (Nashville, Tennessee: Tennessee State Library and Archives and Tennessee Commission, 1979), 811–12.

[12] "Col. Shepard Dead in Lebanon," *Nashville Banner*, June 7, 1917, 14.

[13] *Federal Census of 1860, Wilson County, Tennessee, Civil Districts, 16–25.*

reason I couldn't find verification was that he was soon to be in the Civil War with insufficient legal track record, or maybe records were lost during those years. I could find no trace of a Judge Gooch either. Perhaps, Judge Gooch was not the real name. His daughter said he was certified; I need no more proof.

Fanny and George had a special relationship. Fanny looked up to her older brother and listened to his every word. Then she began to read the papers too and become aware of current events. He became her greatest friend and antagonist, and she his. Fanny always said she couldn't marry because she couldn't find anyone who measured up to her beloved brother, George. She was thirty-seven when she did marry, eight years after the Civil War. Fanny is a big part of the story.

Alice explains how curious George was as a child, how quickly he learned (rose to the top at whatever he tried), what a marksman he was, and what a brave young man he was (the years 1861 to 1865 speak for themselves). He was barely past five when his mother sent him to the store to get some meal. She told him how much it would be. The storekeeper tried to give him the wrong change, probably to see if he was paying attention. George caught him immediately, and the storekeeper complimented him on being such a good "mathematician." George, who wasn't going to school, was excited about the new word (an example of how smart and inquisitive he was). On the way back, he stubbed his toe and broke the toenail off. His mother asked if it hurt; he said it did at first, but then he said he "told the toe, 'You can't hurt an old toe, you ain't hurtin' me,' and it stopped hurtin' me." That supposedly was the day he asked his mother and family to stop calling him "Georgie." From then on, it was "George." Alice used this as an example of how brave he was and the control he had over his feelings and body from an early age—fodder for being a colonel.

Alice answers many questions about George before the war. Before the war, he practiced law, taught school, ran the farm, and was very active in the Baptist church or fellowship. Then the war came—the one that tore the country apart and pitted brother against brother—the one with more casualties than all the other wars combined until midway through Vietnam.[14] He, as well as the other able-bodied men of his area, rose to the occasion—some joined the Union, but most from his state of Tennessee joined the Confederacy as he did.

Of course, Alice takes over after the war by filling in with what she experienced or knew or with what Fanny told her. George left the war behind once the treaty was signed at Appomattox. Neither his daughter nor his granddaughter, both named Alice, said he ever spoke of the war when prompted by his family. He would tell tales and sometimes include something funny about the war.

His granddaughter, Alice Carver Cramer, described what he looked like. There are so few pictures of him. His granddaughter describes an older gentleman. "He was the tallest member of the family," she said.[15] "When six feet meant a man was really tall, he was probably at least six feet two. He was always a head above a crowd of men. Men weren't as tall then as they are now. The Colonel had a dark complexion, black (very black) hair (graying when I last saw him), and blue eyes. He looked Spanish. He had a receding forehead with a sparse area in the back of his head. He was slender without being thin but didn't have an ounce of fat on him. He was big-boned, broad-shouldered, and he had a presence. My father, Dr. William Owen Carver, had presence when he walked into a room, but the Colonel had a more commanding presence. He was always referred to as *the Colonel*. My mother even referred to him as *the Colonel*."

Slavery

Alice, the daughter, answered the question as to whether George believed in slavery. In the book, Fanny and George discussed the events before the war on many occasions. He felt the North–South dissension was mainly "jealousy, greed" on both sides, not just slavery.

"We are not yet welded into a harmonious nation. We have not yet become consolidated," Alice wrote, attributing the statement to George.

---

[14] A. Wilson Green and Gary W. Gallagher, *National Geographic Guide to the Civil War, National Battlefield Parks* (Washington, D.C.: National Geographic Society, 1992), 6.

[15] Alice Carver Cramer, the Colonel's granddaughter, taped telephone conversation with the author, 2001.

"Why do the disagreements usually start with the subject of slavery,"
Fanny asked, "if slavery is not the main issue? George, you don't think
slavery is right, do you?"

"No," he replied and incorrectly predicted, "The abolition of slavery
will come about gradually. The South needs time ... The South as a
whole is not for slavery ... Gradual emancipation is certain to come in
the South ... There are proslavery men in the North." George did not feel
slavery was the sole cause for war. He felt it was economics, a balance of
power in Washington, and rights of the states.

According to his daughter, Alice, one of his first law duties was to
help a Mr. Grant make sure his slave, Silas, and Silas's two children,
Tom and Rose, were set free and would have the necessary paperwork to
prove their freedom after his death. George helped Mr. Grant
approximately seven years before the war and before he was certified.
Alice wrote that George told Fanny, "It was my first venture into any
practical application of law. It wasn't anything to brag about. Just didn't
think to tell it, I reckon."

Both Fanny and George agreed that slavery was an abomination and
should be eliminated. The solution for the elimination was at best
"gradual"—for the good of the South and the slaves.

Alice, the granddaughter, clarified that the Shepards did not have
slaves. It is doubtful they had need for or could afford a slave. There
were slaves in the area who were apparently treated well with the
exception of those belonging to one owner who was cruel.

In one instance, their sister Sallie asked that George prepare the
proper papers for "Aunt Nancy" and "Uncle Reuben" to prove their
freedom in case of a problem. Apparently, the couple had been freed and
worked for Sallie and her husband, but they needed proper
documentation. It appears the whole family was concerned about the
slaves.

Secession

George did not believe in secession, although he believed in the
rights of the South. Alice attributes to him this remark: "This is such a
big country. We ought to be able to have two sides to a question and not
be at each other's throat about it. I think the North would be wise to

allow the South to settle her problems without trying to coerce her too much. The United States have [sic] for years been evolving into two nationalities." (It is interesting to note that at that time in history people thought in terms of states, sections, and nations instead of a nation—a United States.)

But he did believe in one nation—one United States. He said, "Our becoming one nation depends on how much each section is willing to adjust itself to the common good ... Men have a way of trying to tally their beliefs with their financial interests."

George was definitely on the side of the South. "I'd undoubtedly go with the South," he said, when asked by his family. "Why? Because I think there is more right on the side of the South than on the side of the North. Because I'm a Southerner. Besides," he said, "this little fracas will blow over in a few weeks and we'll be home again."

Preparation

George was the type of person to always be prepared. Alice writes that some dozen or more neighborhood bachelors in and near the village, who were taking the war very seriously, asked George to meet with them and help them prepare in case of war. "They met every Saturday afternoon at the village schoolhouse," she wrote. "They discussed war tactics; they planned duties for the following week. Nearly all these boys were farmers. George advised them to put their farms in the best order possible; live outdoors, strenuous lives; walk, not ride, when a journey was to be made; in other words, build a strong physical resistance. They spent part of every Saturday afternoon marching, and learning to carry their bodies in military fashion to accomplish the longest distances with the least outlay of physical effort."

Alice wrote, "When reason and passion walk the highway side by side, the logical outcome is conflict. If reason wins, peace will reign; if passions win, war will come. George had no doubt that reason would win."

George planned to leave the farm in the hands of Jim Burns, a white man, who had been displaced by slaves at John Mason's farm where he had been living and working. Jim Burns had a wife and three children and was thrilled with the opportunity. Fanny was to live with Sallie.

One of the questions that haunted George before he went to war was whether he should become a preacher. Fanny, as well as George, believed that their mother always assumed George would do so. His mother always let George make his own decisions, but he believed she wanted him to be a preacher, not a lawyer.

Now, his life would be that of a soldier—neither lawyer nor preacher.

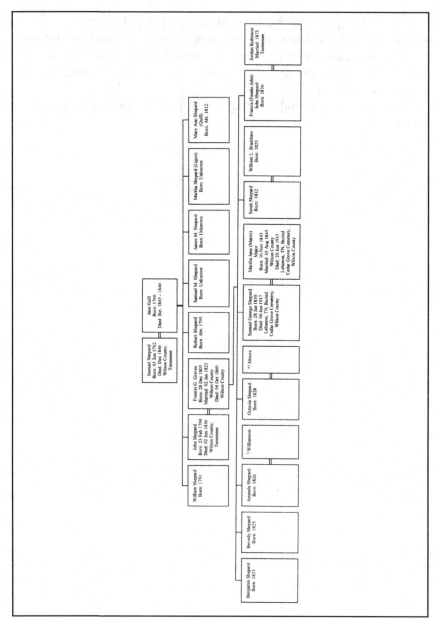

Colonel Shepard's grandparents, aunts, uncles, brothers, and sisters.

1 • Camp Trousdale

During the winter of 1860 and spring of 1861, the men of both the North and the South were being drawn very rapidly into the vortex of war. The secessionists had taken over almost all the forts, arsenals, and troops of the United States. The South, except for ammunition, was fairly well fixed for war. But if the South was to win in this conflict for "freedom" from the North with its larger population and vaster resources, she must have volunteers, many volunteers. The whole South was in a stir. Young men who had never been very far from home before were leaving for camps.

The day Fanny expected and dreaded had come—the day when George and Jake Magruder and the other neighbor boys who had been meeting Saturday afternoons all spring at the schoolhouse would be leaving for Camp Trousdale in Sumner County, Tennessee. Fanny presented George's group with a Confederate flag.[1] It was a hot day that May twentieth when they left for camp.

They headed toward Camp Trousdale. Camp Trousdale was established as a training site for Tennessee Confederate soldiers. It was thirty-five miles north of Lebanon, forty miles north of Nashville, and located conveniently on the Louisville & Nashville Railroad. According to the *Military Annals of Tennessee*, it was here the Seventh Tennessee Infantry was organized on May 25, 1861 and none too soon for Tennessee, the last state to do so, was to secede June 8. It consisted of ten companies of which six were from Wilson, two from Sumner, and

---

[1] John "Bev" Spickard's handwritten note about Company G, Seventh Tennessee Infantry, possibly written or given to him by W. H. Robbins. The note states "Miss Fannie Sheppard [sic] presented to this company a beautiful Confederate flag."

one each from Smith and DeKalb counties. Each company consisted of one hundred men.[2] George's Company G called themselves the "Hurricane Rifles" because of the Hurricane creek near their homes that would rise like a hurricane.[3]

As reported in the *Military Annals of Tennessee*, the Seventh was issued Mississippi rifles, which were different from that of any other regiment in Tennessee. The Mississippi rifles were kept for the first two years but then replaced by the Springfield and Enfield rifles because the Confederacy could no longer procure the ammunition.[4]

Fanny slept very little the night before. She spent the night rolling and tossing or slipping off onto her knees by the bed to pray. After the hard night, she and George were up and out early the next morning. He had things to do at the last hour. The wagons and mules and horses to take the men as far as the river would be leaving at ten o'clock. George was ready by nine. "Why did he get ready so soon?" Fanny moaned to herself. He too was irritated with himself for being in such a hurry. For once, he had overdone his promptness. And now the minutes dragged by like hours.

Fanny would live with their sister Sallie and Sallie's husband, William Bradshaw, while George was away. They were coming for her this morning. George kept looking down the road for them. He went out to the barn to make sure that everything was done that he could do there before leaving. While he was out there, Jake came to say goodbye to Fanny. She had hoped he wouldn't come. She hated goodbyes. When she saw him nearing the gate, she looked around nervously for George. Where on earth was he? Why didn't he stay around where he was needed!

---

[2] John Berrien Lindsley, *Military Annals of Tennesse,* vol. 1, (Nashville: J. M. Lindsley & Co., 1886), 227.

[3] There was a Hurricane creek near their homes. According to John "Bev" Spickard, the creek was named Hurricane because it would come up like a hurricane.

[4] John Berrien Lindsley, *Military Annals of Tennessee,* vol. 1, (Nashville, J. M. Lindsley & Co., 1886), 227.

Jake, the deliberate, never-in-a-hurry man, now seemed to be in a hurry. He came onto the porch with a determined look and clipped words. "Miss Fanny," he began, when he had reached the first step, and with no preliminary greetings, "how many times have I asked you to marry me?"

She wasn't surprised to hear him say it, and the bluntness of his manner and his red-faced, set expression put her at ease. "If you can't remember, Jake, how do you expect me to?" she replied.

Jake smiled and lapsed into his lazy drawl, seating himself on the top step of the porch and leaning against the pillar. "Oh, I guess I could count 'em, the ones I said out loud to you—but the ones I said to myself—well, I guess I couldn't do that."

"Don't you think you better stop that?"

He leaned forward and grinned at her. "Counting them?" he said.

"No. I guess you know what I mean."

"I'm afraid I do—but I can't make no promises about that."

"Well anyhow, don't ask me now. I might say yes, and that wouldn't be good for either of us."

"Maybe not for you, but powerful good for me."

"Oh, Jake, you are all excited now over going to war. Any woman would look beautiful to you today, and desirable. I'm older than you, five years older. A man needs a wife younger than himself. Women get old faster than men. Forget me. Find you another girl. There will be plenty of them when this war is over. A lot of men are going to get killed, I'm afraid. There will be many heart-broken sweethearts and young wives left at home. It's horrible to think about—and terribly unreasonable! Why does it have to be?" She had swept Jake along with her, almost making him forget that he had come to propose once more.

"I ain't letting myself think about that right now," he said. "I hope we won't be long gone. The professor still hopes there won't be any actual shooting. He says 'tain't logical."

"I know, Jake, but I'm afraid my brother's wrong."

"Will you write to me, Miss Fanny, while I'm away?"

"'Course I will, if I know where to find you. I'm glad you're going to be with 'the professor,' as you call him. I feel both of you will be safer being together."

COLONEL S. G. SHEPARD

"So'm I glad. I couldn't hardly go if I couldn't be with him. If he's an officer—as I'm certain he will be—I'll manage somehow to get with his bunch."

"You do that, Jake, and let us know if there is anything we can do for you. I suppose there will be some way to send food or clothing if you aren't well supplied."

"I don't know, but the professor, he'll know. He seems to know purty much everything. He's told us all about companies and regiments and brigades and divisions. Guess I'll learn sometime ... maybe." Reluctantly, he stood up on the porch step where he'd been sitting and turned to go. "Well, goodbye, Miss Fanny. No use hanging around any longer. The flag you gave us is beautiful. I'll always think of you when I see it. Well, our wagon and mules will be going purty soon now." He turned and grinned at her. "If I happen to come back and you are still Miss Fanny, it'll be the same old tale you'll be hearing. Goodbye."

"Goodbye, Jake. God bless you and keep you from harm and danger. Goodbye."

Jake was hardly out of sight when George came in through the back of the house. He was surprised to see Fanny with her head on her arms on the table, evidently much disturbed.

"Fanny, what's the matter?" Fanny didn't cry for nothing.

She raised her head, dabbed her eyes, and gave her nose a vicious swab. "Jake's just said goodbye."

"Well?"

"Oh George, he's so pitiful. I don't know whether I'm just mad at myself because I can't love the man or just sorry for him."

"If you can't, you can't. I wouldn't worry about it. He'll be all right. I'm glad he's going to be with me. I'll try to be his big brother," he said, trying to put a lighter turn to the affair. Fanny stared into the faraway and didn't answer. George cleared his throat. "It's about time Sallie and William were here," he said, looking down the road. "Are you sure there isn't something else you want me to do before I go?"

"Nothing. Nothing, and for pity's sake, go on without saying goodbye. I hate goodbyes." She used her handkerchief again, and said, just to break the tense, awkward silence, "How far is it to Camp Trousdale, George?"

He knew that she knew, but he answered as though he hadn't told her before. "About thirty-five miles. You'll be hearing from us often. Could come over if you wanted to."

"How long do you think you'll be there?" Again, the handkerchief had to be used, this time with determination and finality. She shouldn't be a sissy fool. She wouldn't!

"I haven't much idea. Plenty of time to write home though. We might be there for six months and then come home. The war hasn't started yet, you know. The trouble may blow over before real war ever begins." He gazed down the road. "There they are now," he said, looking relieved, and then added, "Sallie and William. Take care of yourself, Fanny. Don't worry about us, my dear, and write often. I'll tell Sallie and William goodbye at the gate. I'm off now." He looked deeply into her face but didn't offer to kiss her goodbye or even to take her hand. "Don't forget us when you say your prayers," he said, and was gone.

He didn't look much like a soldier as he went down the path. He looked like a man with a very heavy load on his way to a very uncertain duty. And Fanny certainly didn't feel or behave much like a soldier. She hurried into her room, threw herself onto her bed, and sobbed. Then she was off the bed as impatiently as she had flung herself onto it. *You idiot,* she demeaned herself. *Go wash your face. You don't want Sallie and William to see you acting the fool!*

Fanny had a real home at Sallie's. She was conscious of being wanted. She was conscious of being a help to Sallie in running the home and seeing after the babies. Ida and Frank were such adorable babies.[5]

Sallie had insisted on Fanny taking the big, airy room on the second floor, the one with a window looking to the east and out onto the flower garden. There was a western window too and a big fireplace and comfortable furniture, all to give her a feeling of well-being. She was ideally situated, but she missed George sorely, almost tragically. She had

---

[5] The Shepard Genealogy, supplied by Erick Montgomery. According to the genealogy, Sallie and William Bradshaw had nine children: Mary Elizabeth, b. 1854; Ida, b. 1858; Frances (Frank) G., b. 1860; Samuel S., b. 1863; Jack H., b. 1866; Evaline, b. 1867; Ben J., b. 1870; Kate, b. 1873; and Charlie Beverly, b. 1878.

a motherly love for him and adored him as almost perfect, a feeling she kept to the end of her life.

She was afraid to write to him the day after he left for the camp because she was depressed, and she didn't want to depress him. After a lapse of three days, she felt better and decided to try it. He'd be expecting a letter.

May 23rd
Dear George,
  I'm sorry I was such a fool the day you left. I assure you I am fully recovered and feel very proud to have a brother so loyal to duty and so brave about it.
  Of course, you had to go; of course I wouldn't for anything have had you go with the Yankees. Poor old Mrs. Nelson is stricken with an almost unbearable grief. Her only son has gone to the Northern army. Mrs. Samson's two sons have gone, one to the Northern army and the other to the Southern.
  Mr. Lincoln's speech about the "Divided House" haunts me these days. So many homes are being divided now. I wonder which way the country will fall.
  But I'm writing not to philosophize, but to assure you that I'm not altogether bad and am going to be happy here with Sallie and her interesting family. I can see that she needs me, or somebody more capable than her school-teaching sister can possibly be, in running her home.
  It's perfectly amazing how much time children the age of hers take to keep them fed, clothed, and happy. Yesterday, Sallie and I took them out for an airing and went to see Mrs. Underwood. Her only son has gone to Camp Trousdale. Her husband has been dead several years. She made me feel very much ashamed of myself. You would have thought her son had gone away on a triumphant journey and that she had every possible need provided for. If you happen to see her son, Ceph, shake his hand for his mother's sake. I hope he's half as brave as she is.
  Remember me to Jake and let us hear from you as often as you can.
    Your very foolish but very loving sister,
    Fanny

Sallie and Fanny were on the side porch getting ready to hull the plump, green peas that Fanny had just gathered and brought in from the garden. Ida, with her new pink dress and her pink and white gingham sunbonnet securely tied under her chin, was playing in the yard. Frank was asleep in his cradle nearby. Fanny hung her bonnet on the back of her chair, wiped her face on the corner of her apron, and asked Sallie if William had gone for the mail.

"Yes, and it's about time he was back. I hope he brings a letter from George."

"He will, I think—and the papers. I want to see what's happening in Washington and Richmond. Now that George is gone, I don't have the same urge to keep up with the news, except that everything that happens has something to do with him. I do wish I could believe he's right, that no real war will be fought."

"We can only hope and pray, Fanny. I see William coming now."

As William stepped onto the porch, he handed two letters to Fanny.

"One from George, Fanny?" asked Sallie.

"Yes, and one from Jake, I guess. It's from Camp Trousdale, and nobody else there would be writing to me. I'll read George's now, shall I?"

"Please do. Here, let me have your pan. William, you take Fanny's pan and hull while she reads."

Camp Trousdale
May 27th, '61
My dear Fanny,
I was sorry to leave home with you feeling as you do about my going.

"I could kick myself," said Fanny, and then continued reading:

I would be sorry in any case to leave you. But I'm sure you will get on all right at Sallie's. Do, my dear sister, try to be your own bright, cheerful self. But you couldn't be anything else for long. Your vivacity and cheerfulness are not to be subdued by so slight a calamity as that of having an unworthy brother go away for a few weeks. Keep a stiff backbone and look to the future.

We arrived in camp with not too much delay or inconvenience. We had a little trouble in getting started from the schoolhouse on account of Pete Sullivan's mule having one of her stubborn spells. Tommy Jones was in the wagon with Jake and I. When Pete's mule was giving Pete some trouble, I heard Jake say to Tommy, "That's a powerfully handy pole over in the grass there," pointing to a stick by the side of the road near the wagon. I saw Tommy look at Jake and Jake wink at Tommy, and then—but Jake will tell you what Tommy did. I repeat what I said to you on leaving, "Don't worry about Jake." I think he enjoyed the trip thoroughly and certainly helped everybody else to keep jolly.

Much obliged for the lunch I found in the satchel. It was sufficient for Jake and me both for a whole day, and we needed it. Jake's folks had fixed a box for him, but alas, he forgot it! I think he enjoyed sharing mine more, coming from your kitchen and prepared by your lily-white hands! But I desist, remembering how upset you were over his goodbye. Jake's all right. A man's heart is soon mended—or so they say.

By the next letter, the Camp will be in fine running order and I'll be able to tell you more.

Give my love to Sallie and family, and believe me, your devoted brother.

George

When Fanny had finished George's letter, she opened the other one and began to read. Sallie talked to William about allowing Fanny to not read the second letter aloud. But Fanny did.

Camp Trousdale
May 27th, 1861
My Dear Miss Fanny,
    I was a little disappointed that you didn't come to the schoolhouse with the professor last week to see us off.

"Who's the professor?" asked Sallie.

"George. That's what Jake calls him ever since they were having those meetings at the schoolhouse this spring." She continued:

"But I guess it was all for the best. There was a right smart crying among the women and girls who had come to say goodbye to their sons and sweethearts. You wouldn't have liked that. I think you'd have liked

the way Tommy Jones got Pete Sullivan's mule started but I'm not gonna tell you about it.
Tommy Jones was in the wagon with the professor and me. There were ten of us in that wagon.
I'll have to wait to tell you, if you'll let me, about how the professor is now a Captain—huh, Captain indeed! He ought to be a Brigadier General! Now I'm learning to shoot a Mississippi rifle.
    As ever,
    Jake

William said, "And so George is a captain. I supposed you agree with Jake on that subject, Fanny? You too think George ought to be a brigadier general. Wasn't that what Jake said?"

"The war is young yet. No telling what he'll be before it's over," Fanny said with a sigh.

"I think you'd better cultivate Jake, Fanny, if you can get such letters as that from him," said Sallie.

"You don't know Jake. Jake's over-cultivated now."

"What's the matter with him?" asked William.

"Nothing, except he needs to find out that I'm not the only woman in the world."

"Is it hopeless?"

"Absolutely. I could never get romantic about Jake, and I think enough of him to want to see him happy and settled."

"So you won't write him, I guess."

"Once in a while, but not often."

"A pity. Why can't folks be sensible about falling in love?"

"Meaning Jake or me?"

"Both, maybe. Perhaps if he used different tactics you'd fall. Love's a strange animal. You know, Fanny, I think you've got George set up as your ideal, and no man is ever going to please you."

"Too true, my dear sister," Fanny replied. "But let's change the subject. There's a spot out in the flower garden that I want to use for some gladioli bulbs and chrysanthemums and dahlias. I love fall flowers. We are going to need flowers, lots of flowers—all we can get this fall, I'm afraid."

2 • George Reminisces

Preparing for war at Camp Trousdale was a different world for George. When time allowed, he reminisced. His fondest memory was the day he met Martha Jane. He remembered how reluctant he was to attend his cousin's wedding because of the impending "war." Those days played back in his mind as pleasant memories. He could almost hear Fanny's voice.

"George," she'd called, having just come from the post office. She'd had a letter in her hand that she wanted to read to me. She'd called again, "George ..."

"Here," George answered.

"Where's here? I don't see you."

"In the kitchen." He was sitting by the table, absorbed in a newspaper and didn't look up as she came in.

"Dear me!" she said. "What are you doing in the kitchen this time of the day? Hungry? It isn't near suppertime yet." He didn't answer. He kept on reading. She was half-angry, half-amused, and wholly impatient. She shouted at him, "Don't you want to hear the news?"

He laid his paper on the table with reluctance and asked indifferently, "What news?"

She knew that he was not interested in any news she could give him. His mind was still on his newspaper and what he'd just been reading.

"I've a good notion not to tell you! You wouldn't stop reading that old paper if the house was on fire!" She stopped and looked at him reproachfully. "You are so obsessed about a war, you can't even get interested in a wedding."

He grinned at her, and as always when he smiled, she was appeased.

"Anybody getting married?" he said.

"Yes—lots of people. About everybody but you and me." She started to leave the kitchen but thought better of it and sat down. She opened the letter she had in her hand. "This letter that came from Aunt Lina[1] just now says Vic is to be married on the seventeenth of this month, and she wants us to come."

George screwed around in his chair, gave his shoulders a twitch, and recrossed his legs. "Don't see how we can. Everything is so uncertain now. Can't leave home."

"Oh, George, we *need* to leave home. I think I'll go crazy if we don't leave home for a spell." She went on wistfully. "Aunt Lina will be terribly disappointed if we don't come. So will Vic, and so will I," she added and sighed.

George seemed to come back from afar. "Vic getting married?" he asked. "I thought she was sick."

"She isn't really sick," Fanny said. "She's never been able to walk very well since that fall last Christmas. Danced too soon after the accident, they think." She sighed again. "I do wish we could go. You haven't visited our Spickard kinfolks in years—just a few hours' stopover when you've been passing through that part of the country is all you've done for goodness knows when. I certainly want to go but ... if I can't, I can't!" She bounced up and started toward the door in not very good humor.

"See here," said George, "can't you go without me?"

"You know very well that I can't," she said and flounced herself out of the room.

George picked his paper up and tried to read, but only his eyes saw the words. *Fanny does need a change,* kept going through his mind. He'd been powerful poor company for weeks—War! War! War! It was all he could think about. He still did not believe it would actually come, but he couldn't ignore all the talk and excitement that filled the atmosphere; and

---

[1] Margie Spickard Lamb (supplied by) and John "Bev" Spickard (supplied by), Spickard Genealogies. According to the Spickard genealogy, Evaline Graves Spickard was Aunt Lina. Evaline, who was married to Andrew Jackson (A. J.) Spickard, was a sister to George and Fanny's mother. Vic was short for Louisa Victoria Spickard who married Joseph Franklin Huddleston.

then there was Fort Sumter, no denying that. He was doing all he could to be ready if war should come. He had no notion of being drafted. But Fanny now—she was his nearest and dearest. She deserved a vacation if anybody ever did.

At supper that evening, he said, "All right, Fanny, we'll go to the wedding, but we can stay away only two days."

They left home very early on the morning of the wedding and arrived at the home of the Spickards in time for last-minute preparations. The flowers were yet to be arranged in the parlor and dining room. The bride's veil needed some further stitches to make it fit properly. The girls were rushing here and there, all talking at once. Fanny was in her glory. George felt out of place. His uncle and aunt were very quiet and didn't look very happy, it seemed to him.

Maybe it was the thunderclouds of war that hung so threateningly over the land. Maybe they didn't approve of the wedding with Vic so frail. At any rate, he decided to get out of the house to take a walk. He went out the yard gate and across the big lot that separated the yard from the public road. As he neared the gate that opened onto the road, he was caught by the sight of a young girl coming down. She was carrying a basket almost as large as she, filled with flowers. Yellows and whites and greens seemed to envelop her. Her hair, the color of pulled molasses candy, was tied back with a pale green ribbon. Her yellow dress was caught around her slender waist with a sash of the same pale green that held her hair. As she came nearer, he could see that her eyes were very blue and her skin pink and white—very lovely and dainty.

He was not in the habit of seeing in detail the color and style of girls' dresses, eyes, and complexions. He wasn't interested in the subject. But not one item of this child's costume escaped his eyes. As he gazed, he forgot Vic's imminent wedding. He forgot the troubled faces of his uncle and aunt. He even forgot the war. He rubbed his eyes and wondered if this vision that came tripping so airily down the road could be a girl—or was she a fairy coming to grace Vic's wedding?

Just as he decided to find out—and ask to be allowed to carry her basket—she turned toward the gate. He hurried to meet her. Impetuously, he said, "Good morning, little lady. May I carry your basket of posies? You are likely to be smothered with so many, aren't you?"

She stopped, took a long look at him, and replied, "Aren't you Miss Victoria's cousin, Mr. George Shepard?"

"I am," he answered, "but how do you know?"

"Oh, I've seen you before, and besides I heard Miss Vic say that ..." She hesitated for a second, smiled impishly, "that you must be part Indian; you have such straight, black hair and such dark skin."

"You seem to know so much about me, and I don't even know your name."

"I'm Martha Jane Major. I live in that house over there," she said, pointing to a big house across the road, set back among some tall trees. "The one," she said, "with the old locust trees in the yard. Can you see it?"

"Sure I can. I've been there. And so, you are Mr. Sam Major's daughter. Well, well," he smiled broadly. "When did you grow up? You were barefooted and wearing a sunbonnet—let's see how long ago has that been?" he wondered, hoping he'd find out her age, but she didn't gratify him. He caught himself up with, "But here, let me take your basket. I suppose you are taking these flowers to help decorate for Vic's wedding?"

"Yes, I am," she said, handing him her basket. "It isn't heavy. Beck would have brought it for me if I'd have let her."

"Who's Beck? Your sister?"

"Oh no. She's my Negro maid. She's the girl Taylor Spickard, your uncle Spickard's Negro man, wants to marry."[2]

"Is that so? Is she going to marry him?"

"Well not yet. I think she will someday. If," she added, "my father will buy him from your uncle. Right now, she loves to tease him."

"How naughty of her." Martha Jane looked up quickly into George's face to see what his eyes were saying or what she thought she saw.

"I think *you* are teasing now," she said.

"Oh no, far from it. You see, I'm very much interested in weddings right now. By the way, how old did you say you were?"

"I didn't say," she said mischievously, "and I think I won't tell you, sir!"

---

[2] Both the Spickards and the Majors owned Negroes. The Shepards did not. Beck and Taylor are mentioned later in the book.

"Well now—will you tell me this? How many beaux have you?"

"Beaux? Oh, I'm hardly old enough for beaux. At least my mother thinks I'm not."

"I see. Perhaps you and your mother don't agree on this very important subject?"

"I shan't tell you that either, sir. Here we are now. You may give me my basket. I want to surprise and please Miss Victoria."

At the wedding that night, George had eyes only for Martha Jane Major. Victoria was very lovely in her white satin. The house was full of pretty girls and beaux. Martha Jane looked quite the young lady with her hair piled high on her young head.

Fanny saw George's eyes following Martha Jane wherever she went. When Fanny got a chance, she nudged him, "Seeing a ghost, George?" When he paid no attention, she continued, "You are not the only man here who sees she's nearly grown and beautiful. Look at John Davis. He hasn't taken his eyes off her all evening."

"What'd you say, Fanny?"

"Aw—go on! You know what I said. Wake up and pay attention to some of the other girls. Lots of pretty girls here tonight. Doesn't it break your heart," she asked soberly, "to look at Vic? She shouldn't have gotten married. She looks completely worn out, and the evening not more than half gone."

"Why did her parents allow it?" asked George, coming out of his dreams.

"Well, Frank (Joseph Franklin Huddleston) said if she had to be an invalid, he wanted the honor of taking care of her."

Next morning before he and Fanny would be leaving for home, George had to see Martha Jane's garden. Evidently, she knew he'd want to see her garden—or was it one particular flower she knew he'd have to see? At any rate, she was ready to show it to him when he came.

As they went from one flowerbed to another, with him paying such scant attention to the flowers, she said, "You are not looking at my flowers. See these roses? Aren't they gorgeous?"

"Yes," he said, not taking his eyes from hers.

Her little face got very pink. She pouted, "I think we'd better go in."

"Oh no—please. I'll look at your flowers. I'll be going in a little while," he added quietly. "We are leaving right after lunch."

"Why are you going so soon? I thought you'd stay several days."

"Would you like that?" And then he was sorry he had said it and added, "I'd like to stay longer, but business calls us home."

"What business? You are a lawyer, aren't you? Do you have to go to court right away?"

"Yes, I'm a sort of lawyer. No, I don't have to go to Nashville right away—but there are many things to see about on the farm. I'm a farmer too, you know, or I guess you don't know. I want to get the farm in as good shape as possible, in case I have to leave it."

"Leave it? Where are you going?"

"You are too young to bother your pretty head about it. But some folks think we are going to have a war. I don't think so, but I must be ready in case we do."

"Oh!"

"Have I startled you? You've heard of Abraham Lincoln and Jefferson Davis, haven't you?"

"Of course. But they seem millions of miles away—in another world. You see, I have no brothers, and my father is too old. We are so peaceful and happy. I don't think any of our Negroes want to leave us. I just don't want to think of war. Let's forget it."

"I'm afraid we can't do that." He hesitated, seeming so uncertain about what to do. Then he decided. He lifted his shoulders and asked rather timidly, "Would you ..." He hesitated again. She was so young. But it was now or maybe never. He made a new start, "Have you a little picture of yourself—just a tiny one you'd be willing to give me to take ... if I should ever be in line of battle ... if there is to be a war?" He was a little confused. He seemed to himself to be asking for so much.

She looked puzzled, then afraid, and then her face lighted up with a radiant smile. "Oh yes!" she said, "I'm sure mother wouldn't object. You wait here. I'll go get it."

"Captain Shepard," he heard the voice say. He was quickly jolted back into reality at Camp Trousdale.

3 · Enter Jordan Robinson

It was a hot day in June. Sallie was on the side porch knitting and watching the children. Frank was sitting on a pallet, and Ida was playing with him and talking to him. She declared that he could say her name. He was highly amused with her antics and would laugh out loud when she called to him suddenly, "Boohoo, Frank!"

Fanny was coming through the gate with a big package and a bundle of papers in her arms. Her sunbonnet, tied under her chin, had slipped off her head and was hanging down her back. Her round, plump face was flushed. She looked hot and excited.

As she came onto the porch, she dropped her bundles on the table, picked up the turkey-tail fan Sallie had made from the feathers of last Christmas's turkey, and fanned herself before dropping into a chair.

"Fanny, you look tired. Where have you been, besides to the post office?" said Sallie.

"I went to the store for some thread. No letters today. Where's William?" she asked, expecting to see him coming for the papers.

"He's gone to Murfreesboro."

"Oh! I knew he was planning to go but didn't know he was going today."

"It was sorter sudden to him, too. Mr. Robinson was going. He came by for William to go with him. He knew William was planning to go this week if he could get off. I'm glad they are gone. Both of them have had it on their minds so much lately. I hope they get it settled one way or the other today."

"You mean the Mr. Jerd [Jordan] Robinson who had that awful accident here while I was visiting you last summer?"

"Yes. He wants very much to join the army with William. He's been turned down once on account of his eyes. You see, the right eye has been weakened by the trouble in the left eye."

"Did he lose that eye? But of course, he did. I'll never forget the day of that accident. That was no fun. But maybe a lost eye will do him a good turn now—"

"What'd you say, Fanny?"

"I said I'd never forget the day of Mr. Robinson's accident."

"None of us will, I guess. He asked about you this morning. Seemed quite pleased that you are to be with us."

"I didn't suppose he had remembered me."

Sallie was caught by something in Fanny's voice. "Oh yes, he remembers you. Today isn't the first time he's asked about you."

"You never told me."

"Didn't suppose you'd be interested. Are you?" asked Sallie with a twinkle.

Fanny's face got red, and she flared out at Sallie, "Sallie, of all the suspicious women! You see a love affair in every unmarried man and woman who happen to meet under your eye. Shame on you!"

It was Sallie's turn to blush. Fanny's ability to turn the tide of a joke from herself to the other person was a gift. Sallie tried to hide her embarrassment by talking on. "He lost that eye, you know."

"Yes," Fanny replied. "What a pity! He was so brave about it on that hot, awful day. I felt like screaming as we stood by the gate waiting for William to get the horse hitched to the buggy to take him to the doctor. And he joked—said he was glad that 'jumping-jack of a thorn-bush didn't get both eyes.' I imagine he could be lots of fun." Fanny sighed. Her mind was divided between that day a year before and the present.

Sallie was not conscious of Fanny's divided mind. She kept on talking. "Yes, he is lots of fun. I too felt like screaming. William seemed so slow—never saw it take him so long to hitch up. I was thankful Mr. Robinson kept that side of his face well covered with his handkerchief. It must have looked awful."

"Is his face much disfigured?" asked Fanny.

"No it isn't. And he didn't lose his sense of humor either when he knew that the eye was out. He comes to see us right often. The children are very fond of him. I suppose I shouldn't say it because the South needs all the men she can get, but I hope he isn't accepted today."

"I don't think William will be accepted," said Fanny. "They are not going to put men into the army who have small children if they can help it."

"I know that. But we have Aunt Nancy and Uncle Reuben to help us, you know, so that he is much freer to go than lots of men." Aunt Nancy and Uncle Reuben had their papers stating they were free.

"But Sallie, William isn't strong enough. I don't mean he's real sick—he'll probably outlive all of us. But he is so thin, and he looks frail. It takes an awful strong man to take the beatings they are getting at Camp Trousdale, according to George's letters. I don't think you need to worry. William won't be taken. You ought to be thankful. Oh me, I almost wish George had something the matter with him that would take him out of the army."

"Why Fanny! I'm surprised at you. What ails you today?"

"Come on. Let's go out into the garden."

"All right. But we haven't seen the papers yet."

"I don't want to see them now. Come on."

Fanny looked so troubled that Sallie said again, "Fanny, what's the matter?"

Fanny, no longer able to keep her composure, turned to Sallie and blurted out, "The fighting has begun!"

"No! No. Fanny. Where?"

"Fighting near Harper's Ferry with several casualties. A Federal major killed."

Sallie relaxed, "Hopefully, the Confederates are going to hold their own against the Yankees."

"Yes. But somebody said General Lee is very pessimistic about the war. I believe he would stop the whole business now if he could. But that Jeff Davis!" She muttered the Confederate president's name with burning scorn.

"You don't like Mr. Davis, do you?"

"No, I don't. He's in Washington now. And the report goes that he will hear no conciliatory measures."

"Are any being offered?"

"I didn't hear of any at present. But you do know how opposed Mr. Lincoln was to war at the time of his inauguration. I don't suppose he has changed his mind. He's not that kind of man."

"Well, he's president! Why doesn't he stop the trouble?" Sallie, the gentlest, sweetest woman one could imagine, had her moments of intense thoughts also.

"And let the Union go to smash?" exclaimed Fanny.

"Would it do that?"

"Why, Sallie, it already has—unless the southern states can be made to reunite with the Union."

"This is a terribly big country. I can't see why two governments wouldn't be all right."

"Do you believe in slavery?"

"Now Fanny, you know I don't. But the North and the South have always sorter disliked each other, haven't they?"

"Oh yes. Yes, I guess you are right. And little old South Carolina! Dear little old South Carolina! She can't abide the high-and-mightiness of the North. Bless her! I hope she doesn't have to pay too dearly for her aristocratic high-and-mightiness. The great Thomas Jefferson said that a little revolution is a good thing. But I'm powerful pessimistic about this one."

"That's because George is in it, Fanny. Cheer up. I must take the apples in to Aunt Nancy now. Keep an eye on Ida while I'm gone."

It was late that night when William and Jerd Robinson returned from Murfreesboro. Aunt Nancy and Uncle Reuben had long ago gone to their cabin. The babies were asleep. Sallie and Fanny sat up till eleven o'clock, talking, hoping, and praying about the war. Eleven was a very late hour for them. And then they'd gone to bed, but not to sleep.

Fanny was wide-awake—wondering how Mr. Robinson had been disfigured by that awful accident; wondering if he would come in with William and spend the night; wondering whether he really remembered her; and whether he had succeeded today in getting into the army. She wanted to forget the war. She wanted some other thought big enough to hold her mind away from the war. Maybe she had found it in Mr. Robinson. She let him fill her thoughts completely and excitingly. Suddenly, she checked her thoughts with a mental jerk! She was disgusted with herself. Why should she care whether he went to war or not or whether his face was ruined for looks? *Well, he had a nice face,* she thought. Why shouldn't she care? But she knew that her thoughts went deeper than that. If she hadn't seen him, perhaps ... perhaps Jake's case wouldn't be so hopeless. *Why you silly goose,* she said to herself. *He wouldn't know you from Adam's ox if he were to meet you in a strange place. Go to sleep!*

Sallie was sleepless too—wondering what she would do if William had been accepted for service today; wondering how on earth she could manage with him away; and oh, if he should go and not come back! This horrible, horrible war—and the real horrors had not yet begun. Why couldn't John Bell—Tennessee's John Bell—have been elected instead of Abe Lincoln? Then maybe, maybe he could have settled things without war. If the politicians had to take the first ranks in the battle lines, they'd find some way to eliminate the battles ... of course they would. Their lust for power, tempers, and ambitions would cool off with the thought of bullets whizzing by their heads, arms and legs being shot off, and eyes being shot out. On and on her mind raced, till she heard a sound at the door. *Ah, there they are,* she thought to herself. *Mr. Robinson seems to be coming in ... I wonder if William will ask him to spend the night ... If he does, we will be having company for breakfast in the morning ... I'm sure he is interested in Fanny, but she—oh well, who can tell anything about Fanny? She is absolutely unpredictable ... I want to see her settled ... Someday George will get married—if he comes back—if he comes back ... Then Fanny would be bereft ... She can always live with us, of course ... But that would be terribly unsatisfactory for a woman like Fanny ... I wish William would hurry ... What can he be doing so long? I can't go out in the hall ... and I can't wait much longer to know how it went with him today ... and with Mr. Robinson.*

Fanny too had heard Mr. Robinson come in with William and had not heard him go. She was up early the next morning. She was undecided about her toilet for breakfast. She didn't want to "dress up," but—well, she'd wear the blue basque with the full skirt and ruffles. Blue was her color. Blue made her blue eyes bluer and her smooth olive skin more radiant.

When Fanny went in for breakfast, Sallie and William were already seated at the table. Ida was in her high chair. But no Mr. Robinson. She was surprised and much more disappointed than she would have liked for Sallie and William to know. Sallie was not surprised to see Fanny in her prettiest blue morning costume, but William, being a man, was at least surprised enough to notice and remark, "How blooming we are looking this morning! Expecting company?"

"Can't I put on a clean dress without causing comment?" said Fanny, trying not to blush—and not succeeding very well. "Tell us," she said, "how things went yesterday. I judge from Sallie's looks that you were turned down again. I hope your physical examination didn't reveal anything worse than flat feet and a bald spot on your pate!"

"I was turned down with nothing more definite than this little cough I've had for a year or two. My father had it for thirty years. I guess it's nothing really to keep me out of the army. I think they just don't need any more men now. Got more already, according to reports, than they can arm." And there he stopped. Not a word about Mr. Robinson. Fanny was vexed, but she wouldn't say anything. *Men were such stupid animals.*

Finally Sallie said, "They didn't take Mr. Robinson either—his eyes, you know." And then she further relieved the situation for Fanny by saying, "Fanny, suppose you go for the mail this morning. Time for another letter from George."

Going to the post office was exactly what Fanny wanted to do. The walk would allow her to be alone with her thoughts. Well, hadn't she gone for the mail and anywhere else she wanted to go with complete freedom for more years than she'd be telling now? What ailed her this morning? *Oh dear, life can be very complicated,* she thought.

Fanny needed George. She never felt the lack of anything when George was at home. His assurance, his straightforwardness, the feeling of security when he was around—and now all that was gone. She couldn't go through life depending on George. She must get another outlook on life—George might never come back. *Oh no! No, I won't think that!* she cried. *He'll come back, please God ... he'll come back! But not the same George. He'll be getting married, no doubt, and I'll be stuck with William and Sallie. A good home, yes; but not a pleasant thought. Ah well, every question doesn't have to be settled today!*

Fanny got her bonnet and started for the post office, secretly wondering if Mr. Robinson might not be going to the post office too. He wasn't.

4 · War Is On

"**S**allie!" Fanny called. "Here's William with the mail. He must have some letters."

"Coming," answered Sallie.

William came up the steps looking hot and tired. He dropped the papers, letters, and himself on the top step of the porch and fanned himself with his hat. "Whew!" he said. "Hottest July day in years!"

"The war, no doubt," said Fanny as she picked up the letters. "One from George. Want to hear it?"

"Yes," said William. "Long time since a letter from George. "Where's Sallie? She'll want to hear it. He's not much on writing letters, is he?"

"No. Too busy—or thinks he is," said Fanny.

As Sallie came out the door, William said, "Saw Jerd Robinson at the post office."

"What is he doing? Why hasn't he been to see us?"

"He has sold his farm and bought another over in Wilson County, near LaGuardo."

"Is he going to move?"

"Yes. I asked him to come to see us. He said he was leaving today and wouldn't have time, that he was sorry."

"Why William, how strange! Do you suppose he's mad at us about anything? He used to come real often."

"No, of course not. What could he be mad about? I think he's just blue about his eye. Said he's not exactly presentable company for folks since he got his face so marred. I think the army turning him down again has sorter floored him."

"How silly! I wish he'd come to see us before he leaves. Maybe you didn't urge him enough."

Fanny was absorbed in what they were saying, and disgusted, too, that everybody seemed to have forgotten about the letters. "Well," she said, "do you or don't you want to hear the letters?"

"Of course," said Sallie. "Didn't know you were ready to read."

"All right then. I'll read George's first."

Camp Trousdale
July 1861
My dear Fanny,

Been too busy to write very often. But of course, you haven't been uneasy about us. There's no news to communicate. This business of hard drilling would be wearisome to you. The men respond very well to training, and I hope we are prepared for whatever may come.

We are expecting orders any day now. The excitement hasn't abated any, I'm sorry to say, as of course you know. It begins daily to look more like war. But I'm still hopeful that common sense and humanity may prevail, and the trouble will be smoothed out.

The socks came and are greatly appreciated. Thank you and Sallie for your trouble. We'll keep you posted as to our movements.

With love,
George

"What a short letter," said William. "George's letters are not very satisfactory, are they?"

"Not unless you know him—as I do," said Fanny. "His letters are like his conversation. You read much between the lines if you know him. He says so much with so few words—and with his body. I'll read Jake's if you like. Maybe he uses more words."

Camp Trousdale
July 1861
Dear Miss Fanny,

That box of socks came a couple of days back, with three pairs in there for ole Jake—whoops! Company G can run further, crawl faster, jump higher, load guns, and fix bayonets quicker than any company here, and it's because our Cap'n can do all these things like a circus man.

We don't do much shooting, got no ammunition to waste. But we go through the motions in a long drill three times a week. Every man has to learn how to fling his gun on his shoulder according to order, aim, pull the trigger, with one man actually to shoot, and if he hits the bulls-eye, it's a great day for him! But if he misses, it's tough!

We've got one man that can shoot. I say, he can shoot! He came from somewhere up in the Kentucky Mountains. He's tall, lean, gawky, and looks like a first-class greenhorn. He got his pants, hat, and shirt off a scarecrow on the way over. The pants started out brown or maybe blue. Can't tell the patches from pants, and the leg's ain't mates (no uniforms yet). His hat is full of holes, but that comes in right handy. His hair is long and sticks out through the holes so's the wind can't blow it off. I mean the hat.

The boys have laughed at him and tormented him till he's plum hacked. One day I said, "Boys, you'd better let him alone. The Cap'n might step up any ole time. You know he don't kick up no dust when he travels. If he did come stepping up and hear you heckling Abe, he'd give you more fits than Carter had oats."

Well sir, it wasn't but a few minutes till the horn blowed for us to fall in for target practice. When we got to the field and all set to shoot, the Cap'n called, "Private Abe Smith (that's the mountain feller's name), get ready to fire." When the Cap'n calls like that, the man loads his gun as quick as he can and steps to the right place in front of the target. Abe was ready so quick it sorter astonished us. The Cap'n said, as he always does, "Observe closely how this man handles his gun, and if he makes a good shot you'll know how to profit by his example."

The boys began to sorter cough and sneeze, trying to confuse Abe, when the Cap'n called, "Make ready, aim, fire!" Well sir, that Abe hit the bull's-eye all right, all right! We had expected him to miss. The Cap'n said, "We have a man here who knows how to handle a gun and shoot straight. We will now go through the drill." As he'd shout, "Make ready, aim, fire!" like a gun popping off, we'd hustle to keep up. When he had done this till, we was plumb wore out. The Cap'n called out, "Private Abe Smith will now try the target again. We'll see if he's as good as he seems to be, or if his first shot was an accident. Private Abe Smith, make ready, aim, fire!" Again, he hit the bull's-eye. "No accident," said the Cap'n. "Evidently, he's used to taking squirrels out of treetops. Imitate him, and you'll learn to shoot. Dismissed." Now I think the Cap'n knew all the time that this mountain

COLONEL S. G. SHEPARD

feller could shoot. He was just fixing him with his fellers. He's like that—as you know.

A week ago, one of the men failed to show up when the horn sounded to fall-in for a 10-mile march. Come Saturday next at noon mess, the Cap'n announced, "Private Buck, please report at Captain's Headquarters at 2 o'clock sharp."

At 2 o'clock, instead of being out with the fellers playing mumbly peg or pitching horseshoes, it being Saturday afternoon when we have a little time to play, I was hanging around the Cap'n's quarters with both ears hanging out to see what was going to happen.

When Buck reported looking like he'd seen a ghost or something, the Cap'n said, "Private Buck, you will this afternoon take the 10-mile march you missed last Wednesday." Buck began to stammer and try to make an excuse. The Cap'n didn't hear him to all appearances. He went right on "Privates Sullivan, Magruder, Jones, and Turner will time you. See that you make the march in regulation time. Take your gun, knapsack, and blanket as on a regular march. Your route will be from the big cedar at the edge of camp to the milepost down the road a mile away. Make the roundtrip five times. You are fortunate not to be in the guardhouse. Hereafter, see that you report for every call of the bugle. We are learning a serious business. Every man must obey promptly and with all his might. Be ready to march in 10 minutes. Dismissed."

The Cap'n may not believe there'll be any war, but if there is, he'll be ready— if anybody is. And from all the hullabalooing and yelling, "On to Richmond!" since Jeff Davis has been there, it looks pretty serious. We may be gone from here any day. I hope we go further south, but I wouldn't be surprised if we have to go east.

I wish we were going back home. I've had a good time here. I just want to go home, help Pa with the crops, see Ma, and be free! But that's none of ole Jake's business right now, so I'll say goodbye before I get to weeping and moaning.

As ever,
Jake

"Jake writes a good letter," said Sallie. "I like his letters."

"A lot of talk," said Fanny.

"Why Fanny, I don't think you are fair to Jake."

Handing the papers to Sallie, Fanny said, "Here, you read the papers. I'm going to the garden to see what the dahlias and chrysanthemums are doing." She set her mind to think of something other than the war and George's doing. Her thoughts went to Mr. Robinson. *So that's the trouble,* she said to herself, as she poked around in her flowerbeds. *Or is it he just doesn't want to see me? Maybe he has a girl to take to the new home he has just bought. Well! What's that to me! I'm sure I don't care.* But she did care. She wanted dreadfully to see him, to see if his eye was badly damaged for looks. And ... she just wanted to see him. She had to admit it. But he was proving a counterirritant to her worry about George. It was evident that George would be going soon to join the army, ready for action. She'd go dippy if she thought very much of that. She was glad of a diversion in Mr. Robinson, she told herself. However, it wasn't very pleasant to be shunned by one of the opposite sex. It was a new experience for her. She couldn't quite decide whether she was provoked over it or amused. *Never mind,* she concluded, *someday I'll see him.*

As Fanny worked among her flowers, debudding the chrysanthemums, pulling up a late weed or sprig of grass, trying not to think of George going to the front, she heard someone walking toward her. She looked up to see Sallie coming with a newspaper in her hand, looking terribly excited. She ran to her, calling, "What is it, Sallie?"

"See for yourself. I don't really know," said Sallie, handing the paper to her.

Fanny read, "General Joseph E. Johnston is calling for more troops. The Federals are gathering in great numbers in Washington, getting ready for a battle at Manassas Junction, it is believed. Colonel Hatton has been ordered to take his regiment to Virginia as soon as possible. He will leave with his regiment for the front July the eighteenth." She stopped reading and looked at Sallie with white face and deeply troubled eyes. "Why, that's today!"

"Yes, that's today," said Sallie.

"Sallie, George knew it when he wrote his last letter. He could have told us."

"Yes, but he didn't. He was just preparing us. He knew we'd see it in the papers today. Fanny ... don't, Fanny ... don't take it so hard. George will be all right."

"I guess I hoped so hard there wouldn't be any real battles, I believed there wouldn't be," she sobbed.

Sallie walked around from one flowerbed to another, touching this plant and that one, not really seeing any. She came back to Fanny.

"Sallie," said Fanny.

"Yes, Fanny?"

"I think I'll see if I can get a place to teach in the school here this winter. I'll have to be busy, terribly busy. You have your babies and William. George is all I've got."

"Yes, I think that's a good idea. Come on in now and bathe your face. Dinner is about ready. You'll feel better when you've had something to eat. Men have always gone to war," she said, as they walked toward the house, "and strange to say, comparatively few of them get killed. George is too smart and too resourceful to get caught. And always—always, Fanny—there is God, you know."

The newspapers, now more than ever before, became a vital part of Fanny's life. She read about the Federals getting whipped at Manassas and could see George in the thickest of the fight. She and Sally discussed the names of these battles. The battle at Manassas was also called the Battle of Bull Run. The two of them figured out that the Confederates named battles after towns or land areas; the Union named them after water areas. For example, Manassas was the land area and Bull Run was the stream there. After several weeks, she got letters from both George and Jake. George's was characteristically short and to the point. They were "well and happy." Jake's was full of the farce of the Cheat Mountain engagement, which took place in West Virginia in September 1861:

Dear Fanny,

Cheat, huh! That's the right word. We were cheated out of every decent thing a body was ever used to having. And for what? Nothing! We tramped through mud and rain, days on days, with nothing much to eat, and what did we do? Nothing! Only one little brush. The Seventh captured a couple of Yanks and a gun or two, and that was all. Why? Well, some of the Tennesseans said it was all the fault of the Virginians. They just didn't have the pluck to jump into the Yanks. Sent out scouting parties and all such, got ready to attack, and the feller

*who was to lead off with his men never got started. We waited all day,
standing in mud up to our shoe-tops, and never a gun. I'm of the
opinion the Tennesseans ain't loving the Virginians any too much right
now. No fun standing in the rain all day waiting for some feller to make
up his mind. Oh well, I guess it ain't nobody's fault exactly.*

*Yes, Miss Fanny, I'm as sick of this war as you ever said I'd be.
But that's neither here nor there. Ole Jake's in it, and he'll stick all
right, all right. The Cap'n will see to that.*

Jake

The winter dragged by with Fanny teaching and trying with all her
might to keep her thoughts away from the war as much as possible. Yet
she read every line in every paper she could lay her hands on. She knew
that General Joe Johnston was holding the Federals in check around
Manassas Junction with his "Quaker guns." That amused her and made
her feel better. She read how recruits for the Unionists were pouring into
Washington daily. One story had it that a boy threw a stone on
Pennsylvania Avenue and hit six brigadier generals! She had a good
laugh over that, refusing to see what it might mean.

George and Jake spent the winter in the Shenandoah Valley.
Sometime in February, Shepard and then Captain John A. Fite decided to
take a vacation—or Fite decided Shepard and he should do such. The
details of this vacation can be found in Appendix C. Fite started out as
head of Company B. (The only clue as to the exact date of this vacation
is when he mentions hearing the inaugural address of Jefferson Davis.
Davis gave his address to the provisional Confederate States of America
(C.S.A.) on February 18, 1862, and on February 22, he gave his address
to the official C.S.A. Fite heard it on the twenty-second. The Colonel's
official records do not reflect any absence.)

General William Loring hadn't liked it in the mountains. After Cheat
Mountain, the Seventh was put in the divisional command of General
William Loring under the department command of General T. J.
"Stonewall" Jackson.

COLONEL S. G. SHEPARD

George had been very ill on Christmas day in 1861 at Strasburg.[1] The records do not specify the illness. See Figure 4-1. This she learned long after he was well.

Spring was here now. The war news got more terrifying every day. What Fanny didn't know was that George was commander of the Seventh Tennessee Regiment, not just Company G, and had started signing as such in April.[2] See Figure 4-2. Colonel Hatton had been put in command of the First, Seventh, and Fourteenth Infantry Regiments, which were dubbed the Tennessee Brigade. Both were to be promoted because of such. George was promoted to Major (became official in July), Hatton to Brigadier General.

It was predicted there would be a battle near Richmond, and Fanny wanted to go there. George was sure to be in it. If anything happened to George, she wanted to be near him. But going wasn't possible. She'd have to stick it out at Sallie's. After all, George was Sallie's brother too. She must be more help to Sallie. Sallie had gone bad with the winter. She wasn't looking well.

School would soon be out; then she'd do more for Sallie's babies and make a bigger garden. She'd dig and plant and sow.

Then came the last day in May and the Battle of Seven Pines. Fanny read every paper she could buy, borrow, or beg. Papers said the Tennessee Brigade's first major battle was a disaster. According to J. H. Moore in the *Military Annals of Tennessee,* the battle lasted no more than thirty minutes, yet in that short time, Adjutant G. A. Howard, eight out of the ten company commanders, and half of the privates were either killed or wounded. Brigade commander Brigadier-General Robert Hatton was killed.[3]

A few days later, the papers said General Robert E. Lee was put in command of the Army of Northern Virginia after the Seven Pines disaster. According to the National Park Service, thirteen thousand were

[1] *Old Military and Civil Service Records* (Washington, D.C.).

[2] *Old Military and Civil Service Records* (Washington, D.C.).

[3] John Berrien Lindsley, *Military Annals of Tennessee,* vol. 1, (Nashville: J. M. Lindsley & Co., 1886), 231.

killed or wounded that day, and eight thousand of them were Confederates.[4] Although not a major battle, it was a particular disaster for the Tennessee Brigade. Reorganization included Brigadier-General James Jay Archer taking over command of the former Tennessee Brigade under the division command of General Ambrose Powell (A. P.) Hill. (The Seventh was under the commands of A. P. Hill and J. J. Archer for most of the remainder of the war.)

She was frantic. She had no idea how George was. Shepard's pension papers[5] do mention he was "wounded slightly at Seven Pines" but never saw a surgeon, never was incapacitated, and never was admitted to a hospital.

At last, letters from George and Jake came. George's was short and to the point:

> *Dear Fanny,*
> *We succeeded in keeping the Federals out of Richmond. The Tennesseans did their full share of the fighting. Our Bob Hatton was killed—a great loss. No further trouble anticipated from the Federals soon. General Lee has full charge now. General Johnston was wounded. We are well.*
> *Love to all,*
> *George*

> *Near Richmond*
> *June 1862*
> *Dear Miss Fanny,*
> *Maybe some day, I'll get used to killing and being killed, but I doubt it.*
> *You'll know that the Battle of Seven Pines has been fought. That's what I'm crazy about. Bill Smith dead, Jake Willis dead, Joe Hooker dead, our commander Bob Hatton dead, half our regiment dead. When*

---

[4] National Park Service, Department of Interior, Washington, D.C.

[5] Military Records, Civil War (1861-1865), S. G. Shepard, Pension No. 14493, Tennessee State Archives, (Nashville, TN).

COLONEL S. G. SHEPARD

*I think of the boys I knowed alive and well a few days ago now dead
and out in that awful mud on the battlefield, I lose my mind.*

*That awful night after the fighting stopped—because we couldn't
see to shoot and would as likely kill a gray as a blue—we were ordered
to stop, sleep on our guns, and be ready to up and at 'em as soon as we
could see. Sleep? Sleep on your arms in this vile Chickahominy River
mud! But I didn't mind the mud. If I could have buried my head in mud
deep enough to shut out the cries and moans of dying men! If they
would only stop crying for water, or if we could go and give to 'em.*

*Your brother was right there with us, fighting side by side with his
men. I'd seen him grab General Hatton's body and hold him on his
horse when Hatton rode too close to the front and got shot, and then
rush him to the rear and come back to his men before I could load and
shoot three times. The Yankees were not far away.*

*After the battle, your brother was giving water to a dying soldier
who had cried out for water but then said giving him water was no use
because he was gonna be dead in a few minutes anyway. Then he asked
your brother to help him die by praying. Your brother did just that. I
looked at the soldier's uniform. It was blue. I told your brother, "Let's
get out of here."*

Goodbye, Miss Fanny,
Jake

Fanny had a hard time finishing Jake's letter. She had to clear her
throat and swallow several times before she reached the end. Sallie was
frankly wiping her eyes. Nobody spoke for several minutes after the
letter was finished. Then Fanny blurted out, "George is an idiot!"

"What did you expect him to do?"

"Exactly!" said Fanny. "I expect him to do just that, till a bullet finds
him—or worse. Here's another letter from Jake," she said, as she
straightened her face and composed herself.

"Another?" said Sallie. "Hurry. Maybe something has happened to
George."

"No. The one I've just read was a long time coming. This one was
written much later."

1 July 1862
Dear Miss Fanny,
  "Ole Mac" is still hanging around. We call the Union boys Macs, Feds, Federals, Yankees, and sometimes Blues. They call us Grays, Rebs, and Johnny Rebs. But it's my private opinion that that little *"coot"* is just natcherly skeered of us Johnny Rebs. Huh! I hope so.
  Since General Lee has taken over, things are beginning to sorter hum. He's working us mighty nigh to death—that is, all except them Virginians. They just natcherly don't like to dig ditches and build breastworks. Lots of them have got their black men along to curry their horses and black their shoes and bring their breakfasts to them. Huh! One day I said to the Cap'n, "These lazy Virginians ..." He looked me in the eye till I was sorter twisting up and down my backbone, and then he said, "Jake, you'd improve in speech and manners if you'd imitate some of these Virginians a little." Since then, I keep my ole thinker ticking only when he ain't around.
  After supper, "Mars Robert," as the fellers are beginning to call General Lee, lets up on us, and the boys spend the evenings cussing and drinking and fighting musketeers and putting on speech, if the feller who gets nominated can do it. Usually he can't, and the fellers heckle him something awful if he's a private.
  Well sir, that night, right after Tommy and his ole banjo and some of the boys rended, and I do mean rended, "The Girl I Left Behind Me," Pete Sullivan piped up with, "I nominate Major S. G. Shepard as speaker of the evening with 'The Charm and Beauty of Virginia Mud' as his subject."
  Your brother gave a great, funny speech and concluded it with *"Too much dust and we want mud; too much mud and we want rocks; too many rocks and we want soil. It's always best to make the best of whatever we have. It's best to try not to be a fool too often by wanting what is not."* And with that, he grinned at the fellers and stepped off the box. And did the fellers whoop and clap!
  As ever,
  Jake

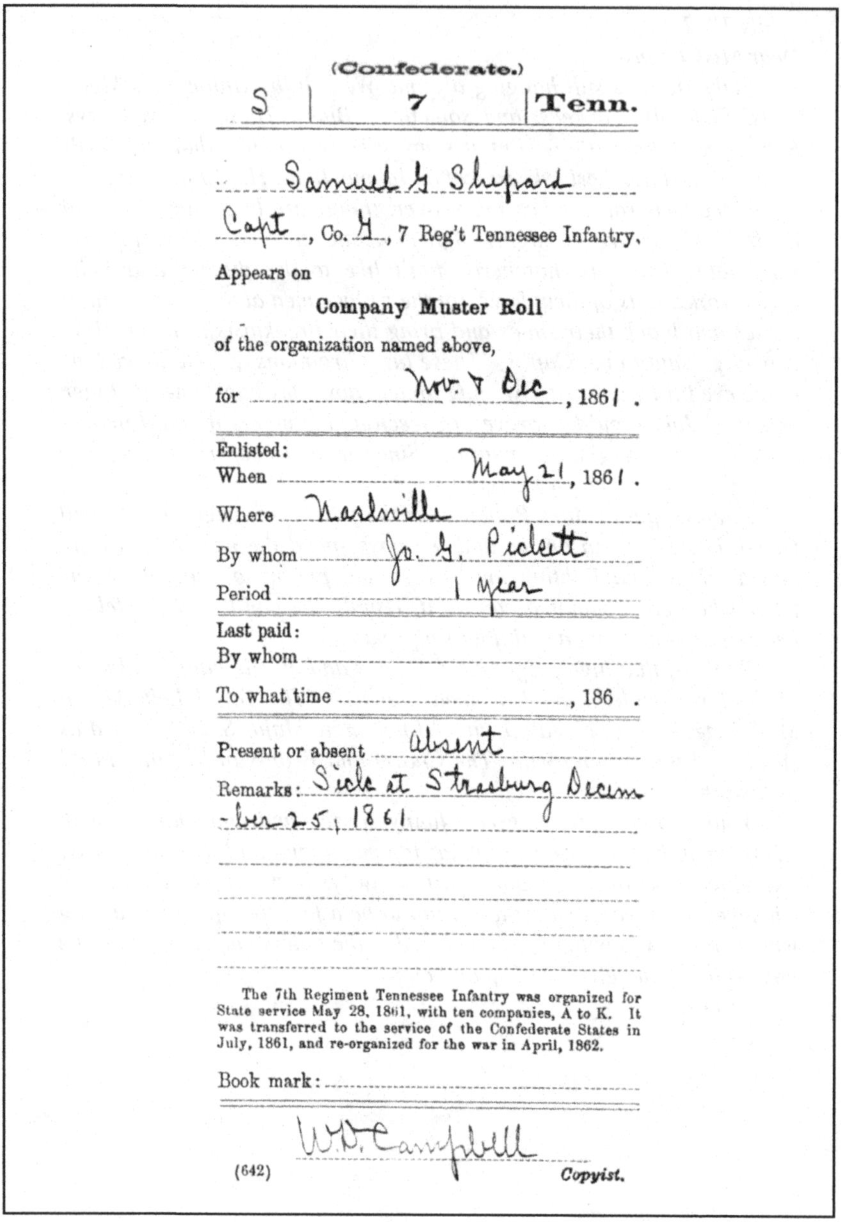

COLONEL S. G. SHEPARD

(Confederate.)

S | 7 | Tenn.

Samuel G Shepard

Capt, Co. H, 7 Reg't Tennessee Infantry,

Appears on

Company Muster Roll

of the organization named above,

for _____ Nov. & Dec _____, 1861 .

Enlisted:
When _____ May 21, 1861 .
Where _____ Nashville
By whom _____ Jo. G. Pickett
Period _____ 1 year

Last paid:
By whom _____

To what time _____, 186 .

Present or absent _____ Absent
Remarks: Sick at Strasburg December 25, 1861

The 7th Regiment Tennessee Infantry was organized for State service May 28, 1861, with ten companies, A to K. It was transferred to the service of the Confederate States in July, 1861, and re-organized for the war in April, 1862.

Book mark: _____

(642) W.D. Campbell *Copyist.*

Figure 4-1. Sick at Strasburg.

· 44 ·

Figure 4-2. Promoted to major and signs as commanding regiment.

5 ▪ George Prays All Night

George didn't write until late September. He had been busy. After the May Battle of Seven Pines, according to the *Military Annals of Tennessee*, there was the Seven Days Around Richmond battle that took place 26 June to 2 July 1862. For the Seventh Tennessee Regiment, the Seven Days battle consisted of the battles of Mechanicsville, Gaines Mill, Frayser's Farm, and Malvern Hill. After this battle, the Thirteenth Alabama Regiment and the Fifth Alabama Battalion joined the Tennessee Brigade under the banner of Archer's Light Brigade. These five units remained together for the remainder of the war.[1]

The battles of Cedar Mountain, Manassas Junction, and the Second Battle of Manassas (Bull Run) occurred in August 1862. The Battle of Antietam, known to the South as the Battle of Sharpsburg, Maryland, followed Harpers Ferry by a day or two in September 1862.

The Second Battle of Manassas was the seventh costliest battle, in terms of casualties, of the Civil War. According to the National Park Service,[2] the Second Battle of Manassas, better known as Bull Run, had casualties, consisting of those killed, wounded, missing, or captured, of a little more than twenty-two thousand of which eighty-three hundred were Confederates. The Battle of Antietam was the fifth costliest and the costliest one-day battle of the war. The National Park Service gave casualty figures, consisting of killed, wounded, and captured for

---

[1] John Berrien Lindsley, *The Military Annals of Tennessee,* vol. 1, (Nashville: J. M. Lindsley & Co., 1886), 229.

[2] National Park Service, Department of Interior, Washington, D.C.

Antietam of almost twenty-three thousand of which a little more than ten thousand were Confederates.

The papers were filled with the casualty information of the battles, but what was capturing the headlines most was the Hill-Longstreet feud occurring after the Seven Days Around Richmond battle. The Longstreet-Hill feud originated from a story supplied to the *Richmond Examiner* by a former member of Hill's infantry. The story complimented Hill's corps in reference to one of the Seven Days Around Richmond battles, and it also excluded any role Longstreet and other commanders might have played. The feud caused Hill, who was under the command of Longstreet, to be relieved of command by Longstreet. The quarrel then accelerated to Hill challenging Longstreet to a duel. Lee stepped in and stopped it all before the duel. Lee restored Hill to commander of his division and transferred him to T. J. "Stonewall" Jackson's wing of the army. Hill's division was under Stonewall Jackson until Jackson's death, at which time a Third Army Corps under the Army of Northern Virginia was established, and A. P. Hill became its commander.

Fanny was frantic. She read everything and to not hear from George or Jake was upsetting to say the least. The first word from either came late in September.

September 1862
Dear Fanny,

> *Nothing much to write that would be pleasant to tell. You know that if anything happens to Jake or me, you'll be notified, so no need for you to worry or be uneasy. We've been very fortunate not to have had any trouble of note.*

> *The Battle of Sharpsburg was bad; not as terrible, however, as the Seven Days Around Richmond. In all the engagements, the Tennesseans have borne themselves worthily. General Lee has been magnificent. General A. P. Hill has always been a man ready to move forward with no explained or unexplained delays.*

Fanny read much between the lines right there. She recalled what she had read in a Richmond paper about A. P. Hill with his "Light Division" bearing the brunt of the first two days in the Seven Days Around Richmond, and how General James Longstreet had been offended at

COLONEL S. G. SHEPARD

Hill's popularity with the Richmond papers and gotten Hill in bad with the higher-ups. Yes, you could read things between the lines in George's letters.

Jake was frank to say Longstreet was "stuck" on himself, and Lee was "partial to him." Oh well, jealousy in the army was no better looking than in private life.

George's letter continued:

> If General George McClellan had half the temerity and sound judgment that General Lee has, the war might have ended with the Sharpsburg campaign. But our General Lee is more than a match for the Federal general in bravery and strategy.
>
> Some amusing stories about General Lee have been going the rounds. All of us know how he hates stragglers. Soon after the Battle of Sharpsburg, he was riding through a woods and came upon a man detached from his company, sitting on the ground. Evidently, he didn't see that the man was removing the shoes from a dead Federal's feet. He accosted the man with, "What are you doing out here? Why aren't you with your company?"
>
> "Oh yes?" said the man, without looking up. "You were hid in a hole all day yesterday, while I fought barefooted. So now, when the danger's over, you come out of your hole, do you? I'm just trying to get myself a pair of shoes. I'll be back with my men in a few minutes. You go on and tend to your own business."
>
> The general rode away laughing. One of his fellow soldiers went to the man. "Do you know to whom you were speaking?" he asked.
>
> "No, but some little old lieutenant. They're always sticking their noses into other folks' business."
>
> "That was General Robert E. Lee," said the man.
>
> "Hooowhat!" said the poor fellow. "On my scissors, I'm a goner now!" And off he ran through the woods.
>
> Don't worry about us. Remember God is everywhere. I have no fears for my safety. Indeed, I have more for yours than mine since the war is almost sure to come to Tennessee. But again I say, remember God is able to do all things.
>
> George

Jake's letter was fuller:

Dear Fanny,
  We are having a little rest after months of awfulness.
*Just imagine if you can a sort of valley running up to a fort, and
that is Harper's Ferry. Well, in this valley, a part of General A. P.
Hill's division was trying to get a night's rest against no telling what
awfulness comes tomorrow.*
  *Between that fort and us was a thing called an abatis. The orders
were that we (Hill's men) were to start the ball rolling in the morning,
before it was hardly light enough to see, to take that fort, because ole
"Mac" was hanging round somewhere close by, and if we didn't take it
early, we'd soon be marching to the tune of "Yankee Doodle" or
getting ready to push up daisies come next spring.*
  *So there we were. And looking at them pine trees on the ground
with them sharpened tops all sticking towards us and guns aplenty
amongst them just didn't look good, as a body could see with one eye
and half a ounce of sense.*
  *Well sir, we were ordered to sleep on our guns, and there we were
with our blankets sorter wrapped around us to—well, not to sleep for
ole Jake. And the Major didn't seem to be drowsy with sleep either.*
  *Your brother slipped away into the pines, and I could see him on
his knees. And, Miss Fanny, he spent the whole enduring night that
way, mostly praying. I wasn't awake all that time—no, sir—but enough
to know that he was doing a powerful lot of praying. And in spite of
wanting him to get some rest, that praying made me feel a whole lot
better.*
  *I'm here to tell you nobody had to have a bucket of cold water
dashed in his face to get him awake next morning. We looked like an
army of ghosts slipping and sliding around swallering a few bites of
bread and gulping a tin cup of cold coffee and getting into position to
make the grand attack. Scared stiff, I was, but getting things done on
the dot. And then the Rebel yell and on! It was like judgment day had
done set in.*
  *And now you won't hardly believe this, but before we got going,
there was a white flag a fluttering from the ramparts of that fort! Yes
sir, done scared plumb to death was them Yanks and surrendering!
Whoops! All over and hardly a man killed! Tell me praying don't do no
good!*

When I got a chance and the Major looked like he was in a frame of mind so I'd dare do it, I asked him what he was praying so much about last night. He flashed his eyes at me, then looked way off like he was seeing over the edge of the world. When he spoke, it was a faraway speech like he was talking to somebody I couldn't see. "I reckon," he said, "I was trying to make a bargain with God. I told Him if He'd get me through that battle next morning, I'd preach ... I wonder ..." I felt kinder creepy. I didn't ask any more questions. I crept off out of sight quick as I could. He didn't see me go. He was still looking over the edge of the world.

But I mustn't stop till I tell you about ole Stonewall. He came loping down the line of prisoners saluting them and they saluting back, looking like he hadn't had a haircut or a new coat since Heck was a pup. The Yankee officer was all decked out, but he didn't look grand like ole Stonewall. One of the Yanks said to his buddy, "He ain't much to look at," speaking of Stonewall, "but if we'd a had him, we wouldn't a got caught in this trap."

Purty soon ole Stonewall was on his way to Sharpsburg with all our men except the two or three brigades he left with General Hill to round things up, get the prisoners sent to the right place, and tend to taking over the guns and things. We hadn't no more than got rested with a night's sleep till here comes a courier lickety-split with a message from General Lee to Hill, telling him to hurry on to Sharpsburg with his men because McClellan was giving him a terrible battle. Of course, Stonewall and all the rest couldn't whip McClellan without us Tennesseans, so off we went down that 17-mile road like the dogs was after us.

Purty soon, I noticed Pete Sullivan limping powerful bad. The Major noticed it too. He rode up by Pete and was down off his horse in a second. He put Pete on his horse. Pete said Abe Smith's foot was nearly shot off and was lamer than him. I was ordered to get Abe. Your brother scribbled a note and gave it to Pete and told him to show it to any officer. The note read: "Pete Sullivan and Abe Smith are riding by order of Major S. G. Shepard.

Pete showed me that note when we got to a stopping place two or three days later. "Pete Sullivan and Abe Smith are riding by order of Major S. G. Shepard." Pete is so proud of that note, I think he'll have it framed and hung on the wall of his house if he ever has a wall in a house.

Now Miss Fanny, maybe you won't think that's so wonderful that your brother walked eight or ten miles so that Pete and Abe could ride. But let me tell you, you'd a had your eyes opened if you'd a been there and seen some of the officers prodding their men with their swords if a man lagged a little. Yes, sir, I saw one poor fellow standing behind a tree sorter leaning up against it just before we got to Sharpsburg. He looked as tired and scared as I felt. His officer rode up by him and whacked him across the back with his sword. And the sword broke! Glory be, if only it had been on that officer's head! Huh!

General Lee sure did need us by the time we got there. And did we stop to cool off a little and rest our poor feet and get us some water? No sir! We were hurled right into the tough spot and fought like killing snakes before we licked them Yanks. But we licked them all right, all right. But it's no fun licking them, and it don't do no good.

Jake

"Fanny, are you keeping Jake's letters?" Sallie asked.

"You'd better believe I am. They are about George, aren't they?" Fanny replied without hesitation.

"Well, I thought you'd keep them. They are a sort of a diary about George and the only one we'll ever see. Jake certainly loves our brother."

"Yes, madam, he does. That's a pretty strong pull for Jake with me but hardly enough to get married on I guess, supposing Jake will be telling the same old tale when he comes home—if he comes home."

"No, that ain't enough, Fanny. Don't let us tease you into thinking so. Oh well, Jake isn't here—nor George. I wonder how soon before that day will come."

"A long, long time, I'm afraid."

"What do you think of that praying all night and promising the Lord to preach?"

"Mother always believed George would be a preacher someday. Jake's letter gives me a very comfortable feeling about George. If Jake is right and George is to preach, then he'll come home."

6 · Confederates Holding Their Own

The year was 1862, the month December. The day was cold. Sallie was deeply troubled and worried about many things. They had not heard from George since the Battle of Fredericksburg (December 13, 1862), which was not so long ago but seemed ages. Christmas would soon be here, and she had made no preparation for it. She must do something for Ida and Frank, but what? Santa Claus would have to come.

The country was full of soldiers. They had upset all the plans and daily routine of living. She and William had had to hide their meat, flour, sugar, meal, and other foods in out-of-the-way places. William had even sacked some hams and shoulders in heavy oilcloth sacks and hung them in trees deep in the thicket near the house. They had hung the sausage and bacon, most of it, from the rafters in the loft. The rest they left in the smokehouse for daily use and for soldiers who came in threes and fours looking for food.

There were no windows in the loft. A trapdoor cut in the ceiling in Sallie's and William's room was the only entrance. No ladder was kept in the house because it might suggest the trapdoor. So the only way to get up into the loft was by placing a chair on William's reading table, mounting it, and going up the wall. A sort of bed was laid up there. Recently, a wounded soldier had spent three days and nights in Sallie's and William's loft. Life had grown hard and troublesome for Sallie.

This morning, she wanted to talk to Fanny about George, about Christmas, about many things. Neither of the sisters had much time for sitting and just talking. Now she thought she'd take her knitting or the buttonholes that had long been waiting for her busy fingers, go in, sit down by Fanny's fire, and talk and work, or let Fanny talk if she would.

On entering her room, she found Fanny bundling up and bustling around, getting ready to go out. She looked at Fanny in surprise. Fanny was always surprising Sallie, always saying and doing the unpredictable, venturesome thing. Sallie sighed with long-suffering patience and resignation, which grew to deep concern before she asked, "Fanny, where are you going? You shouldn't be going out! It isn't safe."

Fanny, busy tying a scarf around her head, said with a broad smile, "Over to see the Whittakers. Jim came home night before last, you know."

"No, I didn't know. Why did he come home?"

"I thought you heard Mr. Whittaker tell me last night. He's been wounded—not much, Mr. Whittaker says, but he was sent home to recuperate."

Another shock for Sallie. She had known Jim Whittaker since he was a boy. She knew that he had joined the army. She knew he went with George to Camp Trousdale—a thousand years ago, it seemed. So many things had happened during these awful months—many things had grown dim and misty in her mind.

"Of course, Fanny," she said, "you have to go. But do be careful, my dear. What would you do if you should meet some Yankees?"

"I'd put on my best smile," said Fanny, bowing and smirking, "and say 'howdy do' to them."

Sallie was almost disgusted with her sister, and looked it. After a pause that lasted long enough to turn Fanny's usually pink cheeks even pinker, she said, "It's a good thing I don't believe you'd do that—smile, I mean. But I do think you are very foolish. Do be careful and hurry back. I'll be terribly uneasy till you get back inside the house."

Sallie *was* uneasy. She watched the road every minute while Fanny was out. The Federals had not been to her house yet to compel them to swear allegiance to the Union, but she'd heard of their being in other homes in the neighborhood. If they should come, she'd need and want Fanny very much. Fanny had joked about it. "Yes," she had said, "I'm afraid I could say a few cuss words if they made me mad enough."

Fanny was not gone long. When Sallie saw her at the gate, she hurried to the door, opened it, and all but pulled Fanny inside. She closed the door quickly, as though Fanny was being pursued by the Yankees, demanding of her to swear allegiance to the Union or be fined or go to jail for treason.

Fanny hurried to get out of her wraps. Sallie came toward the fire, asking many questions. Fanny was excited. "Stand aside, madam," she said. "I saw nary a Yank or Reb, but I've got something." She held two letters up and waved them at Sallie. Sallie looked frightened. She gasped, "Fanny, you haven't been to the post office, have you? What will you do next?" She sank into a chair. "Never mind about the letters; tell me about the Whittakers. How's Jim? Did he know anything about George?"

"Stop stewing while I read you with letters from," she stopped to see Sallie's face work, "Jake and George!" she finished smugly.

Sallie was almost weeping, "Fanny! What? Where?"

"Now listen." And she read from George's letter:

Dear Fanny,

Another terrible battle has been fought and won. At least we've again kept the Federals out of Richmond. According to reports, Richmond is rejoicing. I do not see that a great deal has been gained because it will all have to be done again in the spring. General Ambrose Burnside has dug in across the Rappahannock, and General Lee is trying to settle here for the winter—a dreary prospect.

Many men were killed in this terrible battle but fewer were Confederates compared with the Federal losses. Our generals planned and set a trap for Burnside, and he shoved his men into it till it was a sight I hope never to see again.

I hope this war is not going to leave bitterness and hatred between the North and the South. It has not so far made hatred between the soldiers now engaged in it. At least no hatred is apparent, and I do not believe any exists.

The battle was hardly over and the dead buried out of sight when our men were singing songs with Burnside's men across the river. Men on both sides have built rafts, and, with white flags flying, they row across, our men carrying tobacco to exchange for coffee, sugar, and salt. And the Federals bringing more sugar and coffee to exchange for more tobacco—Kentucky tobacco.

The Federals are well-clothed and well-fed while our poor men are poorly clad and have too little to eat. I hope the South is going to see to it that more food and clothing are sent soon.

Jake and I are all right. Your box came, and we do appreciate it. Also, we are fairly well fixed for sleeping quarters. But Jake will want to tell you about our house. I see he's writing now.

As I've said to you before, do not worry about Jake and me. If we are among the casualties, you'll be notified quickly. I think Jake wouldn't mind being shot up some, if it would get him a furlough home, as it's getting for Jim Whittaker, by whom we are sending our letters.

Take care of yourselves, and remember God is still ruler of the Heavens and Earth, even if some folks do say He's on a vacation at present.

George

Sallie seemed in a sort of a daze. Fanny opened Jake's letter and read:

Dear Miss Fanny,
I'm going to skip all the awfulness and tell you about our mansion. You'd call it a hut maybe, but that would be an insult, pure and simple.

When this last slaughter, the Battle of Fredericksburg, Virginia, this month was over, and we'd cooled off—almost as cold as on the night of the twelfth when one poor fellow froze to death—maybe he was scared to death. I most was. The battle was to be the next day.

Well anyhow, I was like to freeze. I hustled out and found some logs, a few, and a lot of poles and a few planks, and a pile of rocks; and believe it or not, the major and I erected—yes sir, erected—us a house. No floor but the ground, but we got us up four walls almost as high as our heads at the eaves and a foot higher than our heads in the middle, and a sort of roof, and we made us a bed!

The only fault I had to find with that bed was not having nothing between me and them planks but a few clothes. So I got sacks and filled them with shucks and clover hay, not much.

I dream about Tennessee most every night now. And I wouldn't be a-tall surprised if I wouldn't light out from here and turned up in ole Tenny, if it wasn't for your brother. Lots of fellows are lighting out. But it's awful bad if they get caught and brought back. Some have been. And that's another time when ole Jake had to go off behind a tree so as he could cry all by hisself.

Your brother was on the jury to convict one poor fellow. Did he convict him? No sir! No, sir, he didn't do nothing but plead that poor fellow's case till he won. He did some powerful good pleading. Well I just can't go back on a guy like that. Now, I ask you, could I?

Now hold your breath for the super thing we did in erecting our mansion—a chimney! Yes sir, a chimney with a fireplace where we can have us a little fire and cook our bacon and boil us an egg if we ever have an egg. We got us a barrel and put it on top the fireplace so as to draw up and keep the smoke from coming out the wrong end. One night though when it was sorter drizzling, mostly snow, the smoke got to coming out the wrong end anyhow. We tried to look up the chimney but couldn't see nothing. We went outside and was we surprised! Some feller had throwed a wet blanket over the top a our chimney, trying to dry the blanket I guess. Well sir, I grabbed that blanket off our chimney and run to the next hut that had a chimney to give that blanket some more drying. Purty soon the fellers all around was getting a chance to do some drying of that blanket. The whooping and running and yelling helped to warm the fellers up, whether it helped that blanket any or not. The fellers are wonderful—they have to be.

But I'm not going to forget that box you sent. Well, we kissed the last slice of that ham goodbye two days ago. I almost cried. And what do you reckon the Major, heartless wretch, did? He laughed at me! Yes sir, I got plumb mad, and he laughed some more. Oh well, I'd act the fool any ole day to make him laugh. There ain't much to laugh about around here. I wish this war would hurry up and stop. I don't see as we are getting anywhere. But when I begin that sort of stuff, I know it's time for ole Jake to shut his gabber and put up the old goose quill.

As ever,
Jake

When Fanny had finished the letters, she held them tightly in her hands a few minutes, gazing intently out the window. Then she snapped at Sallie, "Well?" Sallie did not respond, and again silence reigned. But not for long could Fanny hold her hands gazing out a window. Fanny was a woman of opinions and actions. Things happened around Fanny. Now she bounced out of her chair and seemed to be looking for something, her knitting maybe. She was happy, very happy to know that George and Jake were still alive and not wounded. But the situation did not look good to her. Two years almost of war and nothing gained by the Confederates, and no giving in on their part. Would they hold out till the last man was killed? What utter stupidity, and yes—crime!

She found her knitting, and her needles began to click viciously. Sallie looked at her with bad, sad eyes, and said, "What do you think is going to happen, Fanny?"

"Maybe General Lee has gumption enough to see it's no use and will stop the war."

"But Fanny, he couldn't stop the war."

"He could do a powerful lot towards stopping it," Fanny said. "There was a piece in the paper yesterday about his freeing his slaves. I hope that means he thinks it's time to give in."

"You mean let Lincoln emancipate the Negroes?"

"Yes. You don't think Lincoln is going to stop short of that, do you?"

Sallie stiffened up. "Well, I'm not so sure of that. The South is not losing so far. There aren't any better fighters or braver men in the whole world than our Southern men."

"For pity's sake!" shouted Fanny. "Who said there are? I'm saying that men can't fight on empty stomachs and naked bodies!"

7 · Martha Jane Gets a Letter

By December 1862, war had entered every home in middle Tennessee. The major's home in Wilson County was no exception. But to see Martha Jane's face as she stood before the mirror on this brilliant December morning combing her pulled-molasses-candy-colored hair, piling it high on her lovely head, one could easily believe that the war had not touched even the hem of her outer garments. She was studying her face appraisingly, her hair, her eyes, her mouth. She felt herself to be growing up—already grown—a new feeling for her and a very pleasant one. She looked radiant.

Her Negro maid, Becky, was bustling about the room, making the bed, dusting the furniture, straightening the chairs, and talking. "Miss Mat, honey, you sure looks powerful smiling this morning. You looks like Christmas done come, and it ain't here yet by two more days. Something in that letter I fetch you yesterday make your eyes look like Christmas candles—huh? What you so happy about? Tell Becky."

It wasn't easy for Martha Jane to have secrets from Becky. Since the day she was born, Becky had been with her. Eight years older than Martha Jane, she was ready to help the old black mammy give Martha Jane her first bath, and on with subsequent baths. When Martha Jane began to toddle, Becky was right there to hold her hand. By the time Martha Jane was old enough to take pride in her room and her clothes, Becky was there to straighten, tidy, and sew. She was now married. She married Taylor Spickard as soon as Martha Jane's father bought him from Major Spickard a year ago. But being married made no difference in Becky's duties and devotion to Martha Jane. She would always be

Martha Jane's maid. Now Becky's voice recalled her from her dreams and problems. "Don't you tell Beck if you don't want to, honey. I'll run along now."

"Oh Beck, something wonderful is going to happen!" She didn't want Beck to go.

"Course there is, honey. Course there is. Always something wonderful gonna happen."

"But I don't understand what it is. I don't quite understand this letter you got for me yesterday. Maybe you can understand it. I wonder ..."

"You just read it to me, honey. I specs I can explain it to you."

"Guess I'd better. All right." She drew the letter from a pocket in the folds of her skirt. She looked at it and held it in her hands tenderly as though it were something too precious to share with anybody. But Becky was waiting. She drew the letter out of the envelope and read:

Dear Miss Major—

"For the Lord, honey! Who calling you Miss Major? You ain't even growed up yet."

"Listen."

Dear Miss Major,
If an old and tired Indian appears at your backdoor asking for bread and a cup of coffee anytime soon, treat him kindly. Ascertain before you turn him from your door whether he carries in his inside coat pocket a daguerreotype of a very beautiful girl. You needn't ask if he carries the original in his heart—you know about that.
Very sincerely yours,
One who treasures in his memory a wonderful day in a May of long ago

"Uh-huh. That is sure purty talk, Miss Mat. And you say you don' know who's a'doing that talking? Course you does, honey. Course you does."

"How do *you* know what he talks like?" said Martha Jane, blushing, knowing she'd given herself away.

"Who? Me? I sure wasn't in the next county that May morning nearly two years ago when you and him was looking at your flowers in the garden. I sure wasn't, honey. Only ... um, he wasn't looking at the flowers cause he was looking at you."

"Well—I'm glad you think it is Mr. Shepard because—"

"Cause you wants it to be—huh? Well, it ain't nobody but him."

"Now listen, Beck. You know how Aunt Sarah hates tramps." She stopped. She looked puzzled and troubled. "I wonder why he would be coming as a tramp," she said.

"To keep them blarsted Yanks from getting him, honey," said Becky, with no hesitation. "Course."

"Oh, Beck, do you think the Yankees might get him?" Her eyes grew frightened. "Only yesterday I saw a group of men galloping down the road toward the Glade. I couldn't be sure whether they were Yankees or Confederates." She stopped again, looking out the window. "I'm glad our house is back off the road," she said.

"So'm I glad. And glad as well we all got that big woods lot back a the horses' lot and them cane breaks along the creek and them sink holes. We all got hiding places enough to hide a army." She stopped to catch her breath and plumped up the pillows on Martha Jane's bed. She looked at Martha Jane, who seemed miles away. Becky didn't like that. She wanted to see Martha Jane smile as she was smiling a few minutes ago. Becky started thinking again. "Dick and the boys is powerful glad a that woods lot. The way they runs them brood mares and horses back there when anybody come galloping down the road be a caution. But someday, I's afeard them Yanks'll catch them too. They done festered up the land, so there ain't no peace nowheres. They oughta go on back up north where they belongs and let nice folks alone. They sure ought."

While Becky was talking, she was fiddling with the curtains, making a slight adjustment here and there, and watching Martha Jane out of the corner of her eye. Martha Jane was having her own thoughts and was hardly conscious of Becky's presence till she said, "But you needn't get scared for that ole Indian man, honey. He too smart to let them Yanks catch him!"

"Oh Beck, do you think so?"

"I sure does, honey."

"And please, Beck, don't let Aunt Sarah run him away when he comes."

"Don't you worry, honey. I'll have both eyes and all my both ears a'hanging out for that ole Indian man, and I'll come galloping to you the minute he arrive at the back door."

8 · The Secret Mission

Jake had begun to wonder what had become of the major. He hadn't seen him since dinner, and now it was about suppertime. Jake had been out himself all afternoon, working hard. He expected to see the major when he got to their hut.

He didn't have long to wait and wonder. Major Shepard seemed to be in a great hurry as he neared their hut, and somewhat excited. He came through the door, if you could call it a door, with a quick gesture and quick words, "Some news for you, Jake!"

Jake caught the excitement. "Yes, sir! What sir? Miss Fanny getting married?"

George relaxed from his high tension to a somewhat lower pitch. He gave his peculiar wink and grinned at Jake. "Is that what you want to hear?" Jake looked so crestfallen, his Major hastened to add, "How'd you like to go home?"

Jake's face underwent a transformation. He dropped the bacon pan he was washing onto the floor with a clatter and bulged his eyes. "Wha-a-at you mean, sir?" He gulped, "Don't be fooling with me, sir; I ain't strong enough to stand it."

"I'm not fooling with you. I mean it."

"Mean I can go home?"

"Yes."

"When? How? Don't keep me waiting, sir."

"Start tonight. The how isn't so easy."

"Going by myself?" he asked, deflating slightly.

"No, I'm going with you." Jake sagged. He looked like a punctured balloon.

"Now, sir, I know you're fooling me."

"You'd better sit down, Jake, and I'll tell you all about it." Jake dropped on his trusty goods box. He sat very stiff and straight. "At ease. Relax," said George. "It isn't that bad."

Jake gulped some more. "I wish you'd hurry, sir."

"All right, I will." George sat down on another box, crossed his legs, and began: "The colonel came to me this afternoon directly from General Lee. He proposed, since I've had no furlough at all nor missed any engagements with the enemy thus far, that I go on sort of a scouting trip down into Tennessee to get a little change and rest, but more to look out the lay of the land down there—food, conditions, etcetera. We are in desperate need of food for men and horses here, as you know—a little better fixed for clothes since the battle (Battle of Fredericksburg, Virginia; December 13, 1862) last week, but still bad enough. General Braxton Bragg, now stationed in Murfreesboro, is in desperate need of men, it seems. He is asking General Lee if he can spare some recruits from Longstreet's division to reinforce his army."

"Why, I thought General Lee was raking heaven and earth for recruits for our army."

"So he was. But since the battle was fought, and it's almost certain there'll be no more fighting before spring, he would like to get some relief in the matter of food for his men and horses. And it's very important to the Army of Northern Virginia that General Bragg succeed. Nashville is now in the hands of the Federals under General William S. Rosecrans."

"Jumping Jupiter! It won't be safe to go into that part of the country, will it?"

"No. We won't be out looking for a safe job. But we won't stick our necks in a noose if we can help it. I haven't much hope we'll be able to do very much toward getting anything like an adequate report for General Lee. But I told the colonel I'd do the best I could." The major shuffled in his chair. "It's a great honor to be so trusted," he said.

"Yes, sir. But where do I come in on this?"

George looked at Jake speculatively. "Well," he said, "the colonel thinks it would be better if two of us go together. He said for me to pick out a man I could trust, one that wouldn't be afraid and would be smart."

"Uh-huh—that lets me out, I guess. I ain't smart, and I'm scare't to death at least half the time now."

"Well, if you don't want to go—I had you picked out as first choice, but—"

"Stop right there, sir. If you really want me—if you think I wouldn't tuck tail and run into a holler log at the first sight of a Yank—"

"I think you'll do all right. So that's settled."

Jake picked up the pan he had dropped, gave a low whistle, and began rubbing the pan on his shirtsleeve.

"Hold on, Jake. Save your shirt, and don't get any more dirt on the pan than you can help. Get your bacon on, and we'll settle the question of clothes while it fries."

"Yes, sir. But we ain't got no clothes to dress up in, if that's what you mean."

"No. We won't dress up. All we'll need will be some pants with patches on the knees and hats about worn out."

"Whoops! That'll be fun!"

"I wouldn't go that far. We'll have to look sharp not to get into a Federal prison or be shot for spies."

Jake again slumped to his box. "Go ahead," he said. "Tell it all. Do we ride, or do we walk, sir?"

"We'll do plenty of both, I guess. Ride and tie a big part of the way." He was referring to a method of transportation used by two people when they have one horse and lots of distance to cover in a hurry. One rides at a good pace while the other sets out on foot. After a while, the rider ties the horse to a tree and commences to walk or run; the first runner reaches the tied horse, mounts it, and races ahead, overtaking the traveling companion and again riding ahead. This alternating ride-and-hike method allows all three participants—including the horse—to rest between markers.

"And get lost from each other, huh?"

"I hope not. We'll stay pretty close together. We'll manage."

"And we start tonight?"

"Yes, we'll leave when the commissary wagons leave for Richmond. We'll have to go by Richmond anyhow to get the clothes. We'll both ride that far. Now here's an address in Richmond," he said, handing Jake a slip of paper. "We'll change clothes there; leave our army clothes till we return. Put that in your pocket and don't lose it. We'll dye our hair there too."

Jake stuffed the paper in his pocket. "Hair dyed!"

"Yes. Gray. We want to look a little older than we are. We don't want to get arrested for army stragglers."

Jake gazed at George and chuckled, "Holy smoke! Won't you be a sight with white whiskers! All that black-as-tar hair turned white! Now me—mine won't be so different, being as it's sorter dingy red anyhow."

"Both of us may have the real thing in gray hair before we get back. We'll have to be smart not to get shot by the Federals for Confederate spies or by Confederates for Federal spies. We'll be just as dead either way."

Jake sobered up. "No, sir—I mean yes, sir." He paused in deep thought. "I don't relish the idea of being shot by either of them boys. How'll we manage?"

"Be smart, as I said. Use our heads."

"Yes, sir. I reckon you'll have to do most of the being smart. I ain't got much head. Now if there's any acting the fool to do, I might tend to that."

George clicked in his throat and shuffled to his feet. "No doubt that will come in handy at the proper place. Now, tie up your blankets in a bundle for the horse." George began folding his own blankets. "Tie another small bundle for the end of a stick. It'll help create the look of an old man on his way somewhere to visit his folk. Think you can work up a limp and mumble like an old man, Jake?"

"Let's see." He started limping and mumbling and hobbling around the shack. George slapped his leg and laughed as he hadn't laughed in many a day.

"That will do, Jake. I see you can do it." George stopped folding bundles. "By the way, where'd that heavy overcoat you've been going around in for a week or more come from?"

"Ask me no questions," said Jake, shaking his head, and then changed his mind. "I'll tell you," he said. "I borrowed it off a Yank that didn't need it no more. You know that night Burnside let us go out and get our dead? Well, I was in that gang." Now he looked like an old man for real—one who had seen things no man should ever have seen. George looked at him intently, traveling with him over that bloody Fredericksburg battlefield in search of the missing. He had seen them too. But time was short and passing. He cleared his throat. "You about ready, Jake?"

Jake stood at attention. "Yes sir!" He smiled sheepishly and turned his attention to the bacon that needed somebody's attention. "You may think it queer, sir, but I was thinking about that feller that tried to get himself a pair of shoes that evening. He could use a pair of shoes."

"Yes? What about him? Did he get a pair?"

"Not then. He had one shoe off the Yank's foot. When he lifted the other foot to take that shoe off, the Yank opened his eyes and looked at him, sorrowful like."

"What did your boy do?"

"He laid that foot down, right careful like, and said, 'Beg pardon, sir; thought you'd gone above.' Then he got away from there in three jumps a kangaroo couldn't a done without extra trying!"

George had to laugh. "I see," he said. "How'd yours come to be *that* color?"

"It started blue, sir. But I couldn't stand it. So I got me about a bushel of pokeberries and dyed it. I'd a used walnut juice if I could a found any hulls. Looks like the fellers eat all the hulls along with the walnuts."

"Well, here is all we have to tie up—not much," said George as he rounded up the bundle.

"You said a mouthful there, sir," said Jake. "I don't exactly relish the idea of going to see Miss Fanny dressed like an old tramp. How'll she take it, you reckon?"

"You'd better forget about Miss Fanny, Jake. She's too old for you."

"That's what she said, sir. But I had a different mind on the subject." He stopped, looked at George, and grinned. "Will you see that little gal whose picture you carry in your inside pocket and look at every night just before you go to bed when you think I ain't looking?" he asked.

George's face got red. He didn't know he'd been so transparent. He started to get vexed but decided not to. He cleared his throat. "Don't know," he said. "Maybe. Better not ... maybe."

Jake chuckled. He set the bacon and a hunk of brown bread on the table. "Supper's ready," he said. "No egg tonight and no butter. But this bacon grease ain't so bad."

"Not at all. We are faring fine."

"I wish that old hen they say lays an egg under General Lee's bed every day would make us a visit."

"You wouldn't have her neglect our general, would you?"

"No, sir, but—well, I guess we'll get plenty of eggs once we get to Tennessee."

"I doubt it. Tennessee has two armies to feed now."

"Yes, sir. I forget. Will you see General Bragg?"

"I expect to."

"Does he know you? Maybe he'll have you shot for a spy."

"I have papers that will take care of that. Here," handing a small paper across their improvised table, "take yours now."

"How'll we carry these papers? Not very big—but too big to swallow in case, huh? If they are found on us by some Yanks, it'll be too bad, won't it?"

"It would. We'll have to be too smart for that."

Next day, two old men could be seen walking on the streets of Richmond on their way toward the canal that paralleled the James River from Richmond to Lynchburg, Virginia. They were setting out on this dangerous, adventuresome trip behind enemy lines to gather facts for General Lee. Being caught could mean being shot as a spy or being condemned as a deserter, depending on which side apprehended them. Even George's family was within the Federal line, which presented complications, as you will read. It was a long, dangerous trip into Federal territory to be taken by any officer under Lee's command. Even the Field and Staff Muster Roll for January and February 1863 indicate he was present and accounted for as shown in Figure 8-1[1]. If it were a furlough, it would reflect such on the muster roll. Figure 8-2 shows his request of forage for his horse for eleven days, starting December 20.

These two were poorly dressed except for overcoats, which were almost new. Their hats were considerably the worse for wear. One of them seemed older than the other in spite of his walk, which was too much that of a soldier to be very convincing that he was an old man, even to a casual observer. He was leading a horse, the bridle over one arm. The other man walked with a cane, carried a bundle on the end of a stick over his shoulder, and limped. He had violent fits of laughter that bent him almost double. His companion would look at him pityingly and walk on, leaving the fellow to straighten up and follow on. They were nearing the canal.

"Well, Jake," said George, leading the horse, "there's the place we will begin our trip to Lynchburg. Do you want to ride Selim or go on the barge?"

"All the same to me, sir. I think you'd get more rest on the barge and maybe find out some things you are trying to find out for General Lee. So maybe you'd better go on the barge, sir."

"Maybe so. Now you can spend the night in some town after fifty miles on the way. You will go faster than the barge. We'll get to Lynchburg about the same time. You go to the station this side of the city and wait there. If the barge gets there first, I'll wait for you." Jake looked so comical when he mounted Selim. George had to laugh.

"I'll be glad to see you, sir, in Lynchburg," Jake said, doffing his hat and bowing with great solemnity as he rode away.

George and Jake met at the appointed place near Lynchburg. Going through the city, they stopped long enough to replenish their ration haversacks and water canteens, eat a bite at a corner tavern, and get feed for Selim. By four o'clock, they were nearing the outskirts of the city. The streets had ended, and a turnpike lay before them.

---

[1] *Compiled Records Showing Service of Military Units in Confederate Organizations, Tennessee, First through Seventh Infantry,* National Archives, the National Archives and Records Service, General Services Administration, 1971.

"Well, Jake, here's where we begin to ride and tie. You ride first."
Jake protested but was overruled. "Keep on this pike for half an hour and
stop," said George. "We'll start on short distances. I won't be far behind.
Don't ride fast."

Jake pulled a tin whistle out of his pocket and blew it. George
winced. "Stop it," he said.

"Sorry, sir. I didn't know it was going to sound so loud. You see, I
got them so's we could call one t'other in case we got separated and
lost." He handed one to George.

"All right. Good idea," said George as he took the whistle. "Now,
move."

"What if I meet some Yanks?" asked Jake, still hesitating.

"You won't. And keep your pistol where it is now. Don't start
anything. Just ride on. Pay no attention."

"What if I'm stopped?"

"Just play ignorant and—well, it might be time to act the fool—but
don't be funny!"

"No, sir—I mean yes, sir. I'll be powerful glad to see you again
soon, sir," he said, still not moving. He looked so troubled the Major was
much amused and a little impatient.

"Oh, go, Jake. Nothing's going to catch you! You act like you
haven't been in some of the worst battles ever fought, and you weren't
afraid then."

"Don't you believe I wasn't! Well, here goes." And he set his face to
the front and his horse to the road.

The days and nights passed pleasantly enough for George and Jake
as they rode and tied their way through Virginia, taking their course in a
southwesterly direction. They were able to get food for themselves and
Selim and places to spend the night. They made good time and actually
enjoyed the trip.

When they came into Tennessee where North Carolina, Virginia, and
Tennessee meet, conditions changed. These folks were Federal in their
sympathies.

George and Jake had been going hard all day. They were hungry and
tired when they approached a farmhouse. They would see if they could

get a cup of coffee, maybe some bread, hay for Selim, and a most-needed place to sleep. Jake wanted to tackle the backdoor job. George was willing.

An old Negro woman answered to Jake's knock. "I say, Auntie," he began, drawing out his voice, drawing down his face, and bending to lean heavily on his cane, "would you give an ole man a bite to eat and a cup a coffee? My friend, he's out at the gate. We been traveling all day going to see our folks down middle Tennessee way. We can pay you," he said as the old Negro hesitated, studying his looks too closely to suit. "We could sleep on the hay in the barn," he whined. "We're powerful tired."

The old woman squinted her eyes at him. "I'll ask ole Mistress," she said. "She's mighty feard a them Yanks. You ain't no Yank, is you? 'Cause if you is, you might as well be on you way. She ain't got no mind to feed no Yanks."

"A Yank? No, course not! And my pap ain't neither. We just poor folks trying to get down to see our people ... if this war ain't killed them all." Jake didn't have to work too hard to be convincing; what he was saying was not far from the truth.

"You wait right there on that step. I tell you, don't you come in till I ask the ole mistress."

They got their supper, feed, a stall for their horse, and a place on the hay for themselves to sleep. Not a bad night for men who had so recently come from General Lee's camp in Fredericksburg.

They were up and away the next morning before the folks in the house were awake. George left a few coins on the kitchen windowsill to pay for their supper. They headed through the foothills of some mountain range, which provided them with another long day. They trudged along together. Jake didn't like it. "I wouldn't call this God's country," he said. "Looks too much like West Virginia."

"We haven't much farther till we reach Knoxville, which, I hope, barring accidents, we'll do in two more days," George assured him.

"Glory be! I'll not object!"

"We'll have to stop soon for the night."

"I'm agreeable to that too, sir."

"I hope we come to a hut and can get a bed for the night. But we may have to sleep on the ground or in a cave. You ride on. I'll walk a little further. Don't go fast. Stop in half an hour—sooner, if you come to a hut. I won't be far behind." Jake rode on, looking almost as tired as he felt. He had had about enough of this trip. These hills—they looked like mountains to him—depressed him.

Jake hadn't ridden more than twenty minutes when he heard the sound of somebody chopping wood. As he came into a sort of clearing, a wider place in the road, he saw an old man chopping what looked to be stove wood. He reined Selim up by the side of the road and greeted the old man, who responded promptly and cordially. "Howdy, stranger," he said. "Light and look at your saddle. Hain't seed nobody in this neck a the woods in so long it sure looks good to see you. Where you from? Come to a powerful poor place if'n you looking for folks. Ain't nobody around here since the boys went off to that dad-blamed war and the old woman kicked the bucket. Where'd you say you come from? Hey? Sorter hard a hearing. The old woman used to say she just about strained her tonsils out trying to make me hear that the stove wood was all burnt out and to go cut some more. Since she took and died, I'm obliged to do my own cooking. Life's powerful hard on a poor old man, stranger. Hey? What'd you say?"

Suddenly, the old man lost his appearance of deafness, snapped his head around, and gazed down the road, alert. He caught himself and resumed his former peculiarities. "Well, I'll be gol-darned if there ain't a man coming a'walkin'! This must be a busy day at Cedar Creek. Maybe the dad-blamed soldiers is coming through here again. They come once and mighty nigh scared the living daylights out'n me. The old woman said, 'Why Pete, they ain't a going to hurt you none if you behave yourself.'"

George came up, and the old man started all over again. Jake hadn't spoken. He hadn't had a chance, and he wouldn't have had anything to say if he had had. The old man had lost all interest in his stove wood on Jake's arrival.

While the old man was repeating his tale to George, Jake was sizing up the surroundings. He wasn't pleased with the old man. He seemed fishy. As he looked about the premises, he saw an old dog stretched out in a spot of sunshine by the side of the hut. There was a sort of shed-barn back of the hut. He couldn't see if there was a cow or a horse anywhere.

The old man began on Jake again. "He your buddy?" he asked, pointing at George. "Don't look a bit alike. Now, my two boys ain't no more alike than a sheep and a goat. John, he was always the good one—just like a sheep, I used ter tell his ma. But look out for that Hiram—regular hellcat he was, always up to some devilment. He's up north now, helping them gol-darned Yanks do their dirty fighting. But John, he ain't going to fight nothing if he can help it. When they drafted him to join that Bragg's army, he cried like a baby. Said he wasn't going to kill nobody—nobody hadn't done nothing to him. This dad-blamed war is right from the old boy down in them hot, lower regions (hell), I always told my old woman."

He stopped and picked up a few sticks of the wood he'd been chopping. George and Jake remained silent. "Better light, strangers," he said, straightening up, "and get a bite to eat before ya'll start on your way again. Got a right smart ways to go, I reckon."

Jake looked at George. George looked at Jake and said, "Well, Jake, if the brother can put us up for the night, I guess we'd better let him."

"Just as you say, bud," Jake said, hesitatingly.

"Get right down and come in, strangers," offered the old man. "I'll give you the best I got and won't charge you a cent. Where'd you say you be going?"

"We are on our way to see our kinfolk in middle Tennessee," said George.

"I do declare!" said the old man, taking his guests back to his shed-barn. "Ain't that interesting! I got kinfolk in middle Tennessee. Up in Jackson County. Purty place, Jackson County. Hills. I says to my old woman, 'Give me hills to live in. I just wouldn't live nowheres else.'" He showed Jake where to put his horse and where the corn feed could be found.

"Why do you like the hills?" asked Jake. He was getting very curious about this old fellow.

"Well now, I'll tell you, stranger—they's more freedom for a man in the hills. Nobody always poking his nose in a body's business."

They went into the hut. As soon as the door was opened, the dog ran in and stretched himself out on the hearth before the few coals in the fireplace. The room had two big beds, four chairs, a small table with a tallow candle on it, and a sort of bureau with a mirror. There was a small adjoining room with a tiny cook stove, a safe (cupboard) for dishes, and a table. A bucket with some water and a gourd stood on a box in a corner. Jake noticed a rifle in a rack over the door.

"Well, I calculate you fellers are hungry, ready for a bite to eat. I'll go out and see what I can stir up."

As soon as the old man left the room, Jake said to George, under his breath, out of the corner of his mouth, "Don't like his looks."

George, nodded, "Keep your eye skinned."

"Too many gol-darns," Jake added.

"We'll get away as soon as we can," agreed George, "after we get something to eat."

"Supper's ready, strangers," called the strange old man. "Set to and help you-selves."

George and Jake ate heartily of the cold cornpone, cold cabbage, and hog jowl. The water seemed clean and was good. They drank plenty.

"Want some 'backy, strangers? I got a couple of cob pipes if you'd like a smoke."

"We have our own pipes and tobacco, thanks," George said. "Do you know anything about this war they say is going on?"

"Now, stranger, you got me there. Don't know a gol-darned thing about it. I'm scared plumb stiff if a soldier comes within four miles a me. Ain't the dad-blamed thing over yet? I'd a thought it had stopped long ago."

After supper, George and Jake went into the big room. The dog was begging for his supper. The old man fussed at him. "Why in tarnation don't you go out and catch you a rabbit? Laziest dog I ever seed. Don't you know I can't keep on giving you the victuals I need for myself? You ain't worth your salt. Now take that and clear out," he said, setting a plate with a sizable hunk of jowl and a chunk of cornpone on the floor. He left the rest of the food and dishes on the table. He came into the big room, closing the door behind him.

It wasn't long till he said to his guests, "Well, I reckon you fellers are powerful tired and want to hit the hay. Now I generally set a spell and doze by the fire before I turn in. Sleep better that way—go to bed too soon and I get restless and have to get up. Don't you fellers wait on me; just turn in when you feel like it. I calculate you got a long trip before you tomorrow? What say?"

George and Jake didn't say. Jake gave a prodigious yawn and said, "I'm just about asleep right now. How about you, bud?"

George said, "I reckon we'd both better get all the rest we can, as long as our good brother is willing." He got up and started removing his coat. He hung it on the back of his chair with his overcoat. "It's so cold," he said, "I think I'll just keep my pants on. All right, Jake. How are you coming on?"

"Okay, bud. I'm practically in the bed and asleep right now," he said, yawning widely again and slipping in on the back side of the bed with all his clothes on except his shoes, which he set beside his bed where he could slam his feet into them on a second's notice. His overcoat he put on the foot of the bed.

It wasn't many minutes after they got in bed till George and Jake were snoring heavily and evenly, each with an eye half open. Jake even mumbled in his sleep and gritted his teeth like he was having a bad dream. In his mumbling, he told his ma they'd soon be there. George was afraid Jake was overdoing it.

The old man by the fire seemed to be dozing too. Before an hour went by, it was all Jake could do to keep from dropping off. But he held on and snored on, wondering who'd do what next. About ten o'clock, the man by the fire began cautiously to move his head so that he could see his guests. With an eye on the mirror but snoring away, George watched him!

Presently, the old man eased himself out of his chair and began to creep towards the chair on which George's coat was hanging. Jake snorted in his sleep. The old man stopped, stooped, and held his breath. Jake and George resumed breathing heavily and evenly, and the old man crept forward toward George's chair. He reached out and slipped his hand into George's coat pocket where the gun was. George was up in a shot and brought the chair down on their host's head. He fell sprawling on the floor, swearing in perfectly correct English—with a Northern accent.

But George had been too late! That Yank had the pistol in his hand and was already scrambling to get to his feet. George threw himself on him and grabbed the wrist of the hand with the pistol in it. Jake was on the job by then. In a flash, they had him tied up and started to ask him questions. "Who are you? What are you doing here?" They couldn't get a thing out of him but swearing—calling them every sort of slaveholder. They fastened a rag around his mouth to gag him—he wouldn't be calling for help any time soon—and prepared to leave.

George put a coin down on a chair to pay for their supper. He said, "We appreciate your hospitality, sir." Jake guffawed. George continued, "We meant you no harm. We mean no harm to anybody. We'll take your rifle, but we'll hide it somewhere you can find it. You'll need it to shoot squirrels with. Jake, get his pistol out of that bureau drawer. We'll put it with the gun."

The old man squirmed, but he was securely tied. Jake did as he was told and then went for their horse. George finished getting their things ready to go, and as he left the room, said, "Goodbye, sir. I hope you don't try to harm innocent people again."

When they got a few hundred yards from the hut, they hid the guns. They rode double until they were well on their way. They didn't talk. They knew the man could not release himself for several hours, so they were not afraid of him. But he might have an ally nearby, ready with the firearms. That was what Jake feared. He could see forms in every shadow. He could hear horses galloping in every rush of the wind through the trees' bare branches. The snapping of twigs in the underbrush sent shivers down his spine. "This is worse than any battle," he thought, sitting behind George. When they had gone a mile or two, he whispered into the back of George's neck, "What do you reckon he wanted?"

"My gun was the first thing he wanted. I think he just wanted to see if we had any papers that would be of value to the Federals. He couldn't have harmed us."

"You think he was a spy?"

"Yes. I think he was put there to intercept any message that might be going through from the Army of Northern Virginia to the Army of Tennessee—from Lee to Bragg—any message of importance."

"What about our papers? Wouldn't they have been important?"

"Well, yes, if he could have found them; but I am sure he couldn't have."

"He might have turned us over to the Federals," said Jake, still shaken.

"Well, he didn't," said George comfortably.

"I'll be powerful glad when we see daylight once more."

"We'll probably have to do most of our traveling in the night from now on—stay hidden during the day."

"Where'll we get something to eat?"

George chuckled under his breath. "Are you hungry?" he asked.

"No, but I'm liable to be. That jowl won't last forever. I've got enough for two more meals where I can lay my hands on it any ole time."

"Where?" asked George, surprised.

"Right here in my pocket. You don't think I was a going to leave cornpone and hog jowl right there on that table and you paying for it, do you?"

George laughed. "Good! That will feed us today. We'll probably have some trouble finding feed for Selim."

"No, sir, not today we won't!"

"How's that?"

"I got four ears of corn, good big ones, for him in my overcoat pocket."

George cleared his throat and grunted. "You got your money's worth then," he said.

Jake thought he detected a slight note of criticism in George's voice. "You got objections?"

"Oh no, not at all. I just should have given the man a little more money, that's all."

"Huh! With what he trying to do to us! More money? Shucks!" Jake muttered.

They managed the next two days on very little food and less sleep and were pretty well worn out when they came to the outskirts of Knoxville on the afternoon of December 24.

George hoped they would be able to get passage on a steamboat to Chattanooga. They could use a couple of days of sleep and rest now. He had Jake wait at the corner tavern while he went two blocks away to the traffic office.

Not many people were around the office. It seemed deserted by both officers and travelers. He finally found a man at the window for cattle boats. George asked, "Can you tell me when there's a passenger boat going to Chattanooga?"

The clerk called to a young fellow in a back office, "I say, Jim, any passenger boat for Chattanooga today?"

"No, sir. No passenger boat till next week."

The clerk said to George, "You heard Jim say no passenger boat. There's a cattle boat going today though, the *Good Will*. You might get standing room."

George bought tickets. "Boat leaves in an hour," he was told, and he hurried away.

"Well, Jake, we'll spend Christmas day on the *Good Will* with a lot of other animals."

"Suits me," said Jake. "Just so they ain't spies a'carrying pistols."

When they reached the wharf, the boat was docked and her cargo being loaded. An officer stood at the foot of the gangplank looking at tickets, giving information, and inspecting. He said to George and Jake as he took their tickets, "You'll find it pretty uncomfortable, I'm afraid. No passenger space. Hardly standing room."

"Do you stop at Chattanooga?" George asked.

"We leave the boat there," the officer replied.

"We are on our way to Murfreesboro, or near there, to see our kinfolk," George said.

The officer had been reading and marking up the tickets. Now he looked at George inquiringly. "Joining Bragg's army?" he asked.

"Oh no," George said. "We are just going to make a Christmas visit."

"You'll find Murfreesboro a pretty crowded place," he said, "if you go there. Bragg is there with fifty thousand soldiers, so the report goes."

"Why isn't he in Nashville?" said George, wanting to get this man's opinion and knowledge, if he had any.

The officer looked surprised. "You must not live anywhere around here," he said.

"No, we don't. Are we running into trouble?"

"You won't miss it. If you are a Yank, the Rebs'll get you; if you are a Reb, the Yanks'll get you. Rosecrans is in Nashville with an army of nearly a hundred thousand, so they say. There are skirmishes and small engagements between Nashville and Murfreesboro all the time now."

"Well, well. That does look bad for us. I didn't know the war had got so bad down here."

"Worse than anywhere on earth, I guess, except maybe in Virginia."

"My people live about ten miles from Murfreesboro. I hope they are not in trouble."

"All depends. Since Andy Johnson has been military governor of Tennessee, the Rebs have been having lots of trouble." (Johnson handled Lincoln's military government from 1862 to 1864 and was headquartered in Nashville.)

"How's that?"

"Even a mother can't protect her own son if he's a Rebel. Johnson's got them swearing allegiance to the flag right and left, all around Nashville. Some folks have been indicted for treason, and I hear some have been condemned to death."

Jake's eyes were getting bigger and bigger. He hadn't said a word, but George was afraid he wouldn't be able to hold in much longer.

"Well, well," he said, "We'd better be getting on board, huh, Jake? Good day, officer. I hope we don't get into trouble."

"Luck to you, sir," said the officer. "I've an idea you are not as old as you'd like to look." That gave George and Jake something of a shock. No time now for their gray beards to fail them! They'd have to practice up on their speech and manner.

The captain of the boat was near the head of the gangplank as they went aboard. George approached him, handing him his tickets. "I hope," he said, "we'll be able to get at least standing room on your boat and food for ourselves and horse."

"Oh yes, I think that can be managed." He took their tickets, looked at them, and slipped them into his pocket, took a keen look at George and Jake, and called to a Negro boy who seemed to be his personal attendant.

"Jackson," he said, "show these gentlemen to that alcove next to my cabin. See that two bunks are made down for them ... and Jackson, have that horse put in an outside stall and fed." He turned to George and Jake, "All right, gentlemen, Jackson will see to your needs." And he dismissed them with a nod and motion of his hand.

Jackson took over. "This way, gentlemens."

To say that George and Jake were surprised would be to put it mildly. Either a cattle boat is a pretty nice place, or the captain is the real thing in a Southern gentleman. When they saw what was to be their cabin, they knew it wasn't the first option. Still, it would be 100 percent better than standing in a stall all night with sheep or cows or mules—or sleeping out on the ground as they had done lately. Oh yes, they were lucky.

Jackson asked, "You gentlemens dwells in Knoxville?"

"No," George said, "we are leaving the boat at Chattanooga. We are headed for Murfreesboro."

"Sure enough! Uh-huh. I'se sorry for ya'll then. Uh-huh. Has you been there lately?"

"Not for nearly two years."

"Things is changed mighty since then. I was up there two months ago before I got this job with Mars Tom. Folks is having a powerful hard time there now."

"Tell us," said George. "Our kin live there, and they haven't written us this bad news."

"You hain't heard? Does ya'll know they's a war going on?"

"Yes. We've heard about that. But that means that men in the armies are having bad times—not regular folk."

"You sure got that a'wrong, boss. Since ole Andy Johnson's been a'running things, ain't nobody been having nothing but a bad time. He all the time trying somebody for treason, and they say he having some kilt."

"What for?" asked Jake.

"Ain't I just been a telling you? For treason!"

"What does a man have to do to make him liable to be arrested for treason?" asked George.

"Well, it's like this, boss. I heard tell of a woman who had a boy in the Southern army, and the Federals tried to make her swear she was a Yankee ... and she wouldn't do it. And they fined her a hundred dollars, but that poor widdy woman ain't got no hundred dollars, so they throwed her in jail."

"Humph! Is she still in jail?"

"No, boss. Her ole colored mammy what nursed her when she was a baby got hold of money somewheres and pay the fine. Yes sir, boss, it's a powerful bad time around Nashville now. The woods is plumb full a soldiers. If'n it hain't Rebs, it's Yanks. Sure enough, boss." He turned to go, repeating the captain's courtesies. "I hope ya'll sleeps well on these bunks. They ain't so good, but I specs they's better than the floor or the ground. When ya'll gets ready to eat, come on out to the deck and holler for Jackson. I'll do the best I can for ya'll."

"Thank you, Jackson. We'll be coming out pretty soon now."

When Jackson was out of hearing, Jake whistled low and gulped, "What do you know about that? Think we'd better turn round and hump it for where it's safer?"

"We'll go on," said George. "I think the officer and Jackson both were exaggerating maybe. We may not be able to stay at home or even see our families. But we'll give it a try."

"See here, you don't mean we've come all the way to Wilson and Rutherford Counties and not see Miss Fanny or anybody? Why I've just got to see Ma and Pa!"

"Not if it would put them in jail or cost them a fortune, would you?"

"No–no, I couldn't do that. But this trip ain't turning out right. No fun, no how. Might as well be back in Virginia fighting Yanks there."

George and Jake didn't have to be told to go to bed on that Christmas Eve night on the *Good Will*. They hit their bunks by eight o'clock and slept straight through till eight the next morning.

They were awakened by Jackson knocking on their door and calling, "Time for breakfast. You gentlemens! Is ya'll awake?"

They both called back, "Okay, Jackson!"

"Might as well get up," said Jake, "though I think I could sleep all day."

George called to Jackson, "We'll be right out," saying to Jake, "We've got to eat. Better be sociable with Jackson."

"Ya'll stay right there," Jackson called. "I'll fetch you something in you cabin." Moments later, he came back with hot bread, a pot of coffee, a bit of bacon, and scrambled eggs, and said, "Ya'll's invited to have dinner with Mars Tom today. He got a box from his wife at Louisville, Kentucky, yesterday, and he wants ya'll to come eat with him at one o'clock."

Jake couldn't restrain a "Glory be! We'll—" But George broke in with, "Tell the captain we'll be delighted. We'll be honored to be with him."

"Yes, sir. I'll sure tell him. Anything else ya'll wants from me now, 'cause I'll be too busy for an hour or two this morning?"

"No, thank you, Jackson. You have served us well. Thank you."

George and Jake did all the getting ready for a holiday dinner possible under the circumstances. They managed to shave and wash up more than at any one time since they left Fredericksburg. Jake was quite excited over the dinner invitation. He wondered what in the world they'd talk about. Couldn't talk about Lee's army, and he didn't know anything else. Couldn't tell about the spy in the hut.

"What'll we talk about?" he asked George.

"We'll have to decide that at the table, I reckon. I think the captain is all right. No harm in him. Maybe we'll learn something about Bragg and Rosecrans from him."

Promptly at one o'clock, Jackson came for them to go to lunch. The table and service were very plain but looked luxurious to George and Jake. And the food all but took their breath. There was a fowl of some sort—not a turkey—just an old rooster, perhaps, but it looked like a feast: plenty of bread and butter, Irish potatoes, hot, canned tomatoes, a pot of hot coffee, a big cake, and a pumpkin pie baked by the captain's wife. The captain was very gracious. He greeted them with, "I think I haven't introduced myself to you. My name is Harris, Tom Harris. And yours?"

George held his hand out cordially with, "My name is George Shepard. My friend is Jake Magruder. You are very kind to invite us to your dinner. We hadn't expected such hospitality and certainly not such food!"

As they seated themselves, the captain kept the conversation going with, "My wife was very much disappointed that I couldn't be at home this Christmas. But not half so much disappointed as I was! We older fellows have to stay on the job now that the young men have all gone to war. My wife did a good bit of scheming to get a box of food to me. I'm glad to have company to help me enjoy it."

"We are the fortunate ones. How's the food situation in Tennessee?"

"About as one could expect, I'd say. So far, neither army has willfully destroyed crops or cattle. But it takes an awful lot to feed an army. Not so many men left to raise crops, and those left are old. Of course there are the Negroes, and so far they are faithful and loyal to their masters."

The captain seemed slightly embarrassed and a little reticent. But with the air of having made a decision, he plunged in. "I don't want to seem to be prying into your affairs, and you needn't reveal anything about yourselves. I know the country is full of spies, and a man has to keep his own counsel. I have two boys in this war. It has been a great grief and cross to their mother and me that they chose to be fighting on opposite sides in this conflict. We have a son in Lee's army in Virginia and one in the Army of the Potomac—Burnside's, at present."

Jake's eyes nearly popped out of his head. "Jumping Jupiter," he said, "you don't say!"

The captain looked at Jake surprised and amused. "My dear sir," he said, "that seems to strike you all in a heap. That's nothing unusual. Lots of fathers and mothers have that grief. A friend of ours has three sons, two on one side and one on the other. It's a common fate to fathers and mothers throughout Kentucky and Tennessee. Where are you from, if I may ask?"

Jake looked at George as much as to say, "If any talking's to be done, you'd better do it."

George cleared his throat, shuffled in his chair, gave the captain a keen look, and decided. "We," he said, "are from General Lee's army in Virginia."

The captain smiled. "I thought so," he said. "Your disguise is not very convincing. I respect your reticence and realize your danger in Tennessee if you are known to be a soldier in the Southern Army. I do not think there is a spy aboard this boat, but they are plentiful all through the country. You'd better brush up a bit on your disguise before reaching Rutherford County. I believe you said you are going to Murfreesboro? I suppose you'll be seeing Bragg?"

"I hope to. My associate here will be seeing his folks in Wilson County."

"Ah! He'll have to look sharp not to get caught if he goes near Nashville."

"What can you tell us about General Bragg?" asked George.

"General Bragg is conceded to be a man of his ability."

"What size army has Bragg now, or do you know?"

"Well, not exactly, but the report is that it's somewhere around forty thousand. He is stationed at Murfreesboro, as you know. His forces reach from Readyville to Triune. In going to Murfreesboro, you are not apt to encounter any Federal soldiers. Your greatest danger will be in being mistaken for army stragglers or shirkers. I suppose you have papers to protect you against that."

George didn't say. Instead, he asked, "What is the prospect of a battle at this time? Will Bragg attack Rosecrans in Nashville or wait for Rosecrans to make the attack?"

"I think the general opinion is that Bragg will wait for Rosecrans. It's pretty well known that the Federals are much stronger in numbers than the Confederates. And Bragg can hardly hope for recruits any time soon."

"What is Rosecrans's strength?"

"The reports vary. The average report is somewhere around seventy thousand. Of course, the scared Confederates think he has at least a hundred thousand. But the general opinion puts his strength at a lower estimate. In any case, he has too many for the comfort of the

Confederates. You are in this war—how do you think it's going? Who's going to win?"

"That's a hard question. Lee's army has repulsed the Army of the Potomac at Fredericksburg, as you know. But the Feds have dug in to await the spring."

"I hear the slaughter of the Federals in that battle was terrific."

"Yes—a sight to forget as soon as possible."

"You didn't say when you think the war might end," the captain said.

"I'll have to confess I don't have much idea. It may be the North will grow weary of the struggle and stop. I don't think the South will give in as long as she has men and means."

Neither the captain nor George said goodbye. When George started off the boat, the captain just tipped his hat with his finger in a respectful salute and said, "Good luck."

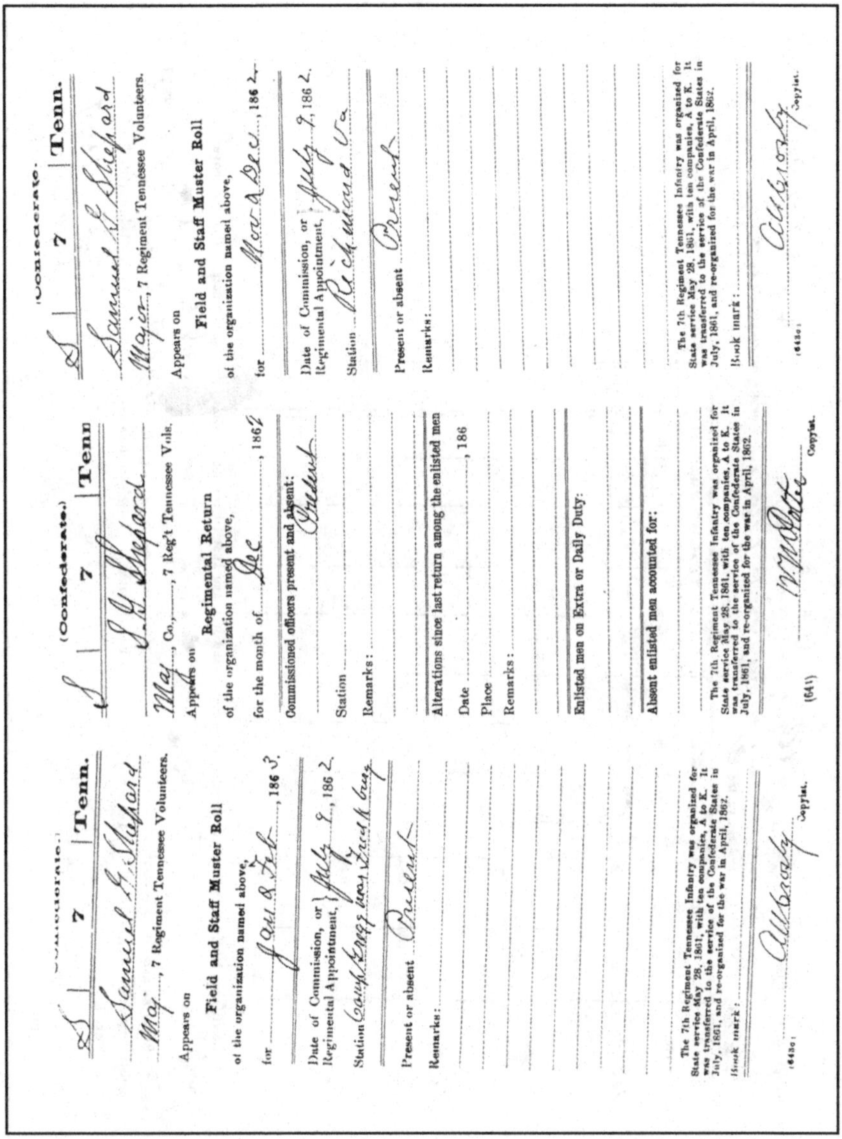

Figure 8-1. Records show Shepard present and accounted for.

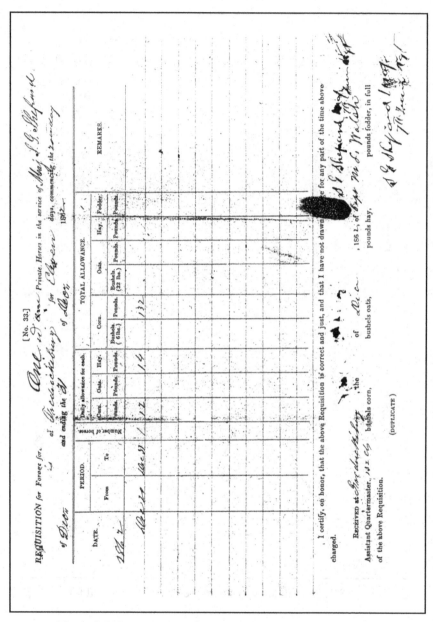

Figure 8-2. Records show forage requisition for eleven days.

9 · The Bradshaws Have Visitors

Christmas Day came and went. It was not a very happy day for Fanny or the Bradshaws. But the grown folks had laid themselves out for the children, and the children had had a good day.

On the morning of the thirtieth about ten o'clock, Sallie saw William coming in the back way with a basket of dishes on his arm. As he came in the door, she said, "William, is a neighbor sick? I didn't know anybody was sick."

"Well! How's the Good Samaritan?" asked Fanny, rounding the yard behind him. "I saw you go off down into the thicket half an hour ago bearing a mound of food. Not feeding the hogs on cake and hot coffee now, are you?"

William could see he was caught. "I don't know as I should tell you," he said. "You probably won't approve, and if the Confederates should learn about it, we might have trouble."

"William, what have you been doing?" Sallie asked, really alarmed.

"I can't stand to see folks starving," he said, "no matter what the color of their coats. I might as well tell you. As I went through the thicket early this morning with a bucket of slop to feed the hogs down in the big woods, I ran up on two bluecoats. They had been hiding there for about thirty-six hours with no food. They thought if they could get some food and a pot of hot coffee to thaw them out, they could make a getaway. So I took some food to them," he ended unhappily.

"Good for you, William," said Fanny. Sallie said nothing, looking doubtful.

That evening, they were all to have another surprise. Sallie and Fanny were sitting in the dining room. There was a knock at the back door. Sallie looked startled. Immediately, she thought of the episode of the morning and wondered if vengeance was at the back door. Fanny bounced up and went to see who was knocking. When she opened the door, she saw an old man with a bowed gray head, holding out his hand for bread, muttering, "Madam—." He stood stooped a second and then lifted his head and grinned in Fanny's face.

"George!" she gasped in a whisper heard well over the house. Sallie, hearing the note of intense excitement but not catching the name, "George," came running. She bent over Fanny, who had collapsed in one of the two entryway chairs, her face in her hands, sobbing.

"What is it, Fanny?" Fanny had no breath to answer with. "Fanny, what is it?" Sallie repeated. In her distress, Sallie had not seen the man standing just inside the door. George cleared his throat.

"Never mind Fanny, Sallie," he said. "She'll recover in a minute." Then Sallie looked up, and she too plunked herself into a chair. George cleared his throat again. "Maybe," he said, "we'd all better sit down. I feel a little wearing myself. But," he added, "maybe you'd better ask Jake in first. He's just outside the door."

Fanny jumped to the door, threw it open, and almost shouted at Jake, "Come in here, Jake Magruder. What are you doing standing out there?"

"Thank you, Miss Fanny. I was just waiting for an invitation." He came limping in, leaning heavily on his cane.

"What's the matter with you? Can't you walk? Are you hurt?" Fanny blazed at him. Jake laid his cane down on the floor and stood straight up.

"For pity's sake. What on earth have you two done to yourselves? I never saw anything so ridiculous in my life! Do your faces just need washing or have you been falling into somebody's can of paint?"

"Now Miss Fanny," said Jake, in a pity-us-lady, ingratiating tone, "we feel bad enough without you fussing at us like that."

"Sit down, you two, and give an account of yourselves."

"We can't stay long," George said.

"What did you say?" Sallie asked, not believing her ears.

"I said … we know that our being here will endanger you, so we'll be moving on after you give us something to eat—if you've got anything cooked."

Sallie looked helpless. She turned to Fanny. "What's he talking about?"

"All foolishness," said Fanny. "He thinks the Yanks would take it out on us if they found them here, and I guess they would. But they won't find them. We'll get William to hide Selim. You fix them something to eat while I show them their *boudoir*. Bring all your plunder," she said to them, "and follow me." She sounded so emphatic, so matter-of-fact, that they followed on meekly enough.

She took them into Sallie's room and explained the intricacies of the trapdoor. "You won't find hotel accommodations up there, but you'll find the necessities. You can leave your door open, and we can talk with you while we sit in Sallie's room. One of us will always be downstairs with an eye out—one out the front and one out the back, watching for soldiers. When and if we see one, we'll call out, 'Scat!' The person upstairs will repeat, and down comes your trapdoor—if you're smart. Now up you go, and I'll fetch your supper to you in a basket with a handle so you can reach when I stand on the table. When you want to come down, tap the little bell you'll see up there. Is all that clear?"

"Miss Fanny, you are wonderful," said Jake.

"Keep that to yourself, Jake, and ascend the stairs, so I can remove the chair and go for your supper."

Before she got away, George asked, "Where are the children?"

"Glad you asked. Had forgotten to mention them in the excitement. Aunt Nancy took them to her cabin for a little while about an hour ago. It's best for them, especially Ida, not to see you. She would be terribly excited over you, and if soldiers should come asking questions, she'd give the whole thing away—whether she opened her mouth or not. We kept a wounded soldier up in your present quarters for three days and didn't let her know it at all."

"All right. I agree. But I'd love to see them."

"Maybe you can before you leave."

"Where's William?"

"He's coming in the door."

After the children were in bed and asleep, George waited for silence and then tapped the bell. William answered.

"Isn't it safe now for us to go for a little walk?" George asked. "Check to see if the soldiers are gone."

COLONEL S. G. SHEPARD

"Yes, it's safe enough this time of day. Soldiers don't prowl around much at night. Besides, there's been pretty stiff fighting today along the Murfreesboro and Nashville pike. Rosecrans seems to be advancing on Bragg. They say—old man Thompson brought the news—that Bragg has got his army entrenched along Stones River, not more than five miles from here."

George and Jake slipped down for a walk but were not gone long.

"See anybody?" William asked.

"Yes, we did," Jake said, "and we thought we'd better crawl back into our hiding place at once."

They hadn't more than got settled, when soldiers in gray coats were at the front door asking for water. William gave them water to drink from the bucket in the kitchen and filled their canteens.

"What's the prospect?" he asked them.

"Battle tomorrow, looks like. We've been fighting more or less all day, but it looks like tomorrow is to be the big day."

"Where are you stationed?"

"About two miles down the road. We are pickets to keep the Yanks from locating our fortifications. Thank you, sir, for the water."

William reported to Sallie and Fanny upstairs. He said, "You can talk to the boys now; I'll keep watch downstairs."

Sallie and Fanny knocked on the trapdoor and reported the news to their guests. Jake let them know he'd be leaving about four o'clock in the morning to go on to Wilson County the following day. George said he'd also be leaving in a few hours to go into Murfreesboro and see General Bragg. "We'll be returning to Virginia in a few days," he added. "I hope I can get an interview with Bragg, so as to be able to report this battle if it takes place tomorrow." The Battle of Stones River was fought December 31, 1862, to January 2, 1863. (The Battle of Stones River pushed General Braxton Bragg's Confederate Army of Tennessee from Murfreesboro in the middle of Tennessee to Tullahoma, which is just south of Murfreesboro. General Bragg was there until June and July of 1863 when Major General William S. Rosecrans' Tullahoma Campaign forced General Bragg to retreat into Georgia.)

"But you can't go through this country. You'll get caught," said Sallie.

"We certainly can't stay here—it wouldn't do for us to get caught in your house."

"No, sir," said Jake. "I'm certainly leaving in the morning. When I get 'howdy' said to Pa and Ma, I'll be for clearing out back to where we came from—where they ain't so much danger!"

"Jake, are you just talking, or are you in less danger in Fredericksburg than here?" asked Sallie.

"I mean it. There, if we get killed, we just get killed and don't have to be hiding out like sneak thieves. I don't relish this hiding out."

"Jake's right," said George. "And that means, Jake, we'll have to plan now about our next meeting place. What say?"

"I'd say ... if you are going down to Wilson County ... "

"What's he going to Wilson County for?" asked Sallie.

"Well now, Miss Sallie, you'll have to ask him about that," Jake chuckled.

"I think I have a pretty good guess," said Fanny. "But really, George, don't you think it's too much risk? Anyhow, she's hardly grown yet!"

"What are you talking about, Fanny? It's all Dog Latin to me."

"We are talking about a certain little girl who lives near our Spickard kin. George met her when we went to Vic's wedding. Don't you remember? I told you about her."

"Oh yes, little Mattie Major. I'd forgotten about her. But George, that's too much risk. Can't you wait till the war is over?"

"Might be too long—or late," he said, and dismissed the subject by saying to Jake, "Suppose we meet in Lebanon at midnight on the night of the third. You remember that grove of tall cedars about half a mile east of Judge Brown's house? (Could that have been Judge Robert L. Caruthers' house on West Main Street? The house was built in 1828.) You remember where he lives, don't you? That house with a big front porch and white pillars."

"Yes, I remember."

"I'll be in that grove some time around midnight. I'll wait for you till morning, in case you are not there before I am."

"I'll be there."

Next morning, Fanny was waiting in the kitchen for Jake when he came downstairs at four. She had a fire in the stove to fix his breakfast

COLONEL S. G. SHEPARD

and to have the room warm for him. She had his haversack and canteen filled. When he had eaten and gotten up to go, she said, "Jake, do take care of yourself, and let us know just as soon as you get safely out of this soldier-infested part of the country. We'll be distracted till we hear."

Jake knew Fanny was right. Union and Confederate soldiers were everywhere. Was not a battle to be fought near by? And he now knew the Union occupied Nashville. He was ready to go back to the Virginia battlefield.

"I'll do that, Miss Fanny." He put out his hand to say goodbye. Much to the surprise of both of them, she threw her arms around his neck and kissed him on both cheeks. Then she turned him toward the door. "Go now," she said, "and may the good God take care of you."

"Miss Fanny, I'll never forget this the longest day I live. No Yank could catch me now."

The door closed behind him. She stood by the window and watched his shadowy form disappear down the path into the woods. She was still standing there an hour later when George and Sallie came into the kitchen. During that hour, she had tried to settle in her mind the bewildering problems of life. Why war? Who is to blame? Why can't God make folks behave better? How's this conflict to end? What'll happen when it does end? It was a relief to her to see George and Sallie. And now George was to have his breakfast and disappear into mercy only knew what. George would be returning by night, he hoped, for one more night of the hiding he detested.

Although it was much earlier than their regular rising hour, the Bradshaws and Fanny did not go back to bed after George left. William had the fires going. They sat in the kitchen talking and waiting for daylight.

Sallie was standing by the window in the parlor, looking out and worrying about George at seven o'clock when Aunt Nancy announced she had their breakfasts ready to serve. But before Sallie could stir, she heard a big *BOOM* and called out: "It's too loud to be a gun." William came and stood by her. Again, the loud *BOOM!*

"It's a cannon," he said. "I guess the battle is on."

Fanny was quaking in her shoes, but she'd die before she'd show it. She had no notion of letting herself or the Bradshaws down. It was going to be her busy day. "Come on," she said, "let's eat breakfast. Aunt Nancy's got some good hot biscuits. I'm hungry as a bear!"

"Fanny, don't you hear the cannons?"

"I'm not interested in cannons now. I'm hungry."

"Fanny, you do beat all. How can you be so—"

"So what? Don't go calling me names, madam, and if you know what's good for you, both you and William will fall to on this breakfast. William, ask the blessing, and let's begin."

There was no resisting Fanny. They even laughed and joked a little at the table, not noticing that Fanny's breakfast was more pretense than solid meal. They didn't see her hide her biscuit in her apron pocket under a handkerchief.

After breakfast, Fanny decided she would give her room a thorough cleaning. She swept and dusted. And then she decided she'd air out the big cedar chest—such an enormous chest—an heirloom from some distant ancestor. She and Sallie kept their quilts and bedcovers in it. She laid out all these on chairs, unfolding each of the piece-quilts to look at them.

Sallie came in. "Fanny, what *are* you doing?" she said.

"I thought I'd air out our quilts and wipe the dust out of the chest. Isn't it strange how so much dust can get in the bottom of a big old piece of furniture as this? I'll leave the quilts out today, and while they air, the chest will dry. I'll just use this damp cloth to wipe it with." She was killing time, trying to occupy both their minds.

"I can't sit still, Fanny. The guns are getting louder and faster all the time. I'm so uneasy about George."

"Don't worry about George. He was going to see General Bragg— you can be sure Bragg is not in the line of fire. George won't be in any danger. Just think of the battles he's been in. You know, Sallie, I think the good Lord is going to take care of George. Remember what Jake wrote us about George's preaching. I'm holding on to that."

"Fanny, you are such a comfort. I'll go now and see what Aunt Nancy can make for dinner. William is standing out in the yard, listening to the guns. I wonder how long it will last. If Bragg surrenders … "

"He won't." Fanny used all her emphasis to convince Sallie—and herself. "He may have to retreat," she continued, "but he won't surrender. Rosecrans may have to retreat."

Fanny went downstairs with Sallie, leaving the quilts folded and piled on chairs. Next, she picked out a storybook and read to Ida. William and Sallie stayed out by the gate with their coats on, Sallie with a shawl over her head, much of the day—an interminable, awful day. Later, Fanny would be glad she had done the chest—she had no idea how glad.

Nobody but the children ate much dinner. Even Aunt Nancy and Uncle Reuben couldn't swallow their food.

"What's we coming to, Reuben?" moaned Aunt Nancy.

"Dear Lord only knows—I sure don't. They going to be a powerful lot o' folks killed today—all for nuttin."

By four o'clock, small squads of bluecoats were already trudging along the road in front of the house. Sallie felt she could not stand another minute of suspense. Fanny, still keeping herself busy, now in the kitchen where she could keep an eye out, saw George first, stealing his way through the trees out back. When he got to the kitchen door, she grabbed him and pulled him in. "Don't ask questions. Come!" She rushed him to her room where no time would be wasted. "Get in," she ordered, almost pushing him into the chest. In less time than it takes to tell, she laid the folded quilts neatly on top of him, leaving no telltale lumps. She closed the lid with a decisive thud and glanced out the window. Five bluecoats were coming through the front gate. Three of them stopped there. The other two, halfway up the walk, were arguing.

"I tell you, sir, these folks are all right. I know. It was this man who gave food to Jim and me yesterday. Don't know what would have happened to us if he hadn't."

"Our orders are to search this house," the officer replied. "The major thought he saw one of Bragg's men ride this way. Come on." He went up to the door and banged on it.

Fanny opened it wide. "Well, gentlemen," she said, smiling and making them a sweeping bow, "what can we do for you today?"

"We've orders, madam, to search this house. Our major saw one of Bragg's men riding in here."

"I assure you, we have not been honored with a visit from one of General Bragg's men."

"We are sorry, madam ... asking you to do this ... but we must obey orders."

"It would seem that killing men on the battlefield would be enough without going in private citizens' homes and frightening the women and children to death. But if you must, come in and search our house."

They came in and went the rounds, looking under beds, opening closet doors, and poking into them. Then they went upstairs with the same routine, looking into every conceivable hiding place. Fanny kept up a running banter about feeding a couple Yanks the other day, saying she hoped they were well, but actually hoping George would hear the men's voices and melt into the cedar. When they raised the lid on the chest, her hands tightened on the back of a chair till the knuckles were white. She stood rigid from head to heel. Had the soldiers looked at her, they would surely have read a tale. They didn't. They took a quilt or two out, poked into the box, seemed satisfied that the box held nothing but blankets, closed the lid, turned, and left the room. She followed them quickly down the stairs as they went out the door without looking back, stopping only long enough to say, "Sorry, madam, to have disturbed you."

That was it. All Fanny's bravado drained out of her. She sat down stiff and straight in an armchair in the parlor, her face set, her hands clasped, and tears streamed from her closed eyes. Sallie had been there the whole time, perched on the edge of the sofa with Frank on her lap and Ida standing by her knee, petrified. Now, she murmured, "You were wonderful, Fanny, wonderful ..."

William was still out by the gate. As the bluecoats went past him, the man whom he'd fed the day before thanked him again for the food.

Fanny didn't go to release George till she was sure no more Yankees would be coming that night. Then she rushed him to the loft and handed him a basket of food.

"Well, Fanny," he said, "I guess you will agree now that it will be safer for all of us for me to get back to Virginia."

"I'm afraid I do. How awful! I think I'm going to howl!"

"I wouldn't—it might fetch in some Yanks."

"Put your door down," she said. "I've stood all I can for one day."

That night when the children were asleep, George opened his door for a family council. William said, "You can't leave tonight, George. The soldiers—Rebs and Yanks—have every road and path picketed for miles around. The battle stopped about five o'clock, but the two armies are ready to fight again in the morning."

This meant another day of hiding for George. He hated it but submitted to a New Year's Day in the attic. On the second of January, another engagement took place, short and fierce. George could abide no longer. He asked William to get Selim. He left that night for Wilson County.

10 · George Visits Martha Jane

George arrived at his uncle A. J. Spickard's home about three in the morning of January the third. He put Selim in a stall and fed him. He climbed into the loft of the barn, made himself comfortable, and went promptly to sleep. Next morning, the sight of him gave William, the stable man, quite a scare, but scares were the order of the day.

"What for didn't you go up to the house, Mars George, when you 'rived last night?"

"Didn't want to rouse the folks."

The Spickard and Major Negroes had a system of communication between the two houses almost equal to a telephone. So George's presence in the Spickard home came to Martha Jane's ears early in the morning. Becky told her that George had spent the night riding and was spending the day sleeping. "And I expect, honey, he'll be coming up here 'bout three or four o'clock. What you going to wear for this here Indian man? You got to look you purtiest."

"How do I know he's coming here at all? I haven't heard from him."

"What's that letter I fetched you some days ago? Course he's coming here! That's what he's head for—you knows that. He'll be here for you hardly knows it. You go do you primping. I'll watch for him."

By the early afternoon, George was refreshed and wearing a borrowed pair of his uncle's trousers and a white shirt and tie when he presented himself at the Major's door—as well groomed as possible.

Becky admitted and announced him when he arrived. Mr. and Mrs. Frances and Samuel Major gave him a glad, cordial welcome. Martha Jane joined them in the conventional greetings and friendly visit until her parents excused themselves, ostensibly to see after various duties, and left her alone with George.

Martha Jane felt panicky. Suddenly and completely, she was just a little girl again. She began talking very rapidly and excitedly. "Aren't you afraid?" she said. "The Feds have been going by all day. I've been watching by the west windows most of the day. I was terribly afraid some of them might come in here."

George didn't seem in any hurry to talk. He was happy just looking at her. She fidgeted.

"You have grown up," he said.

"You said that nearly two years ago," she said.

"Did I? Well, you are more grown up now."

"At that rate, I'll soon be an old woman, won't I?" she giggled.

He shuffled in his chair and grinned. "Hardly that, I reckon. You'll be young a long time, I hope. At any rate, don't get too grown up before this war is over."

"When will it be over?"

"I don't know. Let's not talk about the war."

"You said we'd *have* to think about the war when you were here that May morning more than a year ago."

"You have a good memory. Do you remember everything I said?"

"You didn't say very much, sir."

"No? Maybe I was thinking too much to say much. I've been thinking about the war for nearly two years. I'd like to think of something else for awhile—you." He looked at her so intently and seriously, she rushed on with her talking.

"I'm not important enough to think about with so many people getting killed every day. That awful battle three days ago in Rutherford County! Wasn't that near your sister's?"

"Yes—within five miles of her house."

"Were you there?"

"I was in Murfreesboro the day of the battle."

"Were you afraid?"

"Yes, but a soldier can't stay afraid—and really, we are not afraid when the excitement of the battle is on. It's an awful, terrible thing, and ought not to be." He stopped, changed his position, and looking at her earnestly, said, "Tell me, what have you been doing with yourself these nearly two years since that morning in May?"

"Growing up—you said it." And she smiled at him warmly. She was recovering from her initial excitement and embarrassment.

Becky burst in. "Miss Mat, the Yanks are coming. They are down at the big gate on the road trying to open it."

Martha Jane sprang to her feet. "Mr. Shepard, quick—you must go down in the cane breaks. Come quickly—follow me."

She darted out the kitchen door and across the yard to the smokehouse. He was right behind her, looking very disgusted. *These unspeakable Yanks!* Behind the smokehouse, she pointed to a path that skirted the big woods lot. "Follow that path," she said, "till you come to the cane breaks. They'll be hard to get into, but hurry." And she raced back to the house.

Feds were tramping up the broad path that led from the big gate to the front yard. There were a dozen or more of them. Some of them stopped by the ravine that began some hundred yards down and to the left of the house, ran a hundred or more yards, and turned almost at right angles to the left and on to the spring that supplied the drinking water. Two or three hundred men could easily have been hidden in this miniature canyon. Three of the Feds were looking to see if maybe some Johnny Rebs might be hiding there. Two or three others had ridden to the front gate. Others had gone to the barns.

The boys had rushed the horses into the big woods lot. But the rain the day before had made the ground so soft that the horses had left their hoofprints. The Yankees followed them to the woods and found a dozen brood mares and Martha Jane's saddle pony that she rode every day. Martha Jane did not see that the Feds had found the horses till they were halfway down the road to the big gate.

A Federal officer noticed her pretty dress and decided to question her as she stood on the porch with her parents. "I'll venture," he said, "you have a sweetheart hidden in one of these sinkholes that seem so plentiful in these parts." He was sure they had some Johnny Rebs hidden around somewhere.

She was more angry than frightened, and she looked at him scornfully. "Wouldn't you like to know!" she said. Before her mother could put her hand over Martha Jane's mouth, Martha Jane continued, "Maybe he would take care of my pony your men are stealing!"

"Stealing? That's an ugly word, little miss. This is war, you know."

"It *is* an ugly word, but not as ugly as the deed!" She rushed on, "What good will my pony do anybody? She can't carry a big, heavy man, and she'd be scared to death to go near a battle line."

"Something in what you say, little miss ... Maybe my wife would like her." He wheeled his horse and galloped away.

The Negroes were completely wiped out with the loss of the horses. "Mars Sam, we done the bes' we could. Dem Yanks is the most stealines' folks they is, I guess. We's plumb beat down about it."

"I know you did your best. No use to worry. Go tell the boys I know they did their best. We'll have to get on without our crop of colts next spring. I'm glad they didn't find the workhorses. Maybe they won't ever come back here again. They probably think they've stripped us clean."

From his place in the cane breaks, George had seen the Federals take the mares. His blood boiled, but what could he do? Get caught, and make the Majors subject to indictment for treason and a heavy fine? He could only gnash his teeth and keep quiet. He expected when he got back to the house that he'd find Martha Jane weeping over the loss of her pony and the whole household upset. They were upset but resolved.

"Did you see them get the horses?" asked Martha Jane.

"Yes! I'm sorry I couldn't do anything to stop it."

"Why, what could you have done? There were at least a dozen of them. Oh no, they knew we couldn't do anything—just submit. Couldn't even sass 'em!"

"Did you want to?"

"I most certainly did. I told that officer that he was letting his men steal my pony."

"What did he say?"

"He said 'steal was an ugly word.' I said 'Yes, but it wasn't as ugly as doing it.'"

George laughed.

"You are a spunky girl," he said.

Martha Jane's mother came in to say that supper was ready. "Suppose some Yankees should come while we are at the table, Mother?" Martha Jane asked.

"I think they are through with us for today, honey," said her father, "but if any should come, we'll be able to get George hidden. I've got Tom out the front and Taylor out the back to watch and report. That's one thing about living back off the road. We've time to get ready for them."

"Do you get penalized for harboring a Reb as they do in Rutherford County?" asked George.

"Yes. But we are out of their way here. They don't usually visit us. They stay on the main highway. We've seen more Feds today than we have since the war began."

"You were close enough to the battle three days ago to hear it, weren't you?" asked Mrs. Major.

"I was in Murfreesboro—with General Bragg."

"Tell us—we don't hear much of what goes on."

"There was another engagement on the afternoon of the second—yesterday. Unless General Bragg is retreating, I don't see why so many Federals are spreading through the country. I must find out before I get out of Wilson County. Maybe I'll find out in Lebanon tonight."

"Are you leaving tonight?" asked Martha Jane.

"Yes. I will meet my friend Jake at twelve o'clock tonight close to Lebanon—if both of us are lucky."

As they were leaving the table, Martha Jane said, "You do make short visits, don't you, sir?"

"Weren't you expecting me? Did you get my note?"

"How could I know the note was from you?"

"You did though, didn't you?"

"Well, I guessed it must be—but you don't look like a tramp."

"Don't I? Well, you see—." But he decided not to tell her. Instead he said, "I'm glad you don't think I look too bad."

"Your hair and beard don't look right—not like they did. Have you really turned gray?"

"No—it's dyed—I'm older than you, much older, I'm sorry to say—but my hair isn't gray. We had to look as old as possible, Jake and me, to keep from being mistaken for stragglers. We didn't want anybody to think we were soldiers."

"Why did you come if you aren't going to stay any longer?"

"We were sent. But there is a special reason for my coming by here."

Martha Jane was shy again and felt she must talk. "Did General Lee send you?"

"Yes—it amounted to that. But are you really interested in that?"

"Of course. Why shouldn't I be?"

"There is so little time. I want to talk about something else."

That stopped Martha Jane's flow of words. She was ... frightened? No. But she couldn't think of anything to say. No bright remark came to her at that moment, so she said, "Well?"

"You must know that I'm much interested in you—too much for my happiness maybe."

"Am I that bad?" She refused to be serious.

"You are so young."

"So you've told me—more than once." She sounded resentful. He looked at her with something of a new appraisal.

"Well, aren't you? I'm nearly twice as old as you."

"I don't see how that has anything to do with *my* age. I'm no baby."

"There is so little time—"

"You are always in a hurry when you come here," she said.

"May I come when the war ends and I'm not in a hurry?" he asked.

"We are always glad to see our friends," she said.

"I think you know what I mean. You are no baby, you said."

"I'm not—but I'm not used to guessing riddles. My friends usually say what they mean."

"Your friends? You mean men? How many friends have you in the army?"

"Oh, I have many friends in the army," she said.

"Did one of them take a promise from you away with him?"

"Yes, indeed. I promised Jim to think of him every day. I even promised Bob to pray for him every day. Boys ask for such curious things, don't they?"

"Which one did you promise to marry when the war is over?"

"I didn't promise that to any of them. I told them all if the war lasted very long I might marry a Yankee colonel—if a real handsome one came along and asked me."

"I see you won't be serious. I don't blame you. I—" But he didn't get that sentence finished. Martha Jane's parents were coming into the room. This was one time Martha Jane was *not* glad to see them. She was breathless, waiting for the words that would follow that "I" in George's unfinished sentence.

Mrs. Major was saying, "George, we've come to say goodnight. This has been a hard day for us. I'm not sleepy and shan't go to bed yet, but I know Mr. Major should retire now. I wish you'd change your mind and spend the night with us."

"Thank you. I didn't realize it was so late. I hope your heavy losses today won't keep you awake and troubled tonight."

"Oh no—no," said Mr. Major. "It was a heavy loss—terribly heavy. But at the rate things are going, there'll be nothing left to feed horses on much longer anyhow. If this war lasts two years longer, the South will be ruined. But the greatest loss, of course, is our young men."

"You are right. Well, I must be on my way if I'm to meet Jake. The evening has been all too short." He hesitated and looked embarrassed. "I've asked your daughter if I may come again when the war is over," he said.

"Of course," said Mrs. Major. "We shall be glad to see you. I hope it won't be long."

"I'm afraid it will be. We are doing our best to drive these Northern people back home, but we haven't succeeded so far. I, for my part, will try harder than ever, if possible, since your daughter has told me she may marry a Yankee colonel if the war lasts too long, and a really handsome one comes along." He spoke lightly but added seriously, "I hope you'll use your influence against that."

Mrs. Major pooh-poohed the idea. "She'll never do that while I've any influence with her!" she said.

Mr. Major came more to the point as he said, "Mattie is too young to think of getting married." Everyone called her Mattie.

George offered his hand. "Goodnight then," he said. "Thank you for a good dinner and a very pleasant evening." He turned to Martha Jane. "Goodnight, Mattie." The "Mattie" was so gentle only she heard it. He took both her hands. She thought he was going to kiss her. She was disappointed that he didn't.

When he'd gone, her mother said, "Martha Jane, are you in love with him?"

"What a question, mother! Why should I be? He didn't say he was in love with me."

"That's right, my child. As your father said, you are too young. And *he'll* be seeing a great many beautiful women in Virginia. They say Virginia women are very beautiful."

For George to go across the road to his uncle's barn, change into his tramp outfit, saddle and load Selim, go to the house, and tell his kinfolk goodbye, and be off took less than half an hour. His thoughts as he rode away were a varied mixture. Had he made a favorable impression on Martha Jane—Mattie, as he called her in his mind? She was young, but no baby, as she had said. She had her own mind, and he did not feel at all sure it was turned in his direction. She was beautiful and very desirable. He couldn't deny he was in love. She hadn't asked about the daguerreotype. Maybe his wasn't the only one of her in the Army of Northern Virginia, or in Bragg's army, or—perish the thought—in the Army of the Potomac. He was so absorbed in his thoughts about Martha Jane, he didn't see three men riding toward him till they were too close for comfort.

He turned Selim into a lane that led to a farmhouse back from the road. Without hesitation, he rode up to the fence and dismounted. He'd not be taken without resistance. The men halted at the mouth of the lane, consulted amongst themselves, and rode on. *That was a narrow escape*, he thought. He'd have to be more vigilant. Selim was well-fed and rested. He put his mind on getting to Lebanon and made time, skimming over the ground. He met with no more near adventures.

Around midnight, George passed through the outskirts of Lebanon and on to the pike by Judge Brown's house. He began scrutinizing every corner and dark shadow, looking for Jake. Just before he reached the clump of cedars that was to be their meeting place, he saw a man walking with a cane, slightly limping. He had a bundle on the end of a stick over his shoulder. *That would be Jake*, he thought; but he'd be careful. He rode by him slowly, not looking back.

Before he'd gone many yards, a voice called, "Hello, Bud! If you can't speak, shake a bush!"

George chuckled and was instantly off Selim. "Had to be sure," he said. "Didn't want to kill a man or get killed."

"Jumpin' Jupiter! I *am* glad to see you," said Jake. "Ain't been so glad to see nobody since I left Pa's and Ma's this morning."

"Have you been walking all day?"

"Not walking all the time. Hiding some, resting some, and riding some. A farmer give me a lift on a wagon with some sheep and hogs loaded on it—I rode on the coupling pole. Not so good, but I got my feet rested." He stopped to catch his breath. "Did you see the little gal?"

"Yes. Here, you get up on Selim, and I'll walk beside you. I think we'd better stay together mostly till we get out of Tennessee."

"Yes, sir. But your answer about the little gal don't tell much. Maybe ole Jake shoulda kept his mouth shut."

George gave him his characteristic wink and then the familiar clearing of his throat. "You asked if I saw her. What more do you want to know?"

"Well I'll be dad-blamed ... !"

"Now see here, Jake. Forget that spy's language."

"Yes, sir—all right, sir. But try, sir, not to stir me up beyond my natural-born good nature."

"What do you want to know?"

"Well, I'd like to know if she's as beautiful as ever and—well—have you got any prospects or are you just hanging over the edge ... like some other folks."

"Sort of over the edge, Jake, sort of over the edge. She's more beautiful than ever."

"Well, sir, you've got my full and entire sympathy. I feel powerful sorry for you. But not as sorry as I do for myself. I came away from Miss Fanny treading on air. Didn't hit the ground till the next day. But when I did hit it, I knowed good and well I'd lit for good."

"As bad as that?"

"Yes sir, as bad as that ... but ... well, I'm okay. You see, she told me in the nicest way in the world that I'm just her little buddy, her adored brother George's brother-in-arms, and won't ever be nothing else."

"Sorry, Jake. But you'll be glad of that someday."

"Yes, sir—maybe so, sir. But I've got a powerful far piece to go before I get there."

Three weeks later, George and Jake were back in Lee's camp in Fredericksburg. Because so many men were away on furloughs, they were able to get back into their own hut. They were glad to get back. No more hiding out; no more dodging groups of soldiers, five to their one. Very little danger of a Federal prison now—at least until the next battle.

Union General Ambrose E. Burnside had resigned, and General Joseph Hooker had taken his place. The report was that Burnside had almost lost his mind over the horrible slaughter of his men in the Battle of Fredericksburg. He realized his superior in Lee.

The months went by, somehow, until the first through the fourth of May 1863 when another battle was fought at Chancellorsville, near Fredericksburg. The Battle of Chancellorsville was the third costliest battle, in terms of casualties, of the Civil War. Although outnumbered two to one on the battlefield, the Confederates number of more than ten thousand killed, wounded, missing, and captured was fewer than the more than fourteen thousand the Union had.

Victory was conceded to the Confederates, but A. P. Hill was wounded and Stonewall Jackson killed. General Thomas Jonathon "Stonewall" Jackson was killed by his own men at the Battle of Chancellorsville. General Lee, after the death of his dear friend Stonewall, reorganized the Army of Northern Virginia. General Lee elevated General A. P. Hill to commander of a third army corps. Under Hill was General Henry Heth for division command and General J. J. Archer for commander of one of the brigades, Archer's Light Brigade.

George was promoted, April 8, 1863, from Major to Lieutenant Colonel before the Battle of Chancellorsville and remained commander of the Seventh Tennessee Regiment under Archer's Light Brigade.[1]

---

[1] *Old Military and Civil Service Records, National Archives of Military Service Records* (Washington, D.C.), Lt. Colonel Shepard. The records show that Colonel Shepard was commanding the regiment 30 April to 30 October 1862; May to October 1863; January through March, May through June, and September through October 1864; and January and February 1865. Many records were lost. He was commander of the regiment during the surrender at Appomattox in April 1865.

11 · Gettysburg

At the Bradshaws', things were looking up. Since the Battle of Stones River, soldiers had mostly disappeared. Spring had come and gone and, with it, buttercups, daffodils, cherry blossoms, lilacs, and peach and apple blossoms. Summer had settled in. Sallie and Fanny were in the yard. Sallie, glowing in the sweetness of the flowers, was talking about the peas and beans that were growing in the garden. Fanny was quiet.

"What's the matter, Fanny?" Sallie asked. "You are the one who usually talks continuously about the flowers. You look like you'd lost your best friend. George's last letter hasn't made you blue, has it? I thought it was a very good letter."

"No, George's letter is all right. Nothing in it to be upset about. The death of Stonewall Jackson is a great calamity for us. But maybe it will hasten the end of the war."

"I'll be glad for the war to end, no matter how."

"Yes, I agree. But I'm not thinking about the war for a change. It's Jake's letter."

"What's the matter with Jake's letter? His letters are usually full of fun."

"This one isn't. He says ... here, you read it," Fanny said, handing the letter to Sallie.

Dear Miss Fanny,

When I left you that morning in January, I was just about as happy as a feller could be. I fairly floated through the woods and down that road on to the pike and home. You know why I was so happy! But I guess you knew, too, I'd come to in a day or two. Well, I did—gradually. I wasn't so happy for a spell. I ain't exactly on top the world now, but I've accepted the verdict. I'm just the young brother. I know it.

Now don't think I don't appreciate that. I do. You will always be first with ole Jake, but I promise to keep an eye out for another gal—shucks! Well, I won't have to think about that till the war's over, and who knows what I will be doing by then! Don't you worry about old Jake, Miss Fanny. He'll pull through. And he'll always be thankful he knew you—and loved you—I rather guess he'll do just that the rest of his life, but it won't hurt either of us. And—well, so long, Miss Fanny.
    Jake

Sallie handed the letter back to Fanny and sighed, "Fanny, that letter is enough to make anybody weep. I don't blame you. You know, Fanny, I've sometimes wondered if Jerd Robinson hasn't upset Jake's apple-cart with you."

"My dear madam! When have I ever seen Jerd Robinson?"

"Yes, I know. Well, try not to think too much about Jake. According to George's letter, he won't have much time to think about you or any other girl now before fall."

Sallie was right. George and Jake were on the move with the Army of Northern Virginia, headed for Pennsylvania. The destination was Gettysburg.

July the first, second, and third were three days of the bloodiest battle ever known. The Battle of Gettysburg, according to the National Park Service, totaled fifty-one thousand men killed, wounded, captured, and missing. Of that total, twenty-eight thousand were Confederates.[1] Ken Burns in his Civil War movie called it the "greatest battle ever fought in the western hemisphere."[2] Books would be written about this eventful day in history. History would record Colonel Shepard's part.

Archer's Brigade fired the first shot at Gettysburg and took the first Confederate casualty. Captain J. H. Moore, who fought there in Company B of the Seventh Tennessee Regiment, wrote in a newspaper article entitled "The Battle of Gettysburg:"

On this shoe expedition to Gettysburg, Archer's brigade were [sic] in the advance, and nothing unusual occurred on our march until we

---

[1] National Park Service, Department of Interior, Washington, D.C.

[2] Ken Burns, *The Civil War:* The Universe of Battle, 1863, episode 5 (1990).

got within about a mile and a half of town. Then we were discovered ...
the Fifth Alabama Battalion was deployed ... Archer's brigade formed
line of battle ... on the right of the road ... and Davis's Mississippi
brigade on the left of the road ... Shortly before 12 o'clock ... the battle
of Gettysburg was begun by Archer's Tennessee brigade striking a part
of Gen. Reynolds's corps. General Henry Heth, division commander,
wrote about it for the Southern Historical Society Papers. Heth's
summary of the first day was 'My division—some seven thousand
muskets strong—advanced. I found in my front a heavy skirmish line
and two lines of battle. My division swept over these without halting.
My loss was severe. In twenty-five minutes, I lost twenty-seven hundred
men killed and wounded. The last I saw or remember of this day's fight
was seeing the enemy in my front completely and utterly routed and my
division in hot pursuit. I was then shot and rendered insensible for
some hours.'[3]

General J. J. Pettigrew took over Heth's Division after day one.
Colonel B. D. Fry took over the command of General Archer's Brigade
because of Archer's capture on day one. Colonel Shepard became second
in command to Colonel B. D. Fry of Archer's Brigade. That was
July 1—day one.

Day two, the regiment rested.

Day 3, July 3, was the final battle. General James Longstreet was in
charge of his own division, Pickett's Virginia division, and six brigades
from General A. P. Hill's Corps, one of which was Archer's Brigade.
Later called Pickett's Charge, it was officially referred to as Longstreet's
assault. They were lined up to charge Cemetery Ridge.

There is much contention in the history of Gettysburg about the stone
wall or the stone fence and who went over it. Captain J. H. Moore, who
wrote about Gettysburg for *The Military Annals of Tennessee*, said:

With our line materially weakened by the loss of those that
remained in the road, we pressed on and struck the enemy behind a
fence or hastily constructed breastwork, over which the First and about

---

[3] John Berrien Lindsley, *Military Annals of Tennessee,* vol. 1, (Nashville: J. M. Lindsley
& Co., 1886), 245-247.

one-half the Seventh Tennessee regiments passed. The rest of our command who crossed the second fence had not reached the works because of their horseshoe shape, and because the point that they were to have reached was to the rear and left of where we entered. As we encountered the enemy in his works all was excitement. Our men fought with desperation, and succeeded in driving the enemy from his line. It was a hand-to-hand encounter, lasting but a moment; and as victory was about to crown our efforts, a large body of troops moved resolutely upon our left flank, and our extreme right at the time began to give way, as did our left. Still we in the center held the works, but finally, being unsupported, we were forced to fall back. Those of the second line who reached the Emmittsburg road, never moved beyond that point to our assistance. We fell back to the lane, which was literally strewn with dead and wounded. Around me lay forty dead and wounded of the forty-seven of my company that entered the scene of carnage with me. Col S. G. Shepard and I and the other survivors hesitated in the lane a moment. It was death or surrender to remain. It seemed almost death to retreat. ... We chose the latter alternative, and on we sped through the open field, expecting every [sic] moment to be shot to the ground. [4]

Colonel Shepard in his official report (OR 552) wrote:

Within 180 to 200 yards of his works, we came to a lane inclosed [sic] by two stout post and plank fences. This was a very great obstruction to us, but the men rushed over as rapidly as they could, and advanced directly upon the enemy's works, the first line of which was composed of rough stones. The enemy abandoned this, but just in rear was massed a heavy force. [5]

The two stout post-and-plank-fenced lanes would have been Emmittsburg Road, the rough stones would have been the stone wall, and the heavy force would have been the road at the rear of the angle where the cannons were.

---

[4] John Berrien Lindsley, *The Military Annals of Tennessee,* vol. 1, (Nashville: J. M. Lindsley & Co., 1886), 250–51.

[5] Lt. Col. S. G. Shepard, Report No. 552, Official Report (Lt. Col. S. G. Shepard, Seventh Tennessee Infantry, of Operations of Archer's Brigade, June–August 1, 1863—The Gettysburg Campaign, 10 August 1863, (Washington, D.C.: Government Printing Office, 1889).

Another contention that grew with the years after the war was that Heth's Division was in support of Pickett's Division. Colonel Shepard once again sets the record straight in his official report. He wrote:

> In the engagement of the 3d, the brigade [Archer's] was on the right of our division [Heth's], in the following order: First Tennessee on the right; on its left, Thirteenth Alabama; next, Fourteenth Tennessee; on its left, Seventh Tennessee, and, on the left, Fifth Alabama Battalion. There was a space of a few hundred yards between the right of Archer's brigade and the left of General Pickett's division when we advanced ... by the time we had advanced a little over half of the way, the right of Archer's touched and connected with Pickett's left.

Colonel Shepard's official report of the Battle of Gettysburg is one of the most definitive reports of this eventful battle. It was dated 10 August 1863—just more than a month from the date of the battles. His report establishes that Heth's Division, Archer's Brigade (consisting of the First, the Seventh, the Fourteenth Tennessee regiments and the Fifth Alabama battalion and the Thirteenth Alabama regiment) was lined up with Pickett's Division—not in support of—and it establishes that Confederates other than Virginians and Carolinians went over the stone wall. See Appendix A for OR 552.

Carol Reardon's *Pickett's Charge in History and Memory* states that many a post Civil War tale has stated that only Virginians crossed the stone wall. Reardon, in covering the Virginia–North Carolina clash, brings all up to date with the reiteration of the Southern Historical Society papers, page 357, where it is written:

> It will thus be seen that every one of the official reports, both Federal and Confederate (with the exception of that of Colonel Shephard [sic], of Archer's Brigade, not composed of Carolinians), which refer to the troops who entered the enemy's works, point unmistakably to those of Pickett's Virginians.[6]

---

[6] Carol Reardon, *Pickett's Charge in History and Memory*, (Chapel Hill and London: University of North Carolina Press, 1997), 172.

COLONEL S. G. SHEPARD

Captain Moore and Colonel Shepard both departed Cemetery Ridge at the same time. They ran as fast as they could down that hill and to where General Lee was. Captain Moore years later wrote Colonel Shepard regarding this encounter with General Lee. Moore wrote:

> We fortunately survived, and I now have before me a letter from Col. Shepherd [sic], dated February 8, 1882, relating to the battle of Gettysburg, in which he says: 'I remember very distinctly most of the facts touching the battle of Gettysburg to which you refer. We came out of the fight together. I remember that when we got back to our artillery, we met General Lee, who took me by the hand and said to me: 'Colonel, rally your men and protect our artillery. The fault is mine, but it will all be right in the end.' Whether these were the exact words used by Gen. Lee or not I cannot say but I can say these are substantially his words.' Colonel Shepherd, as I remember, repeats the exact words of Gen. Lee. I was standing within a few feet of them, and remember his using the words 'the fault is mine' at least twice. At this moment Gen. Pettigrew came up to us with his arm black and shattered by a grape-shot, and Gen. Lee addressed him in about the same if not the identical words he spoke to Col. Shepherd, and further said: 'General, I am sorry to see you wounded; go to the rear.' [7]

Colonel Shepard had gone up the hill in command of the Seventh Tennessee Infantry Regiment and second in command of Archer's Brigade. General James J. Archer had been captured day one (July 1), and Colonel B. D. Fry had succeeded him in Brigade command. Colonel Fry was wounded and captured at the stone wall. Shepard was then in command of Archer's Brigade[8] and second in command to General Pettigrew of Heth's Division on the way down from Cemetery Ridge.

---

[7] John Berrien Lindsley, *The Military Annals of Tennessee,* vol. 1, (Nashville: J. M. Lindsley & Co., 1886), 251.

[8] *Confederate Military History*, (Atlanta: Confederate Publishing Co., 1899), vol. VIII, chapt. XI, page 200, states "Lieut.-Col. S. G. Shepard, commanding the Seventh Tennessee, who succeeded to the command of Archer's Brigade after the capture of Col. Fry ..."

Captain J. H. Moore in "Heroism at the Battle of Gettysburg" (See Figure 11-1) wrote:

> Lieut. Col. Shepherd [sic], the 'Old Reliable,' in the center, also did his full duty, and was the only field officer in the entire division that escaped unhurt from the battle. He, for some weeks afterwards, commanded the division.[9]

Pettigrew was in charge of the division because of Heth's injury, and then Shepard was in charge because of Pettigrew's injury. Major J. Jones further verified that Colonel Shepard was in charge of Heth's division in his official report 550. Major Jones wrote:

> I was informed of this condition (General Pettigrew was wounded.), and that I was senior officer of the brigade, subject to the orders of Lieutenant Colonel (S. G.) Shepard, commanding General Archer's Brigade.[10]

The Bradshaws and every other family in the North and South read about Gettysburg in the newspapers. It was all the talk, and all knew that an awful battle had been fought at Gettysburg and that the Confederates had lost. They thought "Gettysburg" every minute of their waking hours and dreamed it in restless, fitful sleep. It would be days before they would hear from George and Jake—if they were still alive and had arms and hands with which to write.

Sallie set another piece of homespun into the loom. Day after day, Fanny would wander in the garden, walk down the road to the post office, visit the neighbors—anything to get away from her thoughts and the bang, bang of Sallie's loom. Even the children were subdued and played quietly with each other or alone.

---

[9] J.H. Moore, "Heroism at the Battle of Gettysburg," *Confederate Veteran,* (Nashville, TN, January 1901), 15 and 16.

[10] Major J. Jones, Report 550, "Twenty-Sixth North Carolina Infantry, Commanding Pettigrew's Brigade, 9 August 1863—The Gettysburg Campaign," *The War of The Rebellion: A Compilation of the Official Records of the Union and Confederate Armies*, ser. I, vol. XXVII, pt. II (Washington, D.C.: Government Printing Office, 1889).

COLONEL S. G. SHEPARD

At long last, a letter came. They had to read much between the lines of George's letter to get anything more than that he was alive and well. They were satisfied with that. They settled down to take plenty of time with Jake's letter. It promised to be a long, full account.

Dear Miss Fanny,

It seems a thousand years since I've had time to do anything but try to keep alive and to shut my eyes and stop my ears from listening to men dying. But a body can't go on seeing and hearing men die and not go stark raving crazy.

Your brother climbed that stone wall with us, and then we had to retreat fast. We had no support and the Union forces came at us. When we reached our artillery, General Lee came to us. He took your brother by the hand and said: "Colonel I am glad to see you alive. The fault is mine, but it will all be right in the end..." Lee looked awful.

Now there's one tale I think ought to be told, and I'm a'going to tell it to you. General Lee had asked your brother to cover his artillery in his retreat. While talking to the Colonel, General Pettigrew rode up, and General Lee told him to go to the rear because he was wounded. Your brother was the only field officer unhurt in Heth's division. Pettigrew and the Colonel were the only field officers left alive in our division

We spent days and days, ten of them, on that retreat, in pouring rain, sloshing through mud, men so tired they'd lie down in mud and go to sleep. We stopped at Falling Waters till pontoon bridges could be fixed to take us across the river. It was too full to ford. As we waited, your brother saw a company of Yanks a'coming. He sent me with a message to General Pettigrew: "A company of the enemy is approaching." Pettigrew sent a message back: "They are our men." I flew with another message to Pettigrew: "Those men have on raincoats. Our men have no raincoats."

By that time, the enemy was upon us, about a hundred cavalry. Pettigrew was mortally wounded. The captain of the Yanks set his horse to ride down Colonel Shepard. He plunged at him. But I'm telling you, Miss Fanny that was one more time when your brother was as supple as a willow and as quick as a flash a lightning. He went under that horse's neck and plunged his sword into that horse's side in one swift movement. The Yank turned in his saddle, had his pistol out— cocked—and a bead on the Colonel. Right then is where ole Jake did the greatest war job he'll ever do if he lives to be a hundred. Before that Yank could pull his trigger, ole Jake's gun spoke and the Yank went to the ground. Before he hardly hit the ground, a hundred bullets riddled him and his horse.

I'm telling you, Miss Fanny, your brother ain't a'going to get killed in this war. He'll never have such another chance encounter as he had at Falling Waters. He'll come home to you, Miss Fanny, some sweet day.

Jake

Fanny crushed both letter and envelope in her hands and lifted her face to the window, her eyes on the horizon. Sallie was sobbing.

After Gettysburg, the Confederacy was in total disarray. Figures 11-2, 11-3, 11-4, 11-5, and 11-6 speak for themselves. Both sides had suffered dramatically, but neither called it quits.

COLONEL S. G. SHEPARD

Figure 11-1 (Page 1 of 2). These articles by Captains J. H. Moore and F. S. Harris, both of Archer's Brigade, relate the heroism at Gettysburg and try to keep the record straight via the *Confederate Veteran*. After the war, bravado was rampant. These two articles appeared in the *Confederate Veteran*, January 1901, pages 15 and 16. Both men were with the Colonel that day.

Capt. F. S. Harris writes from Alabama:

I regret the necessity of a reply to Capt. Turney's article on Gettysburg in December VETERAN. It needs none only for the fact that it appeared in the official organ of the U. C. V., every word of which we want future historians to know is true. . . . But I cannot remain silent at the implied slur against the balance of that grand old regiment, the First Tennessee, whose dead are on every battlefield from Seven Pines to Appomattox; nor the implied accusations against those grand old regiments, the Seventh and Fourteenth Tennessee and Fifth and Thirteenth Alabama Battalions.

Capt. Turney's recollection is so sadly at fault both on the first and third days that it is unnecessary to begin to point out. I have been on that field twice since, in 1899 and 1900. On both occasions I found the lines definitely located. It is true the First Tennessee was next to Pickett, but Capt. Turney's recollection plays him a prank again. Next to the First was the Fourteenth Tennessee. He places the Seventh next, as he says he "cleared the way for Capt. Moore's company to go over," and some of the Fifth Alabama Battalion. Every one in the brigade knows that the Fifth Alabama was on the extreme left of the brigade.

I cannot remember as well as Capt. Turney, but I recollect the gallant Col. George and Capt. Moore far to the front; and I know Col. Fite was captured near there. Col. Lockard, of the Fourteenth Tennessee, was wounded crossing the wall. The Thirteenth and Fifth Alabama Battalions drove to the front as far as any man, and Col. Shepard, Capt. Norris, Capt. John Allen, Bill Young, and others went to the front as far as any Confederate soldier. And they got out with Capt. Allen badly wounded.

But the most serious trouble arising from the publication in so reputable a journal as the VETERAN is that it contradicts that which Archer's and Pettigrew's men have given thirty years to establish. Newspaper soldiers of Pickett's, immediately after the battle, commenced to claim all the glory of this the greatest of the world's battles.

Capt. Bond, of North Carolina, Col. J. H. Moore, before mentioned, and others have established the facts from war records: Fitzhugh Lee's Life of Gen. R. E. Lee and other reliable data. The stones are set at Gettysburg, marking each position attained so different from Capt. Turney's recollection that one would not recognize that gory field from his article. The most unkind shot of all is therefore from the archer in our own camp.

In publishing the foregoing the VETERAN emphasizes afresh its faith in the integrity of any Confederate soldier or officer who was himself in battle. Their devotion to truth and to principle exceeds their partiality for any command over others. We all know by experience that no two will see things alike.

Figure 11-1 (Page 2 of 2). These articles by Captains J. H. Moore and F. S. Harris, both of Archer's Brigade, relate the heroism at Gettysburg and try to keep the record straight via the *Confederate Veteran*. After the war, bravado was rampant. These two articles appeared in the *Confederate Veteran*, January 1901, pages 15 and 16. Both men were with the Colonel that day.

Figure 11-2. The Tennessee Monument is at the staging area of Pickett's Charge (pictures are of both sides). The figures here are for the three Tennessee Regiments and do not mention the casualties for the Fifth Alabama Battalion or the Thirteenth Alabama Regiment, both part of Archer's Brigade. The three stars stand for Middle, East, and West Tennessee. The seven stars on the flag are not understood. The shiny tile base of the monument represents the shape of the state of Tennessee.

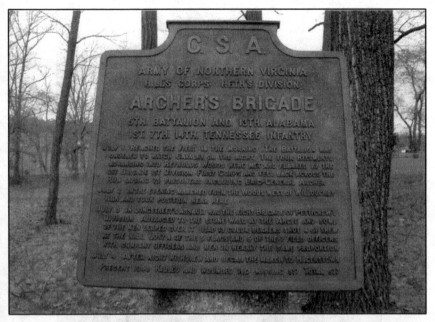

Figure 11-3. Archer's Brigade. Day three statistics for the flags and color-bearers and the totals on this monument were taken from Colonel Shepard's Official Report (OR 552). Colonel Shepard in his OR immortalizes Captain A. D. Norris who saved one of the fourteen flags. Four were left at "the Angle" behind the stone wall along with their flag bearers. Captain Norris tore the flag from the staff and hid it under his coat. Colonel Shepard also mentions the death of General Pettigrew at Falling Waters during the retreat, and his paragraph devoted to the General has oft been repeated. Compared to other official reports, Colonel Shepard mentions few individuals. He concentrates on the facts. Many Confederate reports speak to the gallantry of individuals, which General Lee did not want. General Lee did not like singling out an individual—his soldiers were all heroes, each and every one. The Confederacy didn't even issue medals. The Union did, including many Medals of Honor.

Figure 11-4. A monument with Colonel S. G. Shepard's name on it, near the staging area of Archer's Brigade for Longstreet's Assault (Pickett's Charge) of July 3. Note Colonel Shepard's name is listed under the Third Brigade after Brigadier General James A. (should be J.) Archer, Colonel B. D. Fry, Colonel S. G. Shepard. That was the order of command for the Third Brigade. Archer was captured day one, and his successor Colonel Fry was captured day three at the stone wall. The third day on the monument says, "The Division occupied the position of the day before and was ordered to report to Lieutenant-General Longstreet to unite in the attack of the Union center. The assault was made and failed. The Division returned to its former position."

Figure 11-5. The ominous stone wall. Photo was taken where the oft-referred-to *stone wall*, which runs north and south, meets the wall that runs east. The area boxed in by these two walls was called *"The Angle,"* short for "the Bloody Angle." The east stone wall also ran to the road and met another stone wall, which formed another angle. The road staged many of the cannons. Many Confederates were able to cross the stone wall shown and fight hand-to-hand with the Union forces. There are markers where the North Carolinians made it inside the Angle area and a marker where General Armistead made it. This left the high part (shown) of the wall at the tree for what was left of Archer's Brigade to enter. After entering, the Union reinforcements suddenly came bounding past their own cannons to expel the men in gray. Colonel Shepard wrote in his official report that "Archer's Brigade remained at the works as long as any other troops either on their right or left, so far as I could observe."

Figure 11-6. Photo is taken inside the area referred to as the Angle. From here, one can see Emmittsburg Road and the plank fences framing it on each side. Beyond that, near the trees to the left, is a monument with General Lee on his horse, marking his location after the battle. Colonel Shepard met the general there and Lee said, "Colonel, I'm glad to see you alive. Rally your men and protect your artillery. The fault is mine, but it will all be right in the end."

12 • Grant Goes to Virginia

On the ninth of March 1864, Ulysses S. Grant was made Lieutenant General of the Federal forces in the Civil War; the Federals had charge of the Mississippi River from St. Louis to its mouth. They held all the territory to the northwest, north of the Arkansas River; east of the Mississippi, they had nearly all of the territory north of Memphis and the Charleston Railroad as far as Chattanooga. Nearly all of Tennessee was under Federal control. They held West Virginia and practically all of Virginia, north of the Rapidan River and east of the Blue Ridge Mountains. On the sea coast, they had Fort Monroe and Norfolk in Virginia; Plymouth, Washington, and New Bern in North Carolina; Beaufort, Folly, and Morris Islands, Hilton Head, and Port Royal Islands in South Carolina; and Fort Pulaski in Georgia. One would have thought when the Battle of Gettysburg was lost and Vicksburg had fallen, both in July 1863, that the Confederates would have concluded that it was time to quit. But, no, the war continued.

Fortunately, Archer's Brigade only had two more engagements the year of 1863, and they were minor. One was Bristoe Station and the other Mine Run.

On that same fateful day in March,[1] Colonel Shepard, according to the *Compiled Service Records,* was admitted to the Richmond General Hospital No. 4. The diagnosis was gonorrhea. He was released 28 March 1864. See Figure 12-1. Nowhere else, including his pension papers, is

---

[1] *Compiled Records Showing Service of Military Units in Confederate Organizations, Tennessee, First through Seventh Infantry,* Washington, D.C., The National Archives, National Archives and Records Service, 1971.

there a mention of this disease. Whether the diagnosis was incorrect or not is unknown. There is mention in a later chapter of him having hemorrhoid trouble throughout life.

So thought Fanny, as weary as she was of the whole thing by January 1865. Many things had transpired in the Bradshaw home during the time since George had left them that night in January 1863. Sallie had given birth to her fourth child, Samuel S., not long before Gettysburg. Fanny had spent the winter months teaching the children who could be gathered together at the little, nearby schoolhouse. Jerd Robinson had put aside his pride and timidity about his eye and become a frequent visitor in the Bradshaw home. Letters had come more or less regularly from George and Jake. They wrote very little about war matters. The winters had been hard, food not so plentiful, and anxiety hung with impenetrable gloom over the land.

When Fanny found out that Grant, the victor of Vicksburg, was facing Lee at Virginia, she was frantic with fear and impatience. "Why on earth don't they stop this war!" she wailed to Sallie and William as they read the papers. "How can anybody keep on thinking that Robert E. Lee is the most humane and Christian gentleman ever born?"

"You throw all the responsibility of this war on General Lee," said William. "Do you think that's fair?"

"Why doesn't Abe Lincoln stop the war?" asked Sallie. "He has more power to stop it than anybody else in the world, and yet you never blame him for the terrible slaughter."

"I know," said Fanny. You think Lee is right, and I think Lincoln is right. So there it is! But Lincoln is bound to win."

"I wouldn't be too sure of that," said William. "There is a big part of the Confederacy left in spite of Gettysburg and Vicksburg."

"Yes, but the Confederates didn't follow up that victory to any advantage. It's hopeless. And, William, it all comes back to the question of slavery and preserving the Union. Formal Emancipation Proclamation given January 1, 1863 freed slaves in rebellious states only. Lee is fighting to destroy the Union and keep the Negroes in slavery. As much as I love my precious brother, I can't agree with him—or you—on these questions."

The Battles of the Wilderness, Spotsylvania Court House, and Cold Harbor were to come in the spring of 1864. The Weldon Railroad encounter was in the summer and the battle at Fort Archer was in the spring of 1865 just before the surrender.

"Well, Fanny, after all, I believe you suffer over it more than anybody I know. It will end some day. And, as Jake has always said, George will return to us 'some sweet day.'"

Meanwhile, sickness had come into the Major home in Wilson County. Martha Jane's father was very ill with inflammatory rheumatism and died soon thereafter. They had suffered no recent raids from the Yankees. Martha Jane had heard from George only three times since the Battle of Gettysburg—little notes that she treasured in her jewelry box in the left-hand corner of her top, bureau drawer—precious little notes that said so little and yet so much.

Then, a day came, in April 1865, that set the minds and hearts of every man and woman in both the southern and northern states to throbbing together as one heart and mind in one human body. Strong men wept—some in despair and some in joy. Emotion ebbed and flowed across the land like the waves of some mighty sea. Lee had surrendered! It was 9 April. Lee, the idol of the Confederacy, their hope for "freedom," their infallible hero, the great Lee had cashed in his chips.

What would happen now? What would Jeff Davis do? What would Johnston do? The foundations of the Confederacy crumbled beneath the Southern people.

It wasn't long before they learned that General Joseph E. Johnston surrendered to General William T. Sherman on April 26, 1865 at Durham Station, N.C. After the Confederate armies surrendered, President of the Confederacy Jefferson Davis was imprisoned, awaiting trial for treason. He was freed on May 5, 1867 and was never tried for treason.

In the North, a sigh of relief shuddered through the land. The slaughter was over! Sons and fathers would come home now—those who had not been slain or had not perished. Peace, peace, blessed peace had come at last—at long, long last.

When the news reached the Bradshaw home, William, not stopping to speak to Fanny or Sallie, grabbed his hat and hurried to the post office.

Fanny ran out the gate and down the road to the Whittakers'. Maybe he would have news from George. He had and did.

Sallie went about the house, intensely quiet, doing the housekeeping duties, seeing to the children, and giving Aunt Nancy instructions about dinner.

"What all this excitement about, Miss Sallie?" asked Aunt Nancy.

"General Lee has surrendered the Army of Northern Virginia to the Federals."

"What that mean, Miss Sallie?"

"I guess it means the war is over, Aunt Nancy."

Aunt Nancy shouted, in a subdued and awestruck voice, "Praise the Lord, praise the Lord! Hallelujah! No more killing—no more starving—no more hiding from them Yanks—praise the Lord!"

Fanny called as she burst into the house back from the Whittakers', "Sallie! William! I've letters from George and Jake. Come!" Sallie came. William hadn't returned from the post office.

"Don't wait for William," said Sallie.

"Of course not." Fanny spread the sheets, all crumpled, out on the table.

Appomattox
April 12, 1865
Dear Fanny,

It's all over. An hour ago, we finished the terrible ordeal of stacking arms and signing our paroles. Now we can be on our way to whatever is left for us to go to. I feel stunned. I think most of the men feel stunned and miserable. Now for the first time in months, we have time to think, to remember the friends who have perished in this awful conflict.

This last week has been one of intolerable and needless suffering. I suppose I'm feeling it more keenly because Jake was one of the victims.

Fanny stopped reading and looked at Sallie, her face twisted in pain. "Go on, Fanny. Don't stop to weep. Let's hear the rest." Fanny continued reading.

Maybe there is a man here and there who would like to have fought on; but I believe the men as a rule knew the end had come and were ready to quit. To think that we were so near the end and could go home soon! Well, he's gone to his eternal home.

It was on the retreat from Petersburg to Farmville, where we hoped to get rations after five days of hurried marching, fighting, and starving. Jake was stricken with some intestinal disorder—mostly starvation, I guess. I did all I could to help him. I didn't want him to do as so many of our men were doing, lie down on the side of the road to die or be captured or killed by the Yankees. I managed with one of my men to get him up on Selim. We held him on and rushed Selim along. The Yanks were not far away and coming. Dark came at last, when we'd about given up hope. The Yanks stopped to rest and eat. We stopped, but alas, not to eat. It was then that we found that Jake had stopped breathing. We put his body away as best we could in the short time we had.

I shall miss him terribly, but would miss him even more if the war had gone on. No man ever had a truer friend than Jake was to me. I've had many losses—Archer died [General J. J. Archer died October 24, 1864.] *last fall after rejoining the army after his imprisonment. A. P. Hill was killed* [General A. P. Hill was killed April 2, 1865.] *on our first day of retreat from Petersburg. Nearly all my old company is dead. My Seventh Tennessee Regiment has few of the original men left in it. We've merged and combined till there's not much distinction between companies and regiments. In all my severe losses, I shall miss none more than Jake.*

Forgive my writing so at length on the subject. This is no time to be lamenting losses or looking back. We must look forward and begin the task of rebuilding the fortunes of the South—a bigger task than the one we've just finished. Well, we'll have to learn, maybe in bitterness, to say 'the task that Abe Lincoln has finished.'

General Grant showed every consideration to our great General Lee. But it was heart breaking to see General Lee these last few days. He left just now for Richmond. I think it will be a relief to the men who are still here to have him gone. They cheered whenever he appeared, but their cheers always ended in sobs.

We who were officers were given our horses and side arms. We are under oath, of course, not to take up arms again during this conflict. General Johnston has not yet surrendered, but you know more about that, probably, than I do.

I shall leave today for Washington. Selim has had a good rest and some fodder and oats. I was lucky in that. And thanks to General

Grant, all of us have been fed. I feel equal to the trip, and I'm anxious to see Washington. In two battles, we were almost in sight of the Federal capital. Now I can go in with no danger from the Feds.

I hope to get home soon, but will tarry in these parts till the war is over down there. I've seen enough of war to last several lifetimes. If I'm ever able to blot out the horrors from my mind of these four years—four months, or even the last four days—I shall never want to hear the word "war" again.

I found some scraps of paper in Jake's pockets when I looked to see if he had written to his parents or to you. I found a letter or scraps of paper. I might send them on. Keep his letters and these scraps. I haven't read them. They may be worthless, but I'll want to see them.

Also, I'm sending a tin-type of yours truly—ridiculous. Today, since early morning, the strolling photographers have been busy around the army camp making pictures. They've made hundreds. Some of the men insisted that I sit for one for them. I'm sending you the one that fell into my hands. After all, it will give you some idea of the dilapidated condition your brother is in—so you won't be so shocked when you see him! I hope you are not more disgusted than I am with the ring the "artist" put on my finger. You can soot it out!

I hope to get a barber to trim my whiskers soon and pick up a suit of clothes somewhere before I get home.

Love to the Bradshaws,
George

Figure 12-2 shows that the Colonel was given "two horses" as private property.[2] Alice speaks of only one, Selim. The Colonel kept the penciled terms of surrender addressed to him to read to his troops that fateful day. He later read the terms from the same paper to those attending the June 1897 Confederate Veterans reunion in Nashville.[3] See Figure 12-3.

"Fanny, don't you want just to be happy now over George's safety and wait till later to read Jake's papers?" asked Sally.

---

[2] *Compiled Records Showing Service of Military Units in Confederate Organizations, Tennessee, First through Seventh Infantry*, Washington, D.C., The National Archives, National Archives and Records Service, 1971.

[3] *Confederate Veteran*, (Nashville, TN, August 1897), 405.

"No, I want to see them now," Fanny replied. "You needn't, if you would rather not."

"I'll listen if you feel like reading them," Sallie said quietly, respecting her sister's feelings.

Fanny read:

> *Somewhere in the Wilderness. Papa's pet got shot by his own men last week—just about where Stonewall got killed by his men a year ago. Powerful bad luck, but if "Papa's pet" had got there when Papa told him to, so many of A. P. Hill's men wouldn't have gotten killed.*

"Oh my goodness," said Fanny. "The Wilderness. I read about that slaughter. And Jake is so funny with his 'Papa's pet' as he refers to General Longstreet. What a contrast to the facts." She stopped for a moment and remembered.

The Battle of the Wilderness, May 5 and 6, 1864, was the sixth costliest battle of the Civil War in terms of casualties. Casualties, according to the National Park Service, totaled a little less than thirty thousand of which a little more than eleven thousand were Confederates.[4] General James Longstreet was accidentally shot the first day by his own men. He was back in command in October 1864. It was the first battle for General Ulysses Grant against General Lee.

Fanny read on:

> *In the Wilderness: Wilcox got so scared when Longstreet didn't come as he was supposed to, so he sent somebody at three in the morning to find out why. Heth didn't have sense enough to get scared— maybe that minie ball—maybe born that way. Huh! Lee much upset over Longstreet—but he got over it—Papa's pet.*
>
> *In the Wilderness: Sorter got used to hearing men crying for water after a battle, but in these awful thickets, they had to burn too. Wonder why we keep on. If we had more men and more food, we'd lick em. But old Jeff expects us to lick em one, two, three, and do it half starved. The old dad-blamed hyena.*
>
> *In the Wilderness: Rain, rain, rain. I guess the fire's all out now. A lot of us are still alive—don't see how come! Trees were cut down by*

---

[4] National Park Service, Department of Interior, Washington, D.C.

bullets ... It seems we are to have a run down the road to beat the Yanks to Spotsylvania Court House.

Fanny paused after she read the word "Spotsylvania." The Battle of Spotsylvania, May 8–19, 1864, was the fourth costliest in terms of casualties of the Civil War. Casualties, according to the National Park Service, totaled thirty thousand of which twelve thousand were Confederates.[5] General Grant was fighting against Lee again.

> *Spotsylvania: Well, we beat em all right, and licked em too. Great bunch of fellers. No wonder Lee keeps on. Great General—no wonder the fellers keep on.*
> *Petersburg [June 15, 1864 through April 2, 1865]: Well, here we are between Petersburg and the Yanks to freeze another winter. Archer dead and Hill sick. My Colonel, not so well; I hope and pray he don't go down in this awful fighting he's doing. He won't.*

"Oh, my goodness," George was sick.[6] He didn't say anything in his letter.

> *Near the Crater: Whew! What a hullabaloo! If the judgment day is a bigger belch than that blow up, I'd druther be somewhere else. What a sight! Air full of men and guns and haversacks and logs! May the good Lord deliver me from any more wars. Can't blame men for running away. Would myself, but can't because of my Colonel. I think he'd just about die he'd feel so disgraced if I did. He'd never run from anything. No sir! He sure keeps his face to the front. I think he must feel about hisself as I do about him—that he's not going to get killed. He acts like nothing could hurt him—like the other day when a bullet went clean through his hat and he didn't notice it. It scared me about into fits. What a man!*
> *Heth, huh! He ain't no general. Another one of Papa's pets—a Virginian!*

---

[5] National Park Service, Department of Interior, Washington, D.C.

[6] *Compiled Records Showing Service of Military Units in Confederate Organizations, Tennessee, First through Seventh Infantry,* Washington, D.C., The National Archives, National Archives and Records Service, 1971.

Papa's pet done come back—that shot through his neck didn't kill him! Wonder what he'll do to A. P. Hill now!

Horses eating bark off trees, gnawing through limbs, eating bags and paper—poor horses, poor men. Why on earth don't we stop?

Getting in recruits—boys seventeen to fifty. Won't be no boys and men left by the time the killing stops. Wish I could go home.

Petersburg: Grand day for ole Jake rabbit—yum! yum! The Colonel made me eat it—said he didn't like rabbit. Course I didn't believe that. I was too hungry to hold out. Hadn't had anything for three days but moldy corn bread and not much of that and sour sorghum. One poor fellow got two hard tack biscuits and he was hoarding em—looking at em and nibbling on em. He dropped one in a mud hole. He cussed. Picked it up and ate it, mud and all. Awful winter, but spring's coming, and more fighting. Fighting now. Every day somebody getting killed. Oh, Lord, how long will it last? Forever, I guess-—but not for ole Jake.

Fanny picked up the sheet she had laid aside. She handed it to Sallie. "Sallie, you read this. I'm afraid I can't."

Sallie took it and read:

Petersburg
March 1865
My dear Miss Fanny,

You won't never see this. I'm just writing because I'm tired and lonesome and sick, and want to go home and see Ma and Pa and talk to you.

Miss Fanny, I hope you don't never feel bad about ole Jake. You never caused him no trouble. He ain't never going to stop loving you, but you won't know it. Thinking about you helps me to quit thinking so much about this awful war. I don't much think I'll ever see you again. But I'm glad, terribly glad, I've known you and your brother. He's a great man and a good man. If I'm to cross over before this war is over, I want him close by—and I have a feeling he will be.

Now Miss Fanny, I may sound kinder doleful, but I ain't a feeling that way. I'm just sorter tired. Well, so long, Miss Fanny.
Jake

What neither Fanny nor Sallie nor the whole family knew was George's part in the Wilderness. In fact, there is little known of George's role in the Battle of the Wilderness other than a few articles in the *Confederate Veteran* magazine, which are reproduced here. Apparently, he was a hero in a quiet, never-to-be-recognized kind of way for the saving of many lives. The last sentence (written thirty years after the war) from Captain F. S. Harris in the November 1895 *Confederate Veteran* article puts it most succinctly when he writes: "I can't see how the 'Spaniard' can be any other than Colonel Shepard, and the most convincing proof of all is the modest admission of the Colonel to J. K. Miller that it was he." The articles from the *Confederate Veteran* discussing this issue are reproduced here as Figures 12-5, 12-6, 12-7, and 12-8.

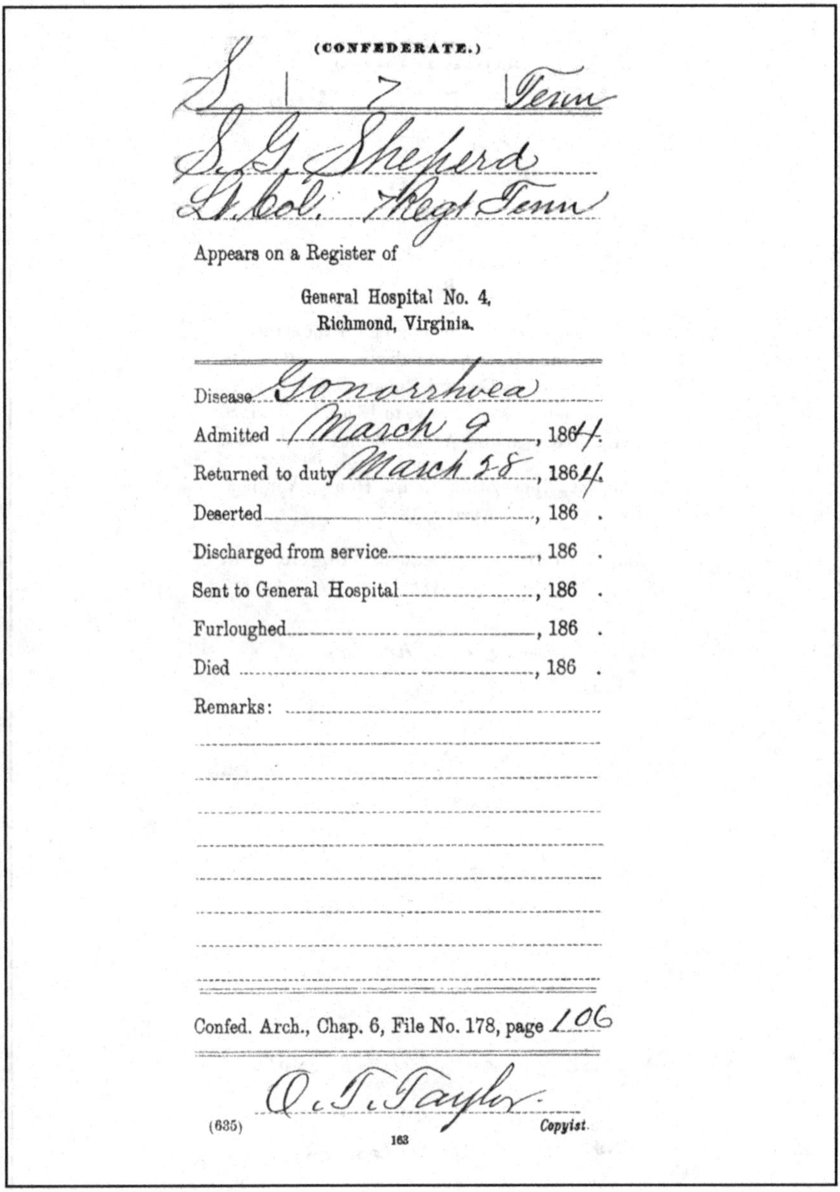

(CONFEDERATE.)

S. G. Shepard
Lt. Col. 7 Regt Tenn

Appears on a Register of

General Hospital No. 4,
Richmond, Virginia.

Disease Gonorrhœa
Admitted March 9, 1864.
Returned to duty March 28, 1864.
Deserted _____, 186 .
Discharged from service _____, 186 .
Sent to General Hospital _____, 186 .
Furloughed _____, 186 .
Died _____, 186 .
Remarks: _____

Confed. Arch., Chap. 6, File No. 178, page 106

O. T. Taylor.
(635)   Copyist.
163

Figure 12-1. Colonel Shepard's record shows he was admitted to General Hospital No. 4, Richmond, Virginia.

(Confederate.)

S | 7 | **Tenn.**

S G Shepard

Lt Col , Co. ...... , 7 Tennessee Regiment.

Appears on a

Roll

of Prisoners of War, belonging to the Army of Northern Virginia, who have been this day surrendered by General Robert E. Lee, C. S. A., commanding said Army, to Lieut. Genl. U. S. Grant, commanding Armies of the United States.

Done at Appomattox Court House, Virginia, April 9, 1865.

Roll dated Hd. Qrs. McComb's Brigade, April 11, 1865.

Private property. *Two horses*

Remarks:

× name cancelled on Roll

Number of roll:

397 *J M Weaver*

(653) Copyist.

Figure 12-2. Colonel Shepard was given two horses at Appomattox.

ABOUT CAPITULATION AT APPOMATTOX.

The following paper in pencil manuscript has been preserved by Lieut. Col. S. G. Shepard, and was in his possession at the Nashville reunion. He commanded the Seventh Tennessee Regiment, Archer's Brigade:

APPOMATTOX C. H., April 10, 1865.

Agreement entered into this day in regard to the surrender of the Army of Northern Virginia to the United States authorities.

1. The troops shall march by brigades and detachments to a designated point, stack their arms, deposit their sabers, pistols, etc., and from thence march to their homes under charge of their officers, superintended by their respective divisions and corps commanders, officers retaining their side arms and their authorized number of private horses.

2. All public horses and public property of all kinds to be turned over to the staff officers designated by the United States authorities.

3. Such transportation as may be agreed upon as necessary for the transportation of the private baggage of officers will be allowed to accompany the officers, to be turned over at the end of the trip to the nearest United States quartermaster, receipt being taken for the same.

4. Couriers and mounted men of the artillery and cavalry whose horses are their own private property will be allowed to retain them.

5. The surrender of the Army of Northern Virginia shall be construed to include all the forces operating with that army on the 8th inst., the date of the commencement of negotiations for surrender, except such bodies of cavalry as actually [Here a line of the manuscript is not discernible] of artillery as were more than (20) twenty miles from Appomattox C. H. at the time of surrender, on the 9th inst.

Signed: J. Longstreet, Lieut.-Gen.; John Gibbons, Maj.-Gen. Vols.; J. B. Gordon, Maj.-Gen.; Charles Griffin, Bvt. Maj.-Gen. Vols.; W. N. Pendleton Brig.-Gen. and Chief Artillery; W. Merrett, Bvt. Maj.-Gen.

A true copy. V. Latrobe, Lieut.-Col. and A. A. G.; R. H. Finney, A. A. G.

Official. Polk G. Johnson, A. A. A. G.

For Lieut.-Col. Shepard, Commanding Seventh Tennessee.

Figure 12-3. Colonel Shepard reads the terms of surrender from penciled manuscript given to him at Appomattox. *Confederate Veteran*, August 1897, page 405.

(CONFEDERATE.)

S | G | 7 | Tenn

S. G. Shepard

Lt Col   7 Regt Tenn

Appears on an

Inspection Report

of Archer's and Walker's Brigades, Heth's Division, 3d Army Corps, commanded by Brig. Gen. J. J. Archer.

Report dated *Camp near Petersburg Va*   *Sept 30*, 186*4*.

Date of muster of organ- }
    ization into service } ----------- , 186 .

Term of service ----------

Absent commissioned officers accounted for :

By what authority *Order Genl Lee sick furlough*

Date *Sept 15*, 186*4*.

Remarks : ----------

Inspection Report P, No. 24; inclosure 19.

M. C. Leonard

(654)   Copyist.

3879

Figure 12-4. Colonel Shepard ordered to take sick furlough.

When that splendid Division, commanded by Gen. Heth, was thrown into confusion by the impetuous Warner's Corps, just at dawn, May 6, '64, at the Wilderness, only one organized command was withdrawn. This was done by the coolness of a Lieut. Colonel, whom Hood's Texans thought to be a Spaniard, owing to his very dark complexion. Was not this Lieut. Colonel Shepard of the 7th Tennessee, Archer's Brigade? The description is the counterpart of that gallant officer, and all who knew him know he was specially qualified for such work.

Figure 12-5. The question was raised about who was the "Spaniard" who acted with such command at the Battle of the Wilderness. *Confederate Veteran*, May 1895, page 145.

COLONEL S. G. SHEPARD

WHAT COMMAND WAS IT?

In publishing the following the VETERAN entertains the parties directly interested without motive of conveying the impression that either side designs discipline in the least.

Capt. F. S. Harris, Nashville: In reply to inquiry from Texas, as to who was the "Spaniard" who brought the Tennesseans "out of the Wilderness in good order," May 6, '64, I think it must have been Col. S. G. Shepard, of the Seventh Tennessee. He was in command of that famous old regiment that morning, and was just the man for such work

However, I admit that I was not one of those so brought out. I got out of the Wilderness in quite a demoralized manner, and just the once from the body of men commanded by the "Spaniard," Col. Shepard.

(Capt. Harris is the author of article in April number about "Sharp-shooting in Lee's Army.")

J. K. Miller, Gallatin, Tenn: Well, Old Comrade, there was an inquiry in May VETERAN from a Texan, in reference to a Colonel who got out "in order" on the morning of May 6th, '64, at the battle of the Wilderness. Col. Shepard, of the Seventh Tennessee, spent the night with me recently, and as it was thought he might have been the "Spaniard," I asked him if he was in command and if his men were in order. He said they were, and went on to speak of the morning surprise, and that as he came out the Texans were deploying, and he passed through their middle. So, you see, he was the man in command of the Tennesseans.

J. K. Cayce, Hammond, Tex., June 14, 1895: In your May issue you speak of only one command of Heth's division retaining its organization when that division was surprised by Warren's corps at the battle of the Wilderness, and you ask if the officer in command thereof was not Lieut.-Col. Shepard of the Seventh Tennessee, Archer's Brigade. The officer was not Col. Shepard, but was Col. J. M. Stone, present governor of Mississippi, commanding that morning the Second and Eleventh Mississippi, Davis' Brigade, Heth's Division. These men saved the army.

Shortly afterwards Gen. Lee rode up, and Gen. Longstreet introduced Col. Stone to him as the man who saved the army. This title Col. Stone modestly declined, saying "My boys did it."

Col. Stone was afterwards rewarded for his bravery by an appointment as brigadier-general, but refused the honor, as he "could not take his boys with him" to his new command.

This bit of history was given me by my father, who was a member of the Second Mississippi, and helped "save the army" on the morning of May 6, 1864.

Figure 12-6. The answers start to come regarding the "Spaniard" who was the hero at the Wilderness. Captains F. S. Harris and J. H. Miller claim it was Colonel Shepard. J. K. Cayce says it was Colonel Stone, based on what his father told him. *Confederate Veteran*, August 1895, page 239.

Page 317   Confederate Veteran October
1895.

SIMPLE JUSTICE ASKED.

J. B. Policy, of the Fourth Texas, Hood's Brigade, writes from
Floresville, Texas: In the May VETERAN appears the following: "When
that splendid Division commanded by Gen. Heth was thrown into
confusion by the impetuous Warren's Corps, just at dawn, May 6, 1864,
at the Wilderness, only one organized command was withdrawn. This
was done by the coolness of a Lieutenant Colonel, whom Hood's Texans
thought to be a Spaniard, owing to his very dark complexion. Was not
this Lieutenant Colonel Shepard, of the Seventh Tennessee, Archer's
Brigade? The description is the counterpart of that gallant officer, and all
who knew him know he was specially qualified for such work."
    Not possessing any information on the subject of inquiry mentioned, I
remained silent, but my pride as a member of Hood's Texas Brigade
prohibits silence in regard to the following which appears in your
August number, from J. K. Cayce, of Hammond, Texas:
    In the May VETERAN you speak of only one command of Heth's
Division retaining its organization when that Division was surprised by
Warren's Corps at the battle of the Wilderness, and you ask if the officer
in command thereof was not Lieutenant Colonel Shepard of the Seventh
Tennessee, Archer's' Brigade. The officer was not Col. Shepard, but was
Col. J. M. Stone, present governor of Mississippi, commanding that
morning the Second and Eleventh Mississippi, Davis' Brigade, Heth's
Division. These men saved the army.
    Shortly afterwards Gen. Lee rode up, and en. Longstreet introduced
Col. Stone to him as the man who saved the army. This title Col. Stone
modestly declined, saying, 'My boys did it.'
    Col. Stone was afterwards rewarded for his bravery by an appointment
as Brigadier General, but refused the honor, as he 'could not take his
boys with him to his new command.
    That two regiments of a Division which had been surprised and thrown
into confusion by an impetuous attack of Warren's Corps, ' 'saved the
army" by withdrawing as an organized command, at a time when the
Confederate army was about to be cut in twain, appears, to say the least,
improbable. Certainly, however, the regiments mentioned held no
ground passed over and recaptured by the Texas Brigade. Certainly too,
Gen. Lee as well as Gen. Longstreet, must have been ignorant that Col.
.Stone and his gallant Mississippians were "saving the army" at the time
of the occurrences narrated in the following, except from a journal
which I kept during the war. Written, as my account was, the day after
the battle, when every scene and incident .was fresh in my memory, it
merits some consideration in any effort to determine what command did
the saying.

Figure 12-7. J. B. Policy says it was Colonel J. M. Stone. Colonel Stone takes
credit and gets promoted to General. *Confederate Veteran*, October 1895, page
317.

Capt. F. S. Harris, Nashville, writes from New Orleans, in reply to J. K. Cayce, of Hammond, Texas, in August VETERAN, as follows:

He insists that the "Spaniard "who "got out of the Wilderness in good order," May 6, '64, was not Col. S. G. Shepard of the Seventh Tennessee, now living at Partlow, Wilson county, Tennessee, but Governor Stone of Mississippi. Col. J. M. Stone was then, and is now, every thing that his legions of admirers claimed, and I have no doubt "came out in good order." However, the gentleman from Hood's old brigade who made the inquiry, states that the man who came out in such perfect order was in command of a Tennessee Regiment—that his complexion was so dark he thought he must be a Spaniard. Col. Stone could not have been commanding a Tennessee regiment, as there were only three Tennessee regiments in the Army of Northern Virginia at that time—the First Tennessee commanded by Col. George, now of Fayetteville, Tennessee, whose complexion was very light; Colonel (afterwards General) McCombs, now of Gordonsville, Va., whose complexion is also light, commanded the Fourteenth Tennessee; while Col. S. G. Shepard, whose complexion was very dark, eyes and skin the regular Castillian hue, with beard and hair long, straight and jet black, commanded the Seventh Tennessee. I can't see how the "Spaniard" can be any other than Col. Shepard, and the most convincing proof of all is the modest admission of the Colonel to comrade J. K. Miller that it was he.

Figure 12-8. Captain F. S. Harris speaks up again for Colonel Shepard. It could not have been Colonel Stone—it had to be Colonel Shepard. *Confederate Veteran*, November 1895, page 334.

13 · The Colonel Goes to Washington

On Saturday, April fifteenth, George disembarked from a barge on the outskirts of Washington. It was six o'clock in the morning and raining. As he left the pier leading his horse, Selim, a sentinel shouted, "Halt!" George stopped, saluted, and asked what the trouble was.

"Where are you from?" the soldier asked.

"I'm just off the barge from traveling all night," George replied.

"Pass," said the soldier, "but watch your step."

George couldn't figure it out. He had been dismissed with so much finality that he automatically walked on, asking no questions. *He thought the war was over—or so he had been led to believe from that last awful day at Appomattox. Why this soldier then? What was he doing? Reconstruction had already begun perhaps. Strange city this—didn't think he'd like it.*

He went a quarter of a mile further before he saw a stable where he could leave his horse. He quickly turned Selim over to the half-asleep stableboy at the front and hurried on, hoping soon to find a place to stop and get some breakfast.

As he passed along a narrow, unfrequented street, he saw an old man standing out on the curbstone in front of an old house whose front door opened right onto the sidewalk. The old man was peering up and down the street, evidently expecting somebody. When his eye rested on George, he gazed at him. As George came within his reach, the old man seized him by the arm, pulled him into the house, and shut the door. George freed himself, ready to defend against what he supposed was a man with too much drink.

"What's troubling you, my friend?" George asked.

"Nothing's troubling me, but something will be troubling you if you try to walk the streets of Washington this morning in that Confederate uniform," he replied resolutely.

"The war's over," George quickly retaliated. "Or haven't you heard?"

"Lincoln's been shot!" was the reply to George. "Haven't you heard? And Seward. And I don't know how many more! Might be Mosby."

"No! Why? How?" George was horrified.

"A man shot Lincoln in the Ford Theatre last night ... Good Friday."

"Who shot him? What are you talking about? Aren't you dreaming, my friend?"

"Absolutely not. That's what they are trying to find out. Who! And the gang he has with him. It's a company of them, they say, and lots of people may get killed. Some already have been. You are in danger, great danger, right now. All Confederates are being arrested. Go up in my attic, and stay till the excitement dies down."

"How do you know I didn't shoot Lincoln?" asked George, inclined to postpone his retirement to the attic, indeed not having much notion of going at all.

"You'll have to explain that to that bunch of Federals coming down the street if you wait much longer! And it might not be so good for me if you're caught in my house. There is a place behind a panel next to the chimney in my attic that they wouldn't find in a year. But if you won't hide in the attic, go on out the back door and don't wait any longer. Now hurry!"

George waited no longer. It wouldn't be right for him to be caught in this old man's house. Besides, he had no hankering to be caught at all by Federals and maybe meet his doom at the end of a rope. He decided on the attic.

It was dark and musty in his hiding place. And he was distressed, appalled at Lincoln having been shot, if indeed he was. What a calamity for the South! The South had all she could stand without killing the man who stood to be her best friend in the terrible days of reconstruction ... Who could have been such a fool? But then maybe the old fellow was lying, thought George. Surely, he'd have heard it on the barge if such a national tragedy had occurred. Well no, he probably wouldn't have heard.

The Federals were on the search. They pounded on the door, calling lustily for the man of the house. Then, they were inside, and George could hear the talking getting louder. Now they were coming up the steps to the attic! Maybe he'd never get home after all. Why on earth hadn't he gone home from Appomattox? Such inordinate curiosity! Washington couldn't be such a great sight—certainly not great enough to get in a situation such as this. If he ever got out of this mess, he'd head for home. But there were Federals there too. Now they were pounding on the very wall behind which he was hiding. His disgust was almost as great as his fear. A mob had no restraint, no reason. Every Confederate would be a criminal if Lincoln were assassinated. Then the mob was gone. George had plenty of time in his musty hiding place to think after the soldiers were gone, before the man, his host, came up with food and water.

Finally, his mental anguish was halted. As he took the tray of food from his host, he asked, "Have you a paper? A newspaper? I'd like to see a paper."

"In a hurry, sir?" the strange old man asked.

George realized that he was acting rather hastily, to say the least. "Pardon me, sir. But, yes, I am. I wonder if there's a paper with an account of last night's shooting?"

"If not already, there will be soon. I'll get one for you."

"Thank you. And will it be all right for me to sit out in the room now? I'll be very careful and go behind the panel if any disturbance is made on the street below."

"I think so. I'll wait for your tray. It wouldn't do for it to be found up here."

"I understand." George gulped his cup of queer-tasting, sweet-potato-and-peanut coffee and swallowed his bread and slice of bacon—not bad.

"Fine, fine," he said. "Now if you'll find me a paper, I'll certainly be obliged to you. I've plenty of Confederate money and a little silver. I suppose the Confederate money is not in use here ..."

"Well, no," his host replied. "I might get a paper with some, though." George handed him a roll of bills, and the old man went out.

At seven-thirty in the morning, George heard the tolling of the bells. They were ringing for Abraham Lincoln, the sixteenth President of the United States, who had died at seven twenty-two, unbeknownst to George at that moment. It was Easter weekend. No doubting any longer or hoping his host was mistaken. Something terrible had happened. He wished his host would come with a paper. He wanted a paper. His patience had about reached the limit when his host burst into the room. Almost too excited to speak, he thrust the newspaper into George's hands and said, "The city is wild. It isn't safe for anybody on the streets now." Then he rushed downstairs and to his front door to watch and listen.

George devoured the papers:

TREASON—A WIDE SPREAD DEMAND FOR VENGEANCE AGAINST THE AUTHORS OF REBELLION FORETOLD

George let that statement soak in while he wondered what had become of Jefferson Davis and his beloved General Lee. It was evident to him now that the city was one wild mob. *Andy Johnson has been made president*, he read. That statement gave him no comfort. He remembered Johnson's military rule in Tennessee. *General Grant has been called to the city to take charge*. That statement gave him some comfort. But he decided that his host was right. He'd better stay in today.

He wondered how it would be if he had some civilian clothes. Perhaps if he got out of uniform, he might venture out. Staying cooped up when things were happening was entirely against the grain with him.

When his host brought him a tray for his midday meal, he asked, "Would it be possible for me to get some civilian clothes? You've been kindness itself, but I feel that I can't continue to impose myself on you. If I had some different clothes, I feel I could get out and mix with the people with very little danger."

"That's for you to say, sir," his host replied. "I'll do what I can for you. I've a suit I might lend you or sell you, if it fits. But I advise you to stay in till tomorrow. By then, the excitement may have died down some. You are welcome in my house as long as you want to stay. They are saying it was an actor, name of Booth, who shot Lincoln. They haven't found him yet. You'll see it in the paper."

"Yes, I have seen. It wasn't he who killed Seward though."

"No. They think that Booth has a regular gang with him. A report has it that Mosby is one of the gang. Do you know him?"

George later learned that John Wilkes Booth also plotted to kill Secretary of State William H. Seward. Booth's accomplice, Lewis Powell, attacked Seward with a knife, but Seward recovered. Vice President Andrew Johnson was also targeted by Booth, but his designated assassin, George Atzerodt, got drunk instead. The speculation that it was the Confederacy or that it was particularly Lieutenant Colonel John S. Mosby, CSA was unfounded.

"No I don't personally know Mosby." George cleared his throat and seemed a little embarrassed, and then, "May I ask why you've been so kind to me? You don't even know my name, nor I yours."

"My name is Simon. I am a Jew; I understand a bit about mobs. And your name?"

"Shepard. I figured you were a Jew when I saw the Hebrew books."

"Colonel, is it?"

"Yes—Lieutenant Colonel. But please, I would like to know ... if you don't mind telling me ... why you have singled me out for your kindness?"

"Well, Colonel, it's a strange story. A man came by before light this morning and stopped at my door. He was in a great hurry—much excited. He announced that Lincoln had been shot. 'There's the devil to pay in Washington today!' he almost shouted and, with that, he dashed off. He was on horseback.

"I was utterly astonished and bewildered. I called my wife. She hadn't heard him at all. She's not very well and sleeps in the back room away from the noise of the street. We talked about this strange fellow till it began to get light, as light as it would get with the clouds and rain. I had a feeling that somebody needed help, somebody that I could and should help. That was what I was doing and thinking when you came. I was looking for somebody I ought to help. When I saw you, it flashed over me: *There's the man you are to help.* Maybe you understand it, sir. I don't."

George was strangely moved. He didn't understand it either. But he was profoundly grateful, and his mind turned to that Eternal Help—the Help he had felt so many, many times during this past four years.

Mr. Simon got a suit for George. It was Easter Sunday. George assured his new friend that he'd be back by dark and sallied forth to see and hear the sights and sounds of Washington. He'd like to find a church. It had been a long time since he'd been in a church, and on this Easter morning, he had a great desire to worship in a house of God. He wandered on, not daring to ask for directions or places or to appear to be unfamiliar with the streets of Washington. Soon, he came to a little church that looked inviting. He went in. All went well enough until the minister made some unfavorable comment on Lincoln in his sermon. Immediately, "veteran reservists" in the audience came to the front, seized the minister, dragged him from the pulpit, and, once outside, arrested him.

George thought it was about time for him to move on. He came to another church—a big, prosperous-looking church. He went in and got seated in time to hear the minister denouncing the ruling classes in the South, saying they must either totally submit or be considered criminals. As the minister spoke, some of the audience muttered, "Hang them!" Altogether, George's morning was not an ideal one for promoting brotherliness and good feeling. He was terribly depressed with the situation, thinking only, *Poor Southland! Poor Southland!*

He wasn't sure after hearing these ministers and seeing and hearing the audiences whether he wanted to see the White House or Lincoln, who would be lying in state. Well, he'd get a bite to eat somewhere; maybe then he'd feel better. In any case, he'd see what he could during the afternoon and leave that night for Tennessee. He'd have to see his new friend, Mr. Simon, once more, to thank him … Strange that Mr. Simon.

As he looked for a café or tavern, Jake, Fanny, and Martha Jane mixed into his somber thoughts and chased each other over and around his mind. He'd be glad to see the folks back home.

So glad and so sorry. Sorry to go home without Jake. Jake's great good humor in words and antics came before him poignantly as he trudged along. How he did miss Jake! Jake would see something funny in all the tragedy and hubbub if he were here now, and he'd make

George see it. Fanny was like that too. He'd be glad to get home to Fanny. But, he couldn't deny it; his most intense desire was to see Martha Jane. He heard directly from her only twice during these nearly two years. He knew through his family that she hadn't married a Yankee Colonel. Maybe she was in love with one though—or a general. He hoped ... maybe she remembered with kindness a certain Confederate Colonel ... That was a very pleasant thought. He'd have to be certain about that very soon. He wouldn't tarry long at Sallie's. All at once, he was seized with a deep impatience to be on his way. He must see Martha Jane soon—very soon.

When he found a place and had a bite to eat and was on his way again, he set his course toward Pennsylvania Avenue. As he passed along streets crowded with excited men standing in groups on crepe-draped corners, he could catch such words as "treason," "rebels," "hang," "vengeance," and "assassination." Was this what the South had spent four years dying to accomplish? He stumbled on with eyes blind to all the sights he'd hoped to see in Washington. If he were on Pennsylvania Avenue, he didn't know it. He failed to see the White House, though he came as near to it as he dared without approaching too close to the numerous guards at all the entrances. It was all one tragic blur. He saw only the tragedy that confronted his beloved Southland.

When he realized that he was utterly weary and was seeing nothing he had hoped to see, he turned his steps to his new friend's house. He would spend the night there and get away early next morning. He could no longer stand the gloom of Washington and his vision of the future for the South, a vision induced by the sights and sounds on every street and in every public building in the nation's capital.

14 · A Wedding

Prior to the war, Colonel Shepard was just called George. During the war, his papers reflected the initials S. G. and Samuel G. After the war, there are a few papers he signed "Samuel G.," but mostly he used only his initials. His family continued calling him George, but everyone else came to call him—with great respect—just "Colonel."

On April 25, 1865, Martha Jane received a letter from Colonel S. G. Shepard asking if he might come for that "longer visit" they had talked about more than two years before.

After his letter, Martha Jane went around as one in a dream. Becky didn't know about the letter, but she heard the lilt in Martha Jane's voice and saw the light in her eyes.

"I'm powerful glad you're feeling so fine, Miss Mat, honey. It makes the house seem like the old times—like before your pa died."

At the hour the Colonel was to arrive, Martha Jane and her mother were seated on the long verandah that ran the full length of the two big front rooms and the hall between them. It was a lovely day in May.

When they saw the Colonel coming, Mrs. Major got up and went into her room. Martha Jane started to follow her mother, then decided not to. "Mother," she called, "please come back."

"Why honey, he's just the George Shepard you've known all your life."

"I know—but he's a colonel now."

By then, the Colonel was coming through the gate. He didn't look too composed himself. But as he stepped up on the veranda, his embarrassment vanished. He shook hands warmly with Mrs. Major and said how sorry he was that Mr. Major had passed away. He then gave Martha Jane the kiss that had been hanging between them for more than two long years. Mrs. Major was shocked. But Martha Jane was not surprised at all.

"Well, George, have a seat ... if you feel so inclined," said Mrs. Major in a sort of twitter.

"Thank you. I will. And I'll state my business and get that off our minds."

Martha Jane flared at him. "Don't you think you are a little premature?"

That seemed to give George a considerable jolt. He sat dejected for a second or two. "Perhaps so," he said. He raised his eyes to hers. "But two years and more is a long time to wait for an answer."

"You haven't asked any questions that I know anything about—not anywhere I'm concerned," said Martha Jane, feigning an icy distance. But her looks belied her words. George looked at her so straight and so long, she began to fidget.

Mrs. Major said, "I think I'd better leave you two alone to settle any question you have between you."

"Before you go," said George, "may I have your permission to ask Martha Jane to marry me?"

"Yes," said Mrs. Major, with something like a sob as she vanished.

"What about it, Martha Jane?" asked George.

"I never heard of such a proposal—if that's what it is!"

"What do you want me to say?"

"Why, you've never said anything about love! I wouldn't marry the highest-up general in the world if he didn't love me." She was almost weeping. Instantly, he was on his feet, and she was in his arms. He just held her. Then he kissed her. When he finished, she had little room left for doubt about his love.

"Is that all right?" he asked.

"That's better," she sank into her chair, sighed, and gazed down the long road to the big gate. George drew his chair close to hers.

"I've talked to Uncle Spickard," he said, "about selling me some land adjoining your family's land to the south and there is a good bit of timber—some well-seasoned cedar, cut and ready for building, three fairly good fields for cultivation, and I think a very good place for building a house. Of course, nothing is settled. I had to ask you first."

"Well," she gasped, "you are fast, aren't you? Is that the way you fought in the army?" She was sorry and deeply ashamed before the words were even out of her mouth. George looked stung to the quick—overcome with utter frustration and depression. "Oh, forgive me, please!" she cried.

"Never mind," he said. "You don't know, and I hope never will know, what this war has meant to us who fought in it. I can't talk about it. I can't think about it and keep my sanity. Maybe someday I can tell you something about it—but not now … not now."

"You don't have to—ever. I'll never ask you again, never!" George stood up, smiled, and reached for her hand. "Would you like to see the place I think would be all right for a house?"

"Oh yes! Let me get my hat."

The summer scurried by for Martha Jane and George alike. But for him, it was too full of backbreaking labor to be altogether satisfactory. He was almost too tired to enjoy his evenings with Martha Jane. On the other hand, the hard work was a relief to his mind—relief beyond all telling. The war grew dimmer as he lifted logs and stones, sawed and hewed and nailed together the house that was to be his and Martha Jane's home. They could have lived with her mother, but he'd have none of that.

At first, they'd have only two rooms—one, a big eighteen-by-twenty-foot great room, and one, a narrow eighteen-by-twelve-foot sleeping room—with a huge fireplace that was six feet high by eight feet wide. That would mean security against the winds that would come as tornadoes in future days. The fireplace was open to both rooms. Though most of the task was on him, friends and neighbors lent a hand in the building. See Figure 14-1.

August was approaching. Martha Jane's wedding dress, fashioned out of her mother's, was about completed. The wedding date was set for August third. Becky was the most excited person in the entire house. Martha Jane's two small sisters, Nannie, who was eight, and Bettie, who was just four, were enjoying the excitement. Eleven-year-old Tom was too much boy to be interested.

On the second of August, Mrs. Eliza Sherrill, a good friend and close neighbor, sent her servant Maria with as many roses as she could carry in two huge baskets to help Aunt Sarah and Becky with decorating the house George had just built for them. The Colonel's Aunt Lina (Evelyn) Spickard sent a cartload of roses from her flower garden. The house was remade into one gorgeous garden of roses: roses festooned over doors and windows, yellow roses in blue bowls, white roses in crimson jars, red roses and pink roses on tables, mantels, cabinets, and bureaus. White roses banked on a wire frame at the end of the verandah made the bridal altar. Roses flamed and perfumed to make a beautiful wedding day for Martha Jane and George. Martha Jane looked radiant. The Colonel looked as though the war was now a thing of the past.

The Colonel and Martha Jane were married on Thursday, August 3, 1865, according to most records and her cemetery headstone. She was twenty years old (10 November 1845), and George was thirty-five (28 January 1830). Figure 14-2 shows the bond for marriage obtained August first. His cousin, friend, and neighbor, Albert Spickard, signed with him.

Figure 14-1. The house still stands. It now has siding. The house was originally built of planks and posts. The upper picture shows the original plus an addition added years later. The original was the part to the right, and it had a "dog run" where part of the porch is shown. A dog run is an opening to the outdoors built like a hall. The picture at the bottom shows the addition, which had a dog run in the middle where the porch is. There are two stone fireplaces, one on each side of the new addition. This photo does not show the original fireplace in the upper photo—too many trees.

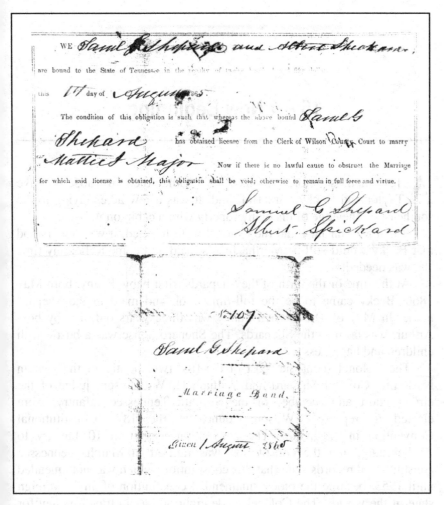

Figure 14-2. License to marry for Colonel and Martha Jane Major (Mattie)—one of the few times the Colonel signed as Samuel G. Shepard. Albert Spickard witnessed the bond. The marriage certificate could not be found.

15 • A New Beginning

A few months before Martha Jane's father died in 1865, he gave Taylor and Becky a tract of land. It was a few acres laying to the southeast on the edge of his own property with a cabin on it.

When Martha Jane and the Colonel were married, it was understood that Becky would still be Martha Jane's maid and come to her any time she was needed.

At the time of the birth of the Shepards' first baby, Fanny, born May 1866, Becky came to be the full-time cook and maid in the Shepard home. In May of 1869, when Fanny was three years old, a baby boy, Arthur, was born to the Shepards. The Shepard house was a bustle with children and happiness.

The Colonel spent the most of the first two months of the year in Nashville. Colonel Shepard and William H. Williamson, judge of the circuit court and member of the Seventh Tennessee Infantry, were elected to represent Wilson County at the 1870 Constitutional Convention in Nashville.[1] The convention was from 10 January to 23 February, and the constitution was ratified in March. Tennessee constitutional records state that this constitution, which was not amended until 1953, became the oldest unamended constitution of any sovereign state in the world.[2] The Colonel made eight dollars in travel money for the fifty miles round trip and $180 per diem for the forty-five days.

---

[1] Ellen Taylor Schlink, *This is the Place, a History of Lebanon, Tennessee, 1780–1972,* (Nashville: Blue & Gray Press, 1972), 39.

[2] *Constitutional Convention Records*, Tennessee State Library and Archives, Nashville, TN.

There were eighty-two men who congregated in Nashville to abolish slavery in the constitution. They also provided for a poll tax that was to be used solely for public, free education. In addition, they reviewed every article and section and made changes as they felt necessary. According to Robert E. Corlew, these "were men of political talent and experience; many had been slaveholders and most were of conservative temperament. Neill Brown had been governor; others, including the chairman, were to hold that office later. A few had served in the United States or Confederate congresses, and more than one-half had been members of the state legislature. Most had fought in Federal or Southern armies, and four had been Confederate generals." Robert L. Taylor in Corlew's book said: "The future should be built upon the enduring principles of free thought, free action, a free ballot, justice, law, order, the education of the masses, the autonomy of the states, constitutional government, one flag, and a reunited republic, and Corlew claims Tennessee with its new constitution was on its way. Not only did these men change the constitution but in so doing they were instrumental in thwarting military rule for Tennessee."[3] See Figures 15-1, 15-2, 15-3, and 15-4.

Arthur died almost a year after he was born during the time the colonel was home from the convention.

After obtaining recognition from the Constitutional Convention, Wilson County elected Colonel Shepard to the House of Representatives, the Thirty-sixth General Assembly, for the years 1871 to 1873.[4] See Figure 15-5.

Less than a year after Arthur's death, and during the Colonel's time as a legislator, Fanny was stricken and died after a short illness.

A death gloom settled over the Shepard home. Martha Jane was pitifully depressed. But the Colonel seemed to have received a heavier

---

[3] Robert E. Corlew, *Tennessee, A Short History*, Second Edition, Updated through 1989, (Knoxville: The University of Tennessee Press), 349.

[4] Robert McBride and Dan M. Robison, eds., *Biographical Directory of the Tennessee General Assembly*, vol. II, 1861–1901 (Nashville: Tennessee State Library and Archives and Tennessee Historical Commission, 1979), 811 and 812.

blow. Always a quiet man, he now became more quiet and absentminded. As the weeks and months went by, Martha Jane almost forgot her own grief in her anxiety and distress for her husband. Too often, he seemed far away, gazing over the edge of the world.

One morning, when the home had been empty of any child for a few months, Martha Jane, on her way to the kitchen to consult with Becky about meals for the day, was stopped at the kitchen door, caught by the sight of a strange Becky. Usually her Becky was lively, jolly, and full of talk. Even when things were not all to her liking, she kept her jovial spirit. Now, she sat dejectedly humped over the pan of potatoes she had on her lap, her elbows on her knees, a potato in one hand, a peeling knife in the other, her eyes out the window. She seemed completely absorbed in what she was seeing. A look of fear was in her eyes. She did not hear Miss Mat approach. Martha Jane hardly dared speak for fear of the shock she might give her. She cleared her throat. Becky came to with a shudder. She straightened up, dropped the knife and potato into the water, clutched the sides of the pan, and blurted out, "Miss Mat, is there anything the matter with the Colonel?"

Martha Jane came into the room and sat down by the table. Her knees were wobbly, her throat dry. "Why do you ask, Becky?"

Becky grew brisk and businesslike. She picked up a potato and began peeling it. "Well, he ain't seem hisself lately. Maybe he need a doctor."

"I've told him that, Becky. But he says there's nothing the matter with him."

"Oh mercy me! Miss Mat, you ain't expect something the matter too, is you?"

"What do you mean? Do you think there's something wrong with him?"

"Just you look out there on that fence right now." She almost whispered it, pointing tragically out the window. "He been out there seem like more an hour, talking to hissef and waving his hands and arms about. What he doing out there?"

"I don't know, Becky. I thought I was the only one who knew he did that."

"Why he been doing that ever since his baby, Miss Fanny, died. Look like he brain sorter went off with her when she died and ain't never come back no more. He took his baby boy dying bad enough but not like Miss Fanny." Shaking her head and mumbling, she repeated, "Not like Miss Fanny."

"Becky, you frighten me."

Becky jerked herself up and took a look at her Miss Mat. Instantly, she regretted her words. "Now, honey chile, don't you worry," she crooned. "I just a ole fool. When he going to Nashville again?" she asked, brightening up and changing the subject. "Maybe he worried about his lawyer business?"

"He has to go to Nashville next week. The legislature meets then. I'm hoping the trip will help him." Martha Jane looked so distressed that Becky was conscience-stricken.

"Course it will, honey chile. I'm an ole fool putting notions in your pretty head. You just go on and have a good time. His sister, Miss Fanny, coming to stay with you whiles he gone?" Miss Fanny was a tonic for Becky as well as for Martha Jane. Becky hoped she would come.

"No, she's too busy—hands too full right now. Nanny will stay with me."

"That's good. Don't you worry no more, honey."

When the Colonel got home from Nashville, Martha Jane could see no change in his actions or his moods. She was desperate. Then something happened.

One morning, he came to her with, "Mat, want to go with me to Fellowship today?"

"To Fellowship? Why are you going there?"

"It's an all-day association meeting and dinner on the grounds. There will be several speakers. I'm to preach the introductory sermon."

Martha Jane almost fainted, but she held on to her chair and kept a straight face. "Preach? I thought you were a lawyer!"

"Well, I am—a sort of one, I reckon." He smiled as she hadn't seen him smile in many a day. "But it won't hurt any in taking a text from the Bible and saying a few words, will it?" He stopped, cleared his throat, and gave his shoulder a twitch. "Coming or not?"

Her mind whirled and reeled. She was afraid he might need her more than he had ever in all their life together. She answered matter-of-factly, "Of course, I'll go with you."

"Be ready by nine-thirty," he said and smiled at her with the old twinkle in his eyes. Then he walked off the porch and down the path, on through the gate, and out into the woods where she had seen him go many times before. Often she had wondered why he went. But she had never had the courage to ask—well it seemed a sort of hallowed place that she could neither enter nor ask about. When he was out of sight, she hurried to the kitchen. "Becky," she called.

"Yes, Miss Mat. I'm right here."

"Becky, the crisis has come."

"Who's that come? Miss Mat, sit down—you all a trembling."

"I can't stop long. I'm going with him to Fellowship at nine-thirty."

"Going with who to what?"

"With Mr. Shepard to a Baptist church five miles from here."

"To a Baptist church? Why he be wanting to go to a church this time of week? It's this a Friday?"

"Becky, he says he's going to preach!"

Becky threw her hands to her head and began to sway her body. She moaned and groaned. Then she threw her head up. "Why didn't' you tell him he be a lawyer?"

"I did, but he said that that wouldn't hurt anything."

"Miss Mat, you better stay at home."

"No Becky, I'll stay with him as long as he needs me. There will be dinner at the church, he says. But I think we'll need something to eat when we get home—if we get home. Have supper for us?"

"I will, Miss Mat. I will, but I sure hates to see you go. I'll be powerful glad to see you a coming home—if you comes home. Goodbye, Mis Mat." She threw her apron over her head and went out the back kitchen door and on down this path to the garden where she grabbed a hoe to work off some of her tension. All the while, she kept looking toward the house to see them go. She knew that they would drive out the road that ran past the garden, and maybe she'd get a look at the Colonel's face, and maybe she could tell whether his mind was all gone or not.

"Po Miss Mat," she moaned, "she sure do love that man. She shaded her eyes with a hand to peer down the road. "There they comes now—he look all shiny like. He's a changed man sure nuff. She watched till they were out of sight, then with a sign she said, "I do hope Miss Mat get by all right." She picked up the hoe. "I believe I'll hoe out the taters whiles I'm out here. And I'll get some corn before it gets too hot. I'll have a corn pudding and chicken pie for supper ifin I ketch one of them young roosters, and some apple dumplins. The Colonel sure do set a hasty tooth in an apple dumplin. Miss Mat she don't care for apple so I'll make some boiled custard for her—bless her pretty self."

When the Colonel left Martha Jane and went into the woods, he had his Bible. She didn't see it because he had it under his arm. In the woods, around the bend of the fence, were many trees, cedars, and hickories, a few walnut trees, and a very big oak. Under the oak was a flat rock, and on the rock was a big log where a tree had fallen. It was George's bethel. Now, he wanted to have a conference with his Lord. He wanted to pray. In the face of what he wanted to do, on this day, he felt weak and helpless. He was afraid. He had made many talks in Sunday school and prayer meetings—but to preach a sermon! That was too big for him.

He'd been working on sermons for weeks, practicing delivery and gestures. He had no idea that Martha Jane and Becky had both seen him sitting on the fence or down by the barn muttering to himself and waving his hand—a sharp little gesture, about the only one he ever made—and thought he was losing his mind. He had worked on many passages in the Bible trying to make sermons.

This morning, after much thought and prayer, he had chosen the fourth chapter of Philippians. Now he opened his Bible and read the chapter again. So many of the verses could serve as texts. But he decided on the thirteenth verse as his text for this morning: "I can do all things through Christ which strengthen me." He needed to remember those words every minute with what was directly in front of him. He felt there would be others in the audience who would need the assurance that that verse gave, not as much as he did, maybe, but everybody needed that verse. His deepest desire was to help his brethren.

COLONEL S. G. SHEPARD

He got down on his knees and prayed the Lord to accept him and give him assurance that he was starting out on the right road, starting out to do His will. "I can do nothing by myself, Lord; I can't help the folks any without your help. They need help. There is much work to do. I'll fail today, Lord, miserably fail, if you don't go with me ..." He left his bethel and went for the horse and buggy.

When Martha Jane and the Colonel reached Fellowship church, there were many horses and buggies already there. Evidently, there would be a big crowd. Martha Jane's heart was pounding. The Colonel was a little more brisk than usual. "We'll hitch right here," he said, "not too close to the church. You can come out and sit in the buggy if you get tired." He unhitched Joe's traces and let him step from between the shafts, but left the harness on him.

Many people said, "Morning, Colonel" and "Morning, Mrs. Shepard" as they picked their way across the yard to the church door.

When they were halfway down the aisle of the church, the Colonel said, "You'd better sit about here. I'll go down to the front where the preachers are."

Martha Jane found a seat and settled herself. She had never before had such a feeling in church as she was having now. Her heart had slowed down somewhat, but her hands were cold and clammy.

The meeting was about to begin. Brother Carter was acting moderator, Brother Russell the secretary. John Adkins had charge of the singing. "Rock of Ages" was announced, and the whole congregation was asked to sing. Jenny Leath was at the organ, and John was standing next to her beating the time. Then there was a prayer, and Reverend Jim Saunders read and then spoke to a set of resolutions that the church make larger appropriations to the Sunday school. In response, Reverend Rice spoke on the greater importance of funding missions as compared to the Sunday school. There were several short speeches, and then it was time for the sermon. The congregation was asked to stand and sing, "Jesus, Lover of My Soul."

Reverend Madison Knight had the job of introducing the speaker at the eleven o'clock hour. He made a rather long-winded speech, in

George's opinion, describing his war record and carrying on about why he was still called the Colonel.

Martha Jane's tension was rising. She didn't take her eyes off George, who was sitting on the rostrum behind the pulpit, his legs crossed.

Finally, Brother Knight turned to the Colonel and said, "Brother Shepard will now speak." The Colonel rose, stepped up to the pulpit, and laid his open Bible on it. Then with his hands grasping the two sides of the stand, he looked out over the audience, sizing up the crowd. Martha Jane calmed down; he looked like he knew what he was doing. He said softly, "Let's have a word of prayer."

After praying with only a few words, he said, "We will take for our lesson this morning the fourth chapter of Philippians. Paul was in prison when he wrote this letter to the church at Philippi. The letter was written for all time. It's a letter to Fellowship Church, to the Powell's Chapel church, to the church at Lascassas at the Glade, to every church represented here today. Listen to the reading of Paul's words as though he had sent the letter to each of these churches."

Then he began to read, reading every verse, stopping at some to comment. "*I beseech Euodias and beseech Syntyche that they be of one mind in the Lord.*" He paused and looked up from his Bible. "I don't know," he said, "if you brethren or sisters have ever had any fallings out ... lately or at any time. But if Paul says to you to 'be of one mind,' he means stop the fuss and get busy doing the Lord's work." Again he read, "*Help those women who labored with me in the gospel ...* Women," he said, "can get into rows and cause trouble. But women are necessary in the Lord's work. They can be a powerful hindrance or a powerful help. Follow after the good women at Philippi who helped Paul, and help your own pastor."

He dwelt at length on verse eight, emphasizing the advantage of keeping the mind clean. He read, "*Finally, brethren, whatsoever things are true ...*" He paused and repeated the word *true*. "Better not say or think things that aren't so. If you don't know what you are saying is the truth, better not say it." Again, he read, "*Whatsoever things are honest ...* Just another way," he said, "Paul had to tell us to think the truth. *As a man thinketh, so is he ... Whatsoever things are just,*" he read, and laid his Bible on the pulpit. "It's powerful easy to think unjust things about neighbors and friends and even about brethren and sisters in the church. Paul says don't do that. Think about things that are just. If we can't think good things about our neighbors, don't think at all—at least don't talk."

He dropped his eyes to his Bible and read the rest of the verse, *"Whatsoever things are pure, whatsoever things are lovely, whatsoever things are of good report; if there be any virtue and if there be any praise ..."* He paused and, as he looked out over his audience, seemed to be searching his own mind and the minds of his listeners. After a second or two, he said, "That means if you've got religion; if you love God and want to do right, think on these things."

He read the next four verses and then paused. He laid his Bible on the pulpit, his hands pressed down beside his Bible. "Now," he said, "we've come to the verse, verse thirteen, that I want to impress on our minds this morning as the text for the lesson today. Paul has been telling us some powerfully hard things we ought to do—things we can't do ... without help. In this next verse, he tells us where to get the help we need: *I can do all things through Christ which strengtheneth me.* Paul told us, in a natural, conversational voice, how Jesus had fed the five thousand down by the sea. He told what a busy day Jesus had had. 'Jesus was weary,' he said. He sent his disciples away, on across the sea in a boat, while He went up into the mountain to pray, a thing Jesus was in the habit of doing when his burden grew heavy. Late in the night, Jesus went walking on the sea to his disciples. When they saw Him, they cried out. Afraid. Peter, who had much self-reliance, said 'Lord, if it be thou, bid me come to thee on the water.' And He said, 'Come.' When Peter got out of the boat into the sea and began walking, he looked down at the waves and was afraid and began to sink. He cried out, 'Lord, save me.' Jesus caught his hand and said, 'Oh thou of little faith, wherefore dids't thou doubt?'

"We think we can do great things. We start out as Peter did, lose faith, and fail. We fail to call on the Lord for help; that's the greatest failure of all. We must have the help of the Lord if we are to succeed in our church work or daily living.

"You remember how on the night of Jesus' betrayal, he said to Peter, 'Simon, Simon, behold Satan hath desired to have you that he may sift you as wheat. But I have prayed for thee that my faith fail not.' And Peter, who still thought he could do anything he wanted to with help from no one, said, 'Lord, I am ready to go with thee both into prison and to death.' When a man thinks that way about himself, he'll soon be in a mighty bad fix. Jesus knew what Peter would do. He said, 'Peter, the cock shall not crow this night before that thou shalt thrice deny that thou knowest me.'

"And when Judas betrayed Jesus, and they brought Him to the high priest's house—the Bible says, 'Peter followed afar off.' Well, if Peter had followed close to Jesus, he wouldn't have made such a failure as he did a few hours later. We get strength from the Lord when we follow closely by Him."

The Colonel had forgotten himself; the extreme nervous tension of the morning had passed. The people were hanging on his every word as he tried to bring to the preachers and deacons and church members the message that so completely filled his own heart and mind, the message that "we can do all things through Christ which strengthen us." George closed the way he began, saying, "Let us pray." His prayer was again short and earnest.

Then the meeting went back into the hands of Brother Knight, who made a few announcements, led a closing song, and pronounced the benediction. The service was then over, and the meeting adjourned. From minutes and leaflets found regarding the Fellowship churches, it is assumed the church he attended was located outside Gladeville in Rutherford County.

While the last song was being sung, many people spoke to the Colonel about the sermon. One of his old war friends said, "Well, Colonel, you can preach 'bout as well as you can fight."

A deacon who had recently declined to pray in public when his pastor had asked him to said, "Mighty good sermon. Looked like you were saying things right at me."

Martha Jane was having a hard time keeping the tears from showing in her eyes. *He can preach,* she thought. *He knows the Lord. He's in his right mind. The Lord has been dealing with him. Why did he ever think he was a lawyer?*

She was saved from thoughts about to completely overwhelm her by Sister Carter and Sister Morris coming for her to have dinner with them. They wanted her to have some of Sister Carter's fried chicken and Sister Morris's chocolate layer cake. Their tables were spread, and they wanted the preacher and his wife to be their guests.

All day, Becky had kept busy sweeping around the doors, wiping up floors, and making things look nice for her Miss Mat. By three o'clock, she began casting an eye down the road on which the Shepards had gone that morning. By four o'clock, she was restless. Everything for supper had been prepared and was ready for the oven. Then she saw them coming. She ran into Miss Mat's room and stood where she could see them but they couldn't see her. She saw that Miss Mat looked happy. She saw that the Colonel still had that shiny look of the morning.

"Mercy me!" she said. "Why don't Miss Mat come on in the house! I is about to explode!"

When the Colonel took the horse and buggy to the barn and Miss Mat came in, Becky met her with her eyes bulged and question marks all over her face.

"Becky, it's all right. It's all right, Becky!" Martha Jane almost shouted.

"He gave a grand sermon. And now he's always going to be a preacher. He isn't going to be a lawyer any more. Oh Becky, I'm so happy!"

According to the *History of Tennessee,* he served his time in the legislature but was ordained a Missionary Baptist Minister in 1872. After he served his time as a legislator, he served as pastor for more than one church at a time. *History of Tennessee* claims in 1886 he had charge of three churches in Rutherford County and one in Canon County at Woodbury.[5] *History of Middle Tennessee* lists all the churches he had from 1873 until 1900.[6]

---

[5] *History of Tennessee*, (Nashville: Goodspeed Publishing Co., 1886), 1 and 116.

[6] J. H. Grime, *History of Middle Tennessee Baptists*, (Kentucky, 1900), pages 36, 77, 91, 101, 533. He was pastor of Big Cedar Lick—Mt. Olivet church in Leeville, Wilson County, 1873–1876 and 1896–1899. He was pastor of Union Church, 10 miles south of

Becky threw her apron over her head and started for the kitchen. "Praise the Lord! Praise the Lord! Glory Hallelujah!" she crooned.

Three weeks, later George's sister, Fanny, arrived.

"Fanny, I'm always glad to see you ... but I don't think I was ever so glad as I am right now," said Martha Jane as Fanny and Jordan Robinson drove up to the front gate at the Shepards' home and Fanny stepped out of the buggy. "Glad to see you too, Jerd," she went on as she kissed Fanny.

"Well now, that's nice of you, Mat—if I'm to call you Mat. I haven't been in the family long enough to know all the ropes," he said.

"Don't you think for a second, Jerd Robinson," Fanny said, "that you'll ever know all the ropes in this family. Besides, if five years dating isn't long enough to know what to say, you'd better hold your tongue." According to the marriage license, Fanny Shepard was married to Jordan Robinson on December 16, 1873 in Wilson County.

"Well, now, maybe someday I'll be smarter than you think I am," he drawled.

"I see she torments you like she used to do me, Jerd. Don't let her get you down," said George. "She's a little hard to manage."

"Uh huh—yes—that's why I married her! I knew then I'd never have another minute's peace. How are you, George?"

"First rate. Why didn't you bring Ida? We'd like to see her too."

"She's spending the night at Sallie's," said Jerd. "Sallie's got a lively bunch. Our Ida loves Sallie's Ida more than she does her own ma." Jerd looked at Fanny expecting a retort. Fanny ignored him. "Come on, George," coaxed Jerd, a little chagrined at Fanny's not rising to his bait. "Let's put the horse up. I want to see your cattle before it gets dark."

Lebanon in Wilson County on waters of Hurricane Creek and better known as "Hurricane Church," from 1880–1889 and "1899 to present" (the book was published in 1900). He was pastor of Woodbury Church, Cannon County, located at the bend of the east fork of Stone's River from 1886 to 1893. He was pastor of Poplar Hill Baptist Church, which was about four miles north of Watertown, Wilson County, and located in a schoolhouse. The Poplar Hill church had merged with Spring Creek Baptist Church and took the name of Linwood Baptist Church by the time Colonel Shepard became pastor in 1896 to Present (1900). The church was six miles east of Lebanon.

"George," said Fanny, "be careful, or he'll buy everything you've got that's of any account. And he'll cheat you out of your eyeteeth." Jerd chuckled.

George answered, "Don't worry about me. I've traded before."

When Fanny and Mat got into the house, Fanny asked, "Mat, what's this I hear about George's preaching?"

"It's true, Fanny. He has preached three times in the past three weeks."

"Have you heard him?"

"Every time. Fanny, he's wonderful! He can preach better than any preacher I've ever heard."

Fanny laughed and grinned at Martha Jane with her peculiarly teasing grin. "Ain't love wonderful?" she said. Martha Jane's face got pink, her eyes big. "That's all right, Mat. I didn't mean a thing. Next to you, I guess, I'm George's most ardent admirer. I've loved him all his life. But it seems a little sudden that he could turn into a preacher overnight."

"I don't think he did that," said Martha Jane. "I think he has been thinking about it ever since Fanny died. I can't see why her death has anything to do with it, but it seems to have had."

"Hadn't he ever said anything to you about preaching before her death?"

"No, not till that morning three weeks ago when he asked me to go with him to Fellowship. That's when he preached his first sermon. You know, Mr. Shepard doesn't tell much."

"Don't I! He's the most closed-mouth rascal in the world."

"Did he ever talk about preaching when he was a boy?" asked Martha Jane.

Fanny sighed and sank deeper into her chair. "Yes, Mat, it's a long story."

"Tell it to me—please now—before they come in."

Fanny told her the tale about how he believed he had disappointed his mother when he became a lawyer. She added the information about Jake's letter after the Battle of Harper's Ferry.

"What a wonderful story. Why did he wait so long to begin?"

"He wanted to be a lawyer! He didn't believe he could be a preacher—wasn't good enough, hadn't the ability. How do you feel about it, Mat? Do you feel he will succeed? He's pretty old to begin now to be a preacher."

"There's no doubt in my mind—nor in his either, I think. Fanny, you must hear him."

"Madam, I've every intention of hearing him at the very first opportunity."

"Fanny, you know, I believe he thinks God took our children as punishment for not starting to preach as soon as the war was over."

"No!"

"Yes, I think he does."

"Well, that seems to be a pretty hard thing to say. Why should a just God punish you for George's disobedience? I can't believe that."

"Why God wouldn't be trying to punish *me*."

"But He would be? Wouldn't He? So none of that makes sense."

"I don't know as much about God as you and Mr. Shepard do, Fanny. But I've read in the Old Testament about how awful it is to disobey God. I've always been afraid of God myself. He seems so terrible."

"He *is* loving—and He's just. And to take your children to punish George isn't loving or just."

"Why, your brother and I are one, aren't we? God can't do *anything* to one of us without doing it to the other. I'm sure I wouldn't want Him to."

"I'm glad you look at it that way. If we are going to think of God in matter at all, we've got to think that He's been pretty patient with George."

"It's all too deep for me," said Martha Jane. "I guess we'll just have to be glad God is God and cares enough about us even to correct us when we need it."

Figure 15-1. This is one of the photos taken during the time he served in the Constitutional Convention of 1870 or during his legislative years of 1871 to 1873. Photo shows his black-black hair and blue eyes (light in picture). (Courtesy of Tennessee State Library and Archives.)

Figure 15-2. There are three photos of the colonel in the Tennessee Constitutional Convention of 1870. They are all taken from one of the three. It appears they took a photo and used the same headshot for the remaining two photos. In this photo, he is in the second row from the bottom, first on the left. (Courtesy of Tennessee State Library and Archives.)

COLONEL S. G. SHEPARD

Figure 15-3. Shows the Colonel in the second from the bottom row, second from left. This figure shows when and where the convention was held and the officers presiding. Two from each county were elected to serve. (Courtesy of Tennessee State Library and Archives.)

Figure 15-4. Shows the same headshot. He is in the top row, second from left. (Courtesy of Tennessee State Library and Archives.)

Figure 15-5. Tennessee House of Representatives. Colonel Shepard served from 1871 to 1873 in the Thirty-sixth General Assembly. The Colonel cannot be identified in this photo. Perhaps he was not there. He had a knack for not being there when a picture was to be taken. (Courtesy of Tennessee State Library and Archives.)

16 • Years Pass, Children Come

From the day he preached his first sermon in the Fellowship Baptist Church, the Colonel—who was still and would always be the Colonel to his old army friends and many others—shaped his plans to end his political life and begin life as a country preacher and pastor. According to his granddaughter, Alice Carver Cramer, Baptists then were more like the Methodists of today. It wasn't easy. His call into political life came from many directions—both from the outside and from his own inclinations. But he was fully convinced that his call to preach was a call from God—the call he had to obey. He was already a public speaker of some ability. He had very good knowledge of the Bible. His mother had been a woman of strong mind and religious convictions and practices, so her son had been taught to read his Bible. Best of all, he knew how to study and loved it, loved to think, and loved to draw his own conclusions.

During the year following his decision to become a preacher while he was touring the country winding up some sort of political business, he would make political speeches during the day at country general stores and preach at schoolhouses or country churches in the evenings. When the Colonel decided to do something, he left no stone unturned to accomplish his purpose. He believed he must learn to preach, and he considered it an opportunity when he could make his own announcements and call his own audiences to listen to a man trying to learn "to tell the old, old story" in his words.

He had many amusing experiences during these weeks of transition from politics to preaching. He particularly loved to tell one of these to other country preachers who would be spending the night in his home on their way to their appointments. He had made his political speech at a

COLONEL S. G. SHEPARD

certain crossroads general store and had asked about and been told that there was a church at Cedar Grove where he could preach that evening. He spent several hours that afternoon riding the lanes and bypaths, making a short talk here and there on the political question involved, till he arrived at Cedar Grove. He was sure he had traveled some five or six miles during the afternoon. That evening, after his sermon and the benediction, a brother spoke to him cordially, saying, "That's a right good little sermon you preached tonight—heard it last night, too."

"How far is it to Pond Lick?" asked the Colonel, naming the place he had preached the evening before.

"About two miles," the brother responded.

He had been going in circles. The transition was hard—but not too hard for the Colonel. Life for him was vivid, full of interest, and fun. Behind the clouds, the sun shone for him, and his bright optimism was very contagious.

On June 5, 1871, another Samuel Shepard was born—Samuel George.[1] Martha Jane insisted that he have his father's full name. The Colonel was called George and never used the name Sam or Samuel until he was in the service because of his grandfather's name being Samuel. Now his son, named Samuel George Shepard, had arrived. The second Samuel George, the son, was always known as "Sam." The Colonel was referred to as the Colonel, S. G., George, Brother, Preacher, Representative, etc., but never Sam and seldom Samuel. A few land deeds show a "Samuel G. Shepard, Jr." signed by Sam and an "S. G. Shepard, Sen.," signed by the Colonel.

The Colonel's reaction to their third child was a blend of joy and sorrow. He'd been terribly uneasy about Martha Jane during her pregnancy, following so close to the death of Fanny. Also Martha Jane had a bad scare from a mean dog when her baby was six months on the way. The Colonel was afraid of the effect it might have on Martha Jane and the unborn child. Birthmarks and old wives' tales had always had

---

[1] *Wilson County Census of 1900 for Districts 11–25*, page 503, also states that Sam was born in June 1871; his death certificate (state file #11760) says he was born 5 July 1872. His headstone says he was born 1871. Alice says June 5, 1871.

little part in his thinking. He had considered them silly nonsense. Now he remembered every one he'd ever heard. It wasn't a happy time for him. If anything should happen to this third child, he would be bereft indeed.

He was filled with profound joy and deep gratitude that Martha Jane had gotten through the ordeal with no unusual trouble, and his boy was born a well-developed and in every way normal baby.

During the three years intervening between Sam's advent and the birth of his sister, Alice, on March 31, 1874, the Colonel had succeeded in finishing the building of two more big rooms. These were in front of Martha Jane's bedroom and divided from it by a hall twenty by twelve feet. Another hall, eighteen by twelve feet, separated the new rooms from the older part of the house. The halls joined each other and formed a cross. Each hall opened to the outside, making a sort of outdoor living room that could be used during eight or nine months of the year. Martha Jane considered these halls priceless, as did visiting friends and relatives.

When Alice was six weeks old, the Colonel's oldest sister, Amanda Williamson, having lost her husband and two sons in Texas, came with her remaining son, Ben, to live alternatively with the Shepards, the Bradshaws, and the Robinsons. The 1880 Census lists Amanda Williamson (54), widowed, and her son Ben (19), B. F. Williamson, as living with the Shepards. [2]

Soon after Amanda's arrival, Fanny and Sallie came for a visit. They had not seen "Sis," as they called her, for years.

Next morning, the four women were on the porch having a lively visit together. Fanny's very appearance was conducive to a jolly good time. Low of stature, she had had as a young girl a pleasing plumpness. With the years, that plumpness had matured into a not unpleasing matronliness. Her high forehead and deep blue eyes, which could be very serious and penetrating, gave her round face dignity and revealed the keen intellect that she possessed. She had a renowned sense of humor, shot through with genuine kindliness. Her laughter was hearty and contagious. There was much laughter on Martha Jane's porch that morning. The sun was shining; the yard was bright with a riot of

---

[2] *Wilson County, Tennessee, Federal Census of 1880, Districts 21–25*, 305.

volunteer petunias and verbena that flourished in spite of the overgrowth of grass that had taken advantage of Martha Jane's spring shut-in condition. Now Martha Jane, who was still convalescing from the birth of baby Alice, was beginning to view the grass in her flowerbeds with impatience. She was also anxious to get out and find the hole in the fence through which a pig had found his way yesterday and destroyed some of her favorite petunias.

"Fiddlesticks, Mat," said Fanny. "Why don't you make George fix that hole?" Just then, the Colonel appeared around the corner of the house. Martha Jane, urged by Fanny, called to him. "Mr. Shepard, there's a hole in the fence somewhere. A pig got in yesterday and ate some of my petunias."

"Don't reckon it'll hurt him," he said, as he went on his way to find and fix the hole.

"Same old George," said Fanny, laughing heartily.

"I'm so no account," lamented Martha Jane. "Mr. Shepard has so many things to do."

"Well what if he does?" retorted Fanny. "They are his children too, aren't they?"

"George seems so well and happy," said Sallie.

"He is," said Martha Jane. "Happy, I mean. He has so much good humor and inner liveliness. The other day, I was sitting in the kitchen door when the little brown leghorn hen went into an old barrel in the backyard, hunting for a nest. I told Mr. Shepard about it and said, 'She ought to have a nest in the hen house.' He cleared his throat like he does, you know, and said, 'Tell her soon as she fills that barrel, I'll set her out another one.' It isn't what he says so much as the way he says it that's so funny," said Martha Jane. "I guess I'd have gotten mad if anybody but Mr. Shepard had said that."

"Ain't love wonderful!" said Fanny. Fanny loved Martha Jane for her own self, but especially she loved her because of the way Martha Jane gave her beloved brother the love he needed to make him happy. But she could never resist the temptation to tease Martha Jane whenever there was an opportunity. This time, however, Martha Jane did not rise to her bait. Instead, she sighed contentedly and said, "Indeed it is, Fanny. Indeed it is."

The Colonel was an experienced farmer. He probably had never heard the phrase "soil preservation," but he knew all about it. He probably *was* familiar with the phrase "rotation of crops." At any rate, he knew all about how it should be done and did it. There was always one field of clover on his farm that was allowed to remain in rotation for two or three years to revitalize the soil. Clover hay was a part of the winter's feed for his animals as well. When the land had had clover long enough, the field would be ploughed under after the mowing of the hay in the fall, ready for a different crop the next spring. If a field seemed to be "good," black-eyed peas would be planted—a crop that was gathered and brought to the house for shelling and the vines turned under as a fertilizer.

The shelling of the peas was a great time. There would be bushels and bushels out in the potato house or meat house ready to be brought in big baskets as the shellers became ready for them. Everybody was a sheller. Much visiting and talking got done during the shelling time. If a neighbor dropped in, she would be given an apron and a pan to shell her peas into. Sometimes, the neighbor would take the peas she'd shelled home with her.

When pea-shelling time was over, there would be peas for the family for all winter and a bushel bag or two to go with the Colonel in his buggy when he went to Lebanon just before Christmas. The bag wouldn't come back empty. Instead of peas, it would be filled with oranges, bananas, lemons, raisins, apples, mixed candies, striped peppermint sticks, and always several packages of firecrackers.

For a good many years, beginning soon after his marriage, the Colonel had a cotton gin. He always ran the gin himself. The ginning during the season would begin on Tuesday morning and end Friday at noon if he had to leave for a faraway church. Friends and neighbors for miles around brought their cotton to his gin. He built the whole set of houses, a big upstairs room below which was the big cog-wheel and levers to which horses were hitched and were driven by two boys around and around in a circle to run the gin upstairs. There was a lint room and a passage from that to the boiler. The Colonel also invented a cotton bailer. The bailer was a big screw and apparatus that pressed the cotton together and then secured it to a bale with thin wire. He should have been able to make money on his invention, but he never tried.

Every fall, he would have five or six bales of cotton that he and Taylor would take to Nashville to sell. It was always a hard time for Martha Jane when the Colonel went to Nashville and returned with so much money in his pocket. He left at least half the money in the bank in Nashville but always brought back enough money to pay for all the cotton he had bought from the neighbors. They knew what day he'd gone to Nashville and that he wanted them to come for their money the day he got home.

One day, when Martha Jane was expecting him to get home from such a trip and he didn't arrive, she got a neighbor boy, Sanin, to come spend the night. Then she decided that Mr. Shepard had been delayed— or waylaid—en route.

When bedtime came, she went to bed but not to sleep. The later it got, the more frightened she became. About midnight, she called Sanin in. He said what he could to comfort her.

"Why no, Cousin Mat, I don't think anything has happened to Cousin George. Taylor is with him, isn't he?"

"Yes, but they were supposed to get here before dark, and now it's after twelve."

"I wouldn't worry about Cousin George if I were you. He's been in too many tight places not to know how to take care of himself. They may have had a breakdown and are spending the night somewhere on the road. You ought to go to bed and get some sleep or you'll be sick tomorrow. Cousin George is all right."

Martha Jane went back to bed but, again, not to sleep. She spent the rest of the night praying and looking out the window. It was a beautiful, moonlit night.

About daybreak, when the moon had slipped away and before the sun had made much light, she saw two men creeping through the barn and cotton gin lot. She couldn't see their faces or tell whether they were white or black. They were sneaking and keeping their faces from the house. They went out onto the road and disappeared. Whether they were up to mischief or not Martha Jane was sure they were waiting for the Colonel to relieve him of his money.

When the Colonel arrived next morning about ten o'clock (Sanin had been right; he'd had a wheel go bad on him and had to spend much time at a blacksmith's shop), he found his neighbors already coming for their money. By noon, the five hundred dollars he had in his pocket was all paid out except for a couple of tens he'd set aside for himself and his family. See Figure 16-1. But Martha Jane had not recovered from her scare. "Mr. Shepard," she asked, "what were those men doing sneaking around in the barn lot if they weren't up to some mischief?"

"Just out looking around a little—seeing the sun rise maybe!" he answered, in his usual good humor. He wouldn't take it seriously until he saw that Martha Jane was pretty badly upset. She wanted him to go to P. Underwood's and borrow a pistol. P. Underwood was one of the Colonel's old veteran friends, and Martha Jane was sure he would still have his army pistol. *Mercy only knew where Mr. Shepard's was*, she thought. So in the afternoon, he went. Really, he was ashamed to ask P. for his pistol, but he couldn't have his beloved Martha Jane staying awake all night for lack of one. He called P. out to the fence.

"P., have you still got your old army pistol?"

"Sure. What's the matter? Going to fight the war over?"

The Colonel grinned, lifted a shoulder, and cleared his throat. "Mat got uneasy about me when I didn't get home till this morning. She was expecting me before bedtime last night."

"Don't blame her! Don't blame her a bit! It sorter made me uneasy this morning when I knew you'd been on the road all night with all that money in your pocket. 'Taint safe. Know you're not afraid of nobody nor nothing, but you'd die just like the rest of us if you got a bullet through your head. Where's *your* old pistol? Why don't you take it with you on these trips?"

"Didn't bring it home. Lost it somewhere after I left Washington."

"Well, you are welcome to mine. I'll go get it."

That night, Martha Jane felt better knowing a pistol was where Mr. Shepard should lay his hand on it. And it would seem that he needed it, for at about two o'clock in the morning, they were awakened by a noise in the hall by their door. The Colonel got his pistol and went to investigate. He opened the door a crack and tried to see out without getting his head in the range of a gun. Martha Jane was sitting up in bed

COLONEL S. G. SHEPARD

almost stiff with fright. She knew she loved her man. She had known that a long time. But she hadn't known how much until she experienced the horror of seeing him facing danger, maybe death. The Colonel opened the door a little wider. The man on the outside saw him and shuffled forward.

"Mars Colonel," he groaned, "is you all got any paregoric? Nancy say if anybody got any, it'd be Miss Mat. I've had toothache all night, and I just had to have some paregoric to put in it. If ya'll got any, please sir, Mars Colonel."

The Colonel relaxed, stowed the gun out of sight, and opened the door wide. "Come in, Jake," he said. "Mat, you know where the paregoric is?"

"It's up on the mantel by the clock," she said, her voice still tight, and dropped back on her pillow, pulling the sheet over her head. She didn't want anybody to see her crying, not even if it was a cry of relief.

Martha Jane woke up with a bad taste in her mouth. She felt nauseated and limp. *It's June,* she thought with a sigh. She wished it were September. *June, July, August—three hot months! Oh well,* she said to herself, *I'll feel better when I get up and wash my face and mouth.* But she knew she wouldn't feel much better. She'd been having symptoms for a week. Well, she wouldn't let Mr. Shepard know—not till she was absolutely certain.

The Colonel had been up and out for more than an hour although it was only six o'clock now. But that's not very early for the middle of June. The days were long and hot. Mr. Shepard was hoeing out the garden.

Becky came in with a bucket of water right from the well, cool and clear. Martha Jane got up and drank a glass. *Oh, that tasted good,* she thought. But she wished she had a lemon—lemonade would help a lot right now.

She counted the months till this baby, if it was a baby, would come. *January, he'll be coming in January. Alice will be nearly five.* She dreaded having a baby. No anesthetics for a woman in travail in those days. Women were supposed to acquire virtue by the pain they bore.

The Colonel came in shortly, and they had breakfast. At the table, he said, "You are not eating much breakfast."

"It's too hot," she replied. "I'll eat later."

"I've got to go to Vesta this morning," he said. "Anything you'd like me to get for you?"

"Yes, lemons. Get me a bag of lemons." She could see he was ready to leave the table, so she quickly asked, "Why do you have to go to Vesta?"

"To try to stop a lawsuit," he said.

"You'll never be left alone about law affairs, will you?"

"Not much law to this case, just a sort of misunderstanding between Jit Jenkins and Simon Jacobs. Their farms join, and Simon claims that the stobs driven into the ground to mark the dividing line have been moved to Jit's advantage of about half an acre."

"What are you to do? Won't Simon and Jit get in a fight most likely? You know they say that Simon is a bad man and carries a pistol."

"No, I don't think there will be any fight. I will find the dividing line by means of a compass, and while I'm measuring, I'll try to pour on a little oil."

"Mr. Shepard, I'm willing for you to pour on all the oil you can produce and to use the compass, but I am not willing for you to take a bullet from one of that low-down bunch!"

"No danger, Martha Jane, not a bit. A loud 'scat' would scare either one of them out of a year's growth. I may not get home for dinner though. Don't be uneasy. I won't get shot."

The Colonel did have a hard day. Simon was determined to get the rich half acre he said Jit was stealing from him. It was plain that no stobs had been moved. The Colonel used the compass and the measuring chains, and his measurements came up to the specifications in the deeds. He told Mr. Jacobs that he couldn't make a case in any court against Mr. Jenkins—that he'd he out money to no advantage. He advised him to accept the facts and live neighborly with Mr. Jenkins. He asked him if he was a church member. Mr. Jacobs said he was a Jew and believed in God and the Ten Commandments. The Colonel quoted the Ten

Commandments to him, emphasizing the eighth and ninth, which referred to not stealing and to bearing false witness.

When he got through with Mr. Jacobs and Mr. Jenkins, the Colonel began trying to think about what Martha Jane wanted him to get for her. All he could remember was it was something yellow. Yellow. He was disgusted that he couldn't remember. Oh well, he'd think what it was when he got in the store.

The first thing that caught his eye as he went in the store was a big section of a huge wheel of yellow cheese. *That's it, I guess. Yellow all right,* he thought. He bought a chunk and started for home. He got home a little before four o'clock in the afternoon. Martha Jane wasn't really uneasy about him, but she was restless and nervous. She wanted those lemons! She felt like she could drink about a quart of good, cold lemonade. She hadn't been able to eat much dinner. She was glad to see him ride up to the front gate.

When he came in, he dropped a bag into her lap, saying, "Couldn't remember what it was you wanted. Yellow was all I could think of. Hope it's all right." She looked in the bag to behold a large chunk of yellow cheese. She felt like vomiting. She sat the bag on the floor, dropped her face onto her knees, and cried. George was shocked, surprised.

"Why Martha Jane, what's the matter? I thought you liked cheese."

"I hate it. You know I do. And I'm going to have a baby! I want lemons."

The Colonel hesitated, looked puzzled, then went to the gate where he hitched the horse, mounted, and rode away. Martha Jane saw him go. Then she was troubled about that. Had she offended him, hurt him, or what?

It was two hours later when he arrived once more at the front gate. Taylor took his horse. He came in and said, "Sorry, Martha Jane, I got mixed up on the yellows this morning." With that, he handed her a bag of lemons, oranges, and russet apples.

"My Mr. Shepard, where did you get them?"

"At Baird's Mill," he said.

"Oh! Oh! I made you go some six miles for a whim of mine!"

"Having a baby is not much of a whim, I reckon. Never had one myself. Couldn't say how I'd stand it. Not very well, I guess." By that time, Martha Jane had her arms around his neck, and he had his arm around her shoulders, patting her on the back.

Fanny had heard that Martha Jane was not feeling so well. She herself was not feeling so well. She wanted to see both Martha Jane and George. She wanted a change from the same old breakfast, dinner, and supper at home to some of Becky's cooking. Aunt Polly Woolen, who lived with the Robinsons, was quite equal to keeping Ida, who was a big schoolgirl now. Jerd had business in Rutherford County. Fanny informed him that he could take her by George's and leave her while he went on to Rutherford to do whatever he had to do. She made Jerd take her through LaGuardo to get her a new hat.

"What on earth do you want with a new hat?" he asked. "You won't be going out much longer."

"Jerd Robinson, I'm going to dress up and go to a picnic, a circus, church, or whatever happens to be on at the time."

Later, while passing through the yard, George heard Martha Jane and Fanny on the porch laughing about the conversation Fanny had had with Jerd while getting ready for this visit.

"It's a beautiful hat, Fanny," Martha Jane said, looking at the new hat. "Maybe someday, *I'll* have a new hat! I certainly need one ... if only to boost my morale."

"Of course, you need a hat! If there's ever a time in a woman's life when she needs a new hat, it's when she's going to have a baby."

This remark struck the Colonel like a slap in the face. He had not noticed that Martha Jane needed a new hat; but as he thought about it, he knew that she was wearing last summer's hat, and this summer was well on the way. *She's got to have a new hat*, he said to himself, wondering how to accomplish the impossible.

A few days later, as he was on his way home from the Glade where he'd been to have Joe and Bob shod, he met Mr. Baggerly in his market wagon. Mr. Baggerly went to Nashville once every two weeks and bought all sorts of merchandise, peddling it out through the neighborhood. It flashed through the Colonel's mind that maybe *he* had a hat. He stopped, greeted Mr. Baggerly, and in the same breath asked, "Wonder if you've got any hats for women?"

"Yes, sir, Colonel, some real pretty ones." The Colonel looked at them very carefully and decided on a sort of blue one—blue was *his* favorite color—a light blue it was, with a quantity of red roses on it. He was a little doubtful about the roses, but Mat could exchange it, Mr. Baggerly said.

By the time he got home, he was feeling a bit squeamish about the hat—so many red roses and they got bigger and grew in quantity the nearer he got to home. Well, he'd tough it out. At any rate, it couldn't be as bad as the cheese had been.

He stepped up on the porch where Fanny and Martha Jane were still having lots of fun. Lizzie Foutch, a neighbor and an ardent fan of Fanny's, was there as well. Fanny had just had a little fall out in the yard. No harm done. Fanny was apt to fall, and she looked very comical doing it, too. Lizzie thought she saw a chance to tease her. But the teasing had gone the other way when Fanny looked at her accusingly, shaking her finger in her face, and said, "Lizzie Foutch, you never fell down in your life!" Fanny made it sound as though Lizzie had broken one of the Ten Commandments.

The Colonel was pleased to find so much good humor. He handed the package to Martha Jane and started for the back hall and the water bucket. Martha Jane pulled the hat out of the bag and held it up. She gasped, but caught herself and assumed a smile of pleased surprise. "Who says I haven't got a new hat?" she said.

Fanny went off into loud laughter. "Where on earth do you suppose he found that thing?" she asked.

Instantly, Martha Jane was on the defensive. "I think it's a nice hat," she said. "I'll take the roses off and keep them for a winter hat. I have a nice bunch of blue forget-me-nots I can put on it. And then, Miss Fanny, it will be just as pretty as yours!"

Fanny subsided into mock solemnity. "Ain't love wonderful!" she murmured.

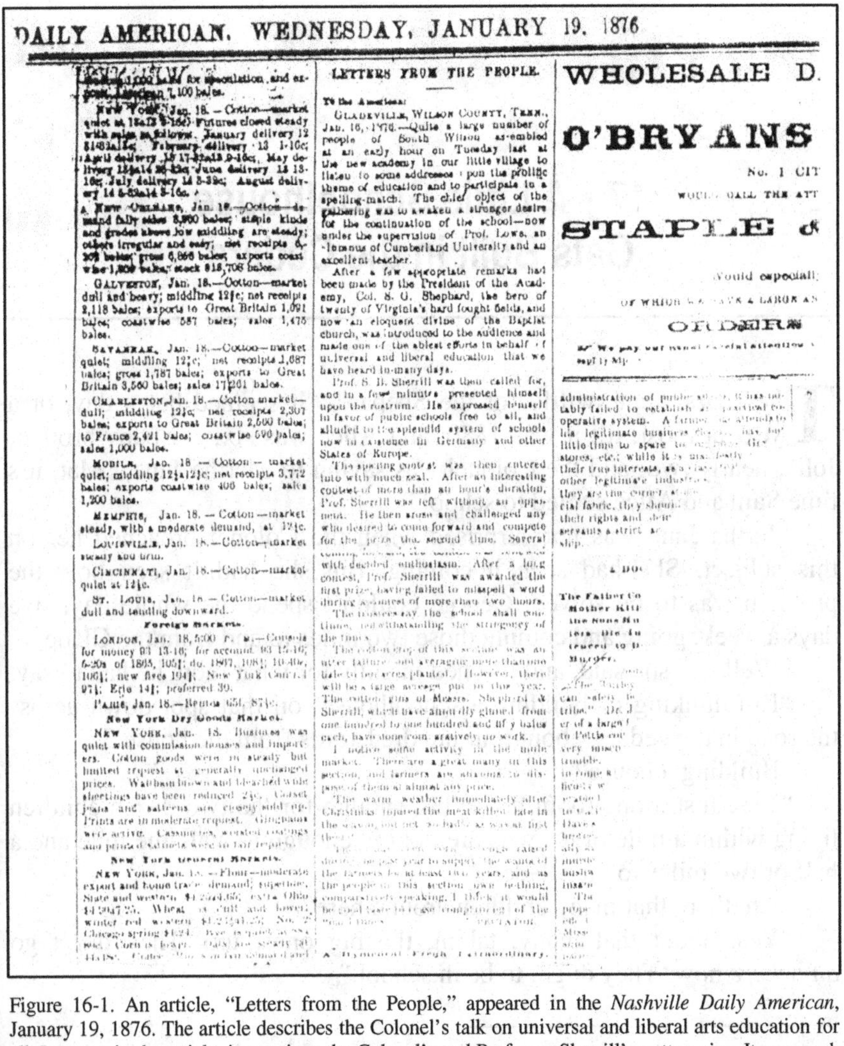

DAILY AMERICAN. WEDNESDAY, JANUARY 19. 1876

GALVESTON, Jan. 18.—Cotton—market dull and heavy; middling 12¾c; net receipts 2,118 bales; exports to Great Britain 1,091 bales; coastwise 587 bales; sales 1,475 bales.

SAVANNAH, Jan. 18.—Cotton—market quiet; middling 12¾c; net receipts 1,687 bales; gross 1,787 bales; exports to Great Britain 3,560 bales; sales 1,201 bales.

CHARLESTON, Jan. 18.—Cotton market—dull; middling 12¾c; net receipts 2,307 bales; exports to Great Britain 2,600 bales; to France 2,421 bales; coastwise 590 bales; sales 1,000 bales.

MOBILE, Jan. 18.—Cotton—market quiet; middling 12¼a12½c; net receipts 3,772 bales; exports coastwise 406 bales; sales 1,200 bales.

MEMPHIS, Jan. 18.—Cotton—market steady, with a moderate demand, at 12½c.

LOUISVILLE, Jan. 18.—Cotton—market steady and firm.

CINCINNATI, Jan. 18.—Cotton—market quiet at 12½c.

ST. LOUIS, Jan. 18.—Cotton—market dull and tending downward.

Foreign Markets.

LONDON, Jan. 18, 5:00 P. M.—Consols for money 93 13-16; for account 93 15-16; ... Erie 14½; preferred 30.

PARIS, Jan. 18.—Rentes 65f. 87½c.

New York Dry Goods Market.

NEW YORK, Jan. 18.—Business was quiet with commission houses and importers. Cotton goods were in steady but limited request at generally unchanged prices. ...

New York General Markets.

NEW YORK, Jan. 18.—Flour—moderate export and home trade demand; ...

LETTERS FROM THE PEOPLE.

To the American:

GLADEVILLE, WILSON COUNTY, TENN., Jan. 16, 1876.—Quite a large number of people of South Wilson assembled at an early hour on Tuesday last at the new academy in our little village to listen to some addresses upon the prolific theme of education and to participate in a spelling-match. The chief object of the gathering was to awaken a stronger desire for the continuation of the school—now under the supervision of Prof. Lowe, an alumnus of Cumberland University and an excellent teacher.

After a few appropriate remarks had been made by the President of the Academy, Col. S. G. Shephard, the hero of twenty of Virginia's hard fought fields, and now an eloquent divine of the Baptist church, was introduced to the audience and made one of the ablest efforts in behalf of universal and liberal education that we have heard in many days.

Prof. S. B. Sherrill was then called for, and in a few minutes presented himself upon the rostrum. He expressed himself in favor of public schools free to all, and alluded to the splendid system of schools now in existence in Germany and other States of Europe.

The spelling contest was then entered into with much zeal. After an interesting contest of more than an hour's duration, Prof. Sherrill was left without an opponent. He then arose and challenged any who desired to come forward and compete for the prize the second time. Several ... with decided enthusiasm. After a long contest, Prof. Sherrill was awarded the first prize, having failed to misspell a word during a contest of more than two hours.

The trustees say the school shall continue, notwithstanding the stringency of the times.

The cotton crop of this section was an utter failure, not averaging more than one bale to ten acres planted. However, there will be a large acreage put in this year. The cotton gins of Messrs. Shephard & Sherrill, which have annually ginned from one hundred to one hundred and fifty bales each, have done comparatively no work.

I notice some activity in the mule market. There are a great many in this section, and farmers are anxious to dispose of them at almost any price.

The warm weather immediately after Christmas injured the meat killed late in the season, ...

WHOLESALE D

O'BRYANS

No. 1 CIT

WOULD CALL THE ATT

STAPLE &

Would especiall

ORDERS

Figure 16-1. An article, "Letters from the People," appeared in the *Nashville Daily American*, January 19, 1876. The article describes the Colonel's talk on universal and liberal arts education for all. Later on in the article, it mentions the Colonel's and Professor Sherrill's cotton gins. It says each once ginned approximately 100 to 150 bales annually but lately had "comparatively no work."

17 · A Little Schoolhouse Gets Built in the Cedars

The years went swiftly for the Shepards. It seemed but a day, or a year at most, till it was 1880, and Alice was six, her baby brother, John, nearly two, and the Colonel was saying to Martha Jane, "Mat, it's time Sam and Alice started to school."

Martha Jane was not surprised when the Colonel broached her on this subject. She had seen it coming. But she hadn't seen how the problem was to be solved. George couldn't spend the whole day, five days a week, going and coming those two miles to and from the Glade.

"Well ..." she said, and listened intently for what more he had to say.

"I'm thinking of building a schoolhouse[1] on that spot down across the road in the cedars, about four hundred yards from the house."

"Building a house?"

"Yes. Just a one-room house big enough for the two dozen children living within a mile of us, who are not big enough to walk the mile and a half or two miles to the Glade."

"Are there that many children around here?"

"Yes, about that many, taking the big ones, too. They don't go *anywhere* now. They ought to be in school."

---

[1] In 1909, when the Shepards sold part of their farm, which included their house, to J. B. Barrett, measurements were used such that the description included mention of the schoolhouse. Measurements stated: "Beginning on a cedar corner in Bettie Taylor's west boundary line east of the Schoolhouse and running 12 poles west to 3 cedars _____ [word not distinguishable] North West corner of Schoolhouse ..." Was this the schoolhouse that was later moved and then added onto to start the new Baptist Church in Gladeville?

"But Mr. Shepard, how can you build a schoolhouse with all the other work you do?"

"Odd times. The neighbors will help."

"Will they help furnish the materials?"

"There's enough cedar on that lot across and beyond the garden already cut and seasoned to be sawed into planks and posts to do the job."

"Was this house project why you had those big, wonderful cedars cut a year ago?" Martha Jane was puzzled at the time, but she didn't get her curiosity satisfied.

"Well, I sort of had that in mind. Sort of looking to the future."

"How'll you get it sawed?"

"Tom Saunders is running his mill right now. He'll saw it for nothing. He wants to send his two children to school too."

"Oh, I see! So, you've already made all the arrangements." The Colonel grinned sheepishly.

"Same old George," Fanny would have said, but Martha Jane just smiled, her knitting needless flying over a new pair of socks for him. After a few moments, she said, "Sam certainly needs to be in school. Alice could wait a little longer ..."

The Colonel cleared his throat. "Alice needs it bad as Sam. She's getting too big to be running all over the place with him." But he added, with a joking chuckle, "she can't get lost if she stays home."

Martha Jane hadn't thought of that. Now she agreed fully with the Colonel that Alice needed to be in school.

"Sam," he continued, "has a lot of things to do. His time's not wasted. He can chop the stove wood now and help Taylor feed the stock—learn a lot about farming."

"Alice does all of that, too," said Martha Jane.

"Yes, yes—but she ought to stay in the house and yard more. I wish she could have some kind of music lessons."

"She's too young for that, Mr. Shepard."

"I reckon so. Well," he said, standing up and brushing his hands on his trouser legs, "I must go now—I want to see Jake Harris."

"Is he going to help build the schoolhouse?" Martha Jane asked.

The Colonel grinned. It was good to have a woman agree about things so readily. Fanny would have argued. He said, "He's going to make the benches. He wants to use white ash. Too fancy—but Jake's a good carpenter."

"What do you mean, fancy?"

"He wants to make the seats with five strips instead of just one broad plank. I've decided to let him." He went out the door and down the steps.

Martha Jane called after him. "You'll be home for dinner?"

"Yes, won't be gone long."

It was a matter of only a few days before the arrangements had been completed and the building begun. It proved to be a great time for Alice. She adored her father and dogged his steps whenever he was working about the place. She sat on ends of planks to hold them steady when he sawed. She handed the hammer and nails to him when he nailed. She loved to stir the mortar with the hoe when he was daubing on the filling between the logs.

Once, a wasp lit on the spot due for the next daub of mortar. On went the mortar with the remark from the Colonel, "There now! Gone in a hole and pulled it in after him!" Alice rammed her small fists in the pockets of her pink and white, checked, gingham apron, reared back on her heels, and laughed uproariously. What a smart joke her papa had played on that old wasp! Was there ever as smart a man as her papa!

Now that the schoolhouse was finished, there was no obstacle left for Sam and Alice to start up the ladder of learning but to find a teacher. According to *Goodspeed History of Wilson County*, the Colonel was a superintendent sometime during 1873 to 1886.[2] The Colonel found one. And so Miss Rebecca Powers came to be a very important member of the Shepard household. She was a spinster of uncertain age. But one could be certain that she would not again see forty. She had dyed coal-black, bobbed hair, which she wore in ringlets that barely reached the bottom of the white linen, turnover collar that was a part of her daily attire. One felt that Miss Rebecca would not feel properly dressed without her white-linen cuffs and collar. She wore gold-rimmed spectacles and a very dignified air. She had a super-abundance of religion that was an

---

[2] *Goodspeed History of Wilson County* (Nashville: Goodspeed Publishing Co., 1886), 22.

ever-present factor. She was a strict disciplinarian, a perfect lady, and a sore trial to Sam and Alice's good nature. She was the children's governess as well as their schoolteacher. She had full charge of them in the home as well as in the schoolroom. She supervised their table manners, their clothing, and their general behavior. She was supposed to be a Mary Sharp graduate, but she wasn't listed as a graduate in the limited number of classes with records.

Martha Jane had heard about Miss Rebecca many times but had never seen her until the morning she arrived in the Shepard home. The Colonel was a little nervous about what Mat would think of her. As soon as Miss Rebecca was settled in her room and the Colonel had an opportunity to see Martha Jane alone, he said, "Well, how do you like her?"

Martha Jane's eyes twinkled. "I won't ever need to be jealous of her, will I?"

The Colonel shuffled and grinned. "Wasn't looking for a pretty gal," he said.

"Needn't tell me that," said Martha Jane.

"She's smart—graduate of Mary Sharp,"[3,4] he said, on the defensive.

Raymond Finney in his book on the college claims Mary Sharp College, Franklin County, Winchester, Tennessee, was *the* college for women, starting as "Tennessee Female Institute" in 1848. The college reached its peak before the Civil War and closed in 1896. When the college first opened, there was Wesleyan College in Georgia, established in 1839, and it wasn't until Vassar in New York was established in 1861, that there was any competition. Mary Sharp College conferred the Liberal Arts degree to three women in 1855, Vassar four degrees in 1861. The college was established to provide the same quality of education and thus curriculum "afforded men at Brown, University of Virginia, and Amherst College." Dr. Z. C. Graves, president of the

---

[3] Raymond Alfred Finney, "A History of the Private Educational Institutions of Franklin County, Part I: Mary Sharp College," *Franklin County Historical Review* 22 (1991), 24-33. Tennessee State Library and Archives, Nashville, TN.

[4] James Waring McCrady, "The Mary Sharp Superlative: Claims Made for Mary Sharp," 19-20. Tennessee State Library and Archives, Nashville, TN.

college, said, "Educate your daughters, and then the elevation of the whole family will follow."

According to Finney, the college was a result of the foresight of Mrs. Mary Sharp who incidentally was "Miss Corn" before her marriage to Mr. James Sharp. When Mr. Sharp died, she freed eighty Negroes and paid their way to Liberia, Africa. Her bequest to the Mary Sharp College was the nucleus out of which the Mary Sharp College grew.

McGrady's *Mary Sharp Superlative* states that "following Mary Sharp College of Tennessee, in addition to Vassar, were Wellesley College, founded in 1870 and opened in 1875, and Smith, organized in 1873 and opened in 1875, both in Massachusetts."

"How old is she?"

The Colonel saw that Martha Jane did not dislike Miss Rebecca. He relaxed. "Didn't ask her that," he said. "Can though."

"Shucks, Mr. Shepard, you can twist things around so."

"Ask her, if you say so," he continued, seeing that Martha Jane was teased.

"No, you needn't ask her that, nor if she's ever been in love, nor if she expects ever to get married," Martha Jane said, clicking away on her knitting needles. The Colonel decided that the teasing had gone far enough. He said, "Hope you like her. If you don't, we'll look somewhere else for a teacher."

As the weeks went by, it became generally known that Miss Rebecca could lead in public prayer as well as any man and speak from a text in the Bible equal to almost any preacher. A Sunday school was organized to meet on Sunday afternoons in the little new schoolhouse. The average attendance was about twenty-five. The capacity of the house was about fifty.

The Colonel's time was already filled for Sundays. He was away from home, as a rule, from Friday to Monday. But he was always able to be present for Sunday school at the schoolhouse on those afternoons when he was preaching in the Glade. On other Sundays, if some other preacher was not present, Miss Rebecca was not the least hesitant in taking charge. For that matter, she was not loathe to take charge of any performance, public or private, that seemed to need a leader or, as Fanny would say, "a boss."

On one of Fanny's visits to the Shepards' during Miss Rebecca's reign in their home, Fanny gave Martha Jane some private advice on the subject of this "boss." "Mat, I wouldn't have that woman bossing my children around like she does Sam and Alice! Why don't you put a stop to all this foolishness?"

"That's what Mr. Shepard got her for!"

"Fiddlesticks! You are too easy. I'd give George a piece of my mind, if I were you!"

"Why Fanny, he got her to relieve me. You see, I'm not very strong, and Johnny is about all I can manage. She has nothing to do with Johnny."

"Well, she could help without being such a boss, couldn't she? The way she sent Sam from the table this morning to wash his face and hands! Umph!"

"They needed washing, didn't they?" said Martha Jane.

Fanny looked at her in utter astonishment. "Well of all things!" she said. "That beats anything I ever heard!" She looked around for her knitting. She needed something on which to vent her feelings. When she didn't see her knitting anywhere, she subsided and continued. "The way you and George sat there this morning at the table and talked on like nothing was happening! I nearly exploded!"

Martha Jane laughed. "She doesn't hurt them, Fanny. Having her is a great relief to me. The children need to be in school. We couldn't send them to the Glade—it's too far for Alice to walk."

"How long will she be here, running the ranch?"

"I don't know. As long as the children need her, if things go along all right."

"Do the children like her?" Martha Jane paused to pick up a dropped stitch before answering.

"Well, I don't suppose they exactly enjoy her," she said.

"I should think not!" exploded Fanny. "George is a queer one. Always was. Gets a notion and nothing on earth can stop or change him. Where did he ever get the notion of a Miss Rebecca and where did he ever find her? Of all the queer-looking women!"

"She has a good reputation as a teacher. She's a college graduate. She's a gentlewoman in every sense of the word. We certainly want our children well brought up and a foundation laid early for their future education. That's one of the things Mr. Shepard is set on."

"Of course! But why did he have to get *her*! Of all the … guess I'd better hush!" She got up with a grunt of disgust and went back toward the dining room looking for her knitting. As she was nearing the dining room table, she heard Becky and Alice in a conversation in the kitchen. She stopped to listen. Becky was saying, "You better run along now, honey, and get your ma to give out them spelling words to you again. If you don't, Miss Rebeccy be keeping you in again."

"Miss Rebeccy's not ready to go to school yet," Alice said. She's curling her hair and putting on perfume to make her smell good."

"Uh-huh! I'm just the ole black Becky, and she's the white Miss Rebeccy—but she sure do smell—not good no how!"

"She does smell bad, doesn't she? I heard Papa tell Mama that she's got a guitar that makes her smell so bad."

"Hush your mouth, chile. A guitar is something you makes music on—like a banjo. What she's got ain't no music making thing. I think she totes a bag of something round her neck to keep off bad colds and all such. Only her bag's got Limburger cheese in it!"

"Cheese don't smell bad," said Alice.

"You ain't never smelt no Limburger, have you? Run along now about them words—I don't want you keep in your mouth."

When Fanny got back to the porch with Martha Jane, Alice had gone to school having been prepared by her mother so as not to be kept in after school. Martha Jane was ready for Fanny's tale of what she had heard in the kitchen. When Fanny had told the conversation, she said, "Becky's got sense. Becky and I see alike about Miss Rebecca. But I see your side too. No doubt, she is good for the children. George is usually right. I can see why Becky can't like the boss. I don't see how she stands to have her in the kitchen so much. She's forever ironing those white cuffs and collars when she isn't teaching or bossing Sam and Alice. Have the irons been cold since she's been here?"

"I'm afraid she does annoy Becky. But Fanny, how could she get on without her white collars and cuffs!" Mat grinned at Fanny. "I guess Becky's thankful she washes and irons them herself and doesn't ask her to do it."

"You've certainly got the house full o' folks, Mat. Don't see how you stand it."

"Yes, we've got a houseful. But we like it. Mr. Shepard told Mother before she died that we wanted Bettie, Martha Jane's sister, to live with us. It was a wonderful relief to Mother. Bettie seems happy here. Since Ben's (Amanda's son) death, I think Amanda would be lonely without Bettie. They were almost the same age."

"Mat, you're wonderful!"

Martha Jane was very much surprised at Fanny's outburst. "Why Fanny, there's nothing wonderful in what I do. Now Mr. Shepard ..."

"Yes, yes, I know. George does everything."

"Well, he does. You should have seen how he worked on that schoolhouse, never neglecting his other work either. He's never idle. I've seen him come in from work and drop on the top step in the door and be asleep almost by the time he's stretched out. He works too hard all the time. I suppose he does get a little rest on Saturdays and Sundays though I wouldn't consider preaching a sermon much rest." Martha Jane snipped off the thread from the hem of the dress she'd been lengthening for Alice.

"Do you think he has ever regretted giving up law for preaching?" Fanny asked.

"Never. He seems perfectly happy in his church work. His people love him so much."

"Does he ever talk about the war?" Fanny's mind was racking back to the time just before the war when the subject of preaching had given George some bad days and to the letter from Jake after the Battle of Harper's Ferry.

"Oh, no," said Martha Jane, whispering out of George's earshot at the bedroom desk. "I never mention war to him. I did one time—that was enough! He never talks about the Yankees like you hear some people talk."

"I should say not. I give him credit for having that much sense about the war."

Martha Jane wasn't any too well pleased with this speech from Fanny. She didn't see eye to eye with her about the war. "Fanny, are you a Democrat?"

"Yes. Sure!" Fanny answered emphatically, and added, "But I'd never let a child of mine speak disrespectfully about Abraham Lincoln or teach one to hate the Yankees. Why?"

"Well, you don't talk much like a Democrat. I just wanted to know."

"I suppose I don't. It's true I didn't believe in the war. I did believe in Mr. Lincoln. I was rebellious about George and Robert Lee joining up with Jeff Davis, whom I never could tolerate. I was in a strait betwixt two, you might say, before the war was fully on—and during much of that awful four years. George was always my ideal of a man, and it hit me pretty hard to have him spend four years of his life trying to do two things I didn't want done."

"What two things? Did you want to be bossed by the North?"

"Of course not. I don't want to be bossed by anybody. I just wanted the Union to be preserved and the Negroes freed."

"Well, you got it—if you can call it preserved. I think the South hates the North more now than it did before the war."

"I'm afraid you are right. But there is some hope now of a Union someday. But not a ghost of a chance if the Confederacy had won."

"Maybe you are right. But I can't forget what the Yanks did to my father's property."

"Well, Mat, you have a comfortable home, lovely children, and a right nice husband, if I do sound contrary. And that's about all any of us can hope for in this generation, I guess."

They were having their little visit in the hall in front of the Shepards' bedroom. Martha Jane watched Johnny and Fanny's William, three months older, building pens with blocks on the floor between them. Certainly, Martha Jane had to agree on that last point.

Presently, Alice came running in from playing, calling, "Mama, a Dutch peddler is coming! I saw him way down the road!" When she reached the hall, she ran into the bedroom where her father was working at figures. She slowed, sensitive to his work mood, and put her hand on his knee, looking up at him sympathetically. "You'd better go out in the lot, Papa," she said.

Fanny overheard Alice. She was amazed, and interjected, "What do you mean, Alice: 'Go out in the lot'?"

"Papa doesn't like Dutch peddlers. He says they say 'yah' for 'yes' and 'nine' for 'no,' and they cheat."

Fanny gave a big laugh. The Colonel looked uncomfortable. "This young one, now—surely her ears are too big!" He shuffled, crossed his knees, and cleared his throat; his eyes twinkled. "I think I'll stay and see this one," he said. "I broke my specs yesterday. Maybe he'll have some."

Alice was delighted. She liked nothing better than to see a Dutch peddler open his big square pack done up in black oil-cloth and expose his wares, red-checkered tablecloths, laces, shoestrings, pillowcases, and maybe a tray of toys. Also, there would be hairpins, ribbons, and fancy combs for the back. She danced with joy that her papa was to see the sights.

The women were also glad to see the peddler. They cordially invited him in and offered him a seat. He wasted no time, after a dipper of cold water, in opening his pack. Soon, Fanny had bought a tablecloth and a boy doll for William. Martha Jane bought yards of lace for petticoats and pillowcases, some ribbons for Alice's hair, a Barrow pocketknife for Sam, and a toy dog for Johnny. The tray of spectacles was near the bottom of the pack. When the peddler reached it, Alice sang out, "Here they are, Papa. Here are the specs!" The Colonel reached for a pair. Soon he had tried on a dozen or more pair and found a pair that suited him. When he had paid for them, the peddler took another pair, slipped the lenses out, and gave the empty frames to Alice, who was, as usual, close by her father.

As the peddler passed through the gate on his way out, Pete Bond, a neighbor with a bucket on his arm, came in through it. No less than three neighbor families got their drinking water from the Shepard's deep, bored well with the wonderful, clear, ice-cold water. When the Colonel saw Pete coming for his, he said, "Here, Alice, let me have your specs a minute. I want to fool Pete."

As Pete came up on the porch, the Colonel, handing him Alice's empty frames, said, "Just bought me some new specs." Pete took the specs, put them on, looked out at the trees and the sky, held up his hand, and gazed at it, then, handing the empty frames back to the Colonel, said, "Well, George, them's the best specs I ever had on."

Alice danced around laughing. Fanny laughed. Martha Jane shook her head and smiled, making a few stitches in the shirt she was making for Sam, and said softly to the Colonel, "Why, Mr. Shepard!"

After a few seconds, Pete joined in the laughter. "George up to his old tricks," he said. "I was suspicious of them specs all the time."

Amanda had gone home with Sallie for her annual visit. Miss Rebecca was away on a visit for the weekend. It was the Colonel's week to be with his church at the Glade.[5] Hence, he was at home for Saturday and Sunday, a very happy time for Martha Jane. But trouble disturbed her peace of mind that Saturday morning. She almost wished Miss Rebecca had not gone away. Sam and Alice were feeling their freedom. Alice had borrowed Sam's knife to get a small nail out of a board she was using to make another flower box for her mother and broke the little blade. If it had been the big blade, no telling what might have happened. As it was, Sam was punishing her. Johnny, not big enough to really know what it was all about, was helping his big brother. Martha Jane was sewing by a window in the parlor and saw the end of the fracas. She didn't interfere since nobody was really getting hurt. But she was troubled. It was only a few minutes till the dinner bell rang.

When the children had finished eating and left the dinner table, and Martha Jane and the Colonel were folding their napkins, Martha Jane said, "Mr. Shepard, the children have too many quarrels."

"What's the matter now?"

"Didn't you notice how smug Sam looked at the table, and how worried Alice seemed when she finally got here? Sam had that 'dare-you-to-tell' look."

---

[5] Wylene Pafford, local historian, said the church at Gladeville lists S. G. Shepard as pastor from 1901 to February 1912. The Colonel and family moved to Lebanon February 1912. Ms Pafford added, "Probably fifty years ago a woman told me she could remember hearing Brother Shepard preach and he preached a long time." This was taken from Ms. Pafford's letter, addressed to me, dated 8 May 2003. She also sent a picture of the original church with an unidentifiable article stating that the church was originally a one-room schoolhouse built in 1878. "A schoolhouse was her home. Two years later, she (the little schoolhouse) moved to 'town' (Gladeville) and grew up in a log house. She soon built a little house of her own and lived right where she sits today." The church today consists of a large brick structure that in the year 2000 had 1,200 members. Was this the schoolhouse the Colonel built for Sam and Alice?

"Didn't notice. Noticed Alice was late."

"She was troubled."

"Sam teasing her again?"

"Yes—but she got even this time."

"That's good," said the Colonel. He shuffled and grinned.

"She can throw rocks too well," said Martha Jane.

"Huh?" The Colonel was rising from his chair.

"Do you want to hear about it, or do you want to go feed those nasty little pigs?" The Colonel settled back in his chair. Martha Jane continued, "The first I knew about it, Sam was holding Alice at the front steps and making John whip her. Of course, Johnny is too little to hurt her, but she was awful mad. He had a little switch tickling her around the legs. Sam was laughing, urging Johnny on. Sam had his arms around Alice so she couldn't use her hands. She twisted her head over and got her teeth in his arm. He yelped and dropped her and ran. But before he rounded the corner of the house, she hit him between the shoulders with a rock and knocked him down." The Colonel shuffled and clicked in his throat. "But," Martha Jane continued, "Sam wasn't hurt. He scrambled up and ran on around the corner of the house. So I came back to the kitchen to see if Becky had dinner ready."

"Well, no damage done, I reckon."

"But Mr. Shepard, I think you ought to speak to them. Alice might hit him in the eye someday."

"He ought to let her alone. Maybe this will teach him a lesson."

"You ought to speak to her. She'll do anything you say."

"You speak to her. You saw it."

"You were as close to them as I was. You could have seen it. Why didn't you?"

"Looking the other way," said the Colonel, and hurried away to feed the "nasty little pigs."

Martha Jane sighed. "He expects me to do all the spanking," she said.

18 · A Father–Daughter Bond Grows

It was now the year 1882. At eight, Alice was old enough to walk to the village school. Miss Rebecca's reign of two years in the Shepard home was at an end. She had departed to new fields of activity. The Shepards drew a deep breath of relief and started happily on the new regime. The Colonel was especially glad because a music teacher had been added to the teaching force of the village school. He was anxious for Alice to begin lessons as soon as she was big enough. At that time and place, music lessons for boys were unheard of so Sam would escape.

The Colonel was doomed to disappointment, however. When the teacher was consulted and came to the Colonel's home to talk matters over and see if Alice was mature enough, had hands big enough, had sense enough, etc., she decided against taking the small girl as a pupil, giving the excuse "hands too small." Alice shed no tears over the verdict, and Sam got a good laugh out of it.

But next spring, when the school at the Glade was closed for four weeks in March to let the big boys help their fathers on the farms, the Colonel had better luck finding music lessons for Alice. The young organist of the Fellowship Church where the Colonel was pastor was soon to be married. Adelia Morris was her maiden name, and she owned the only organ in any private home for miles around. She was willing to give music lessons for four weeks to several children in order to augment the cost of her trousseau. The Colonel was quick to take advantage of the opportunity. Both Martha Jane and Alice spent a night in the Morris home so Alice could get acquainted with Miss Adelia and feel at ease there. After all, she wasn't quite nine yet, and her mother felt she might be homesick away from home five nights and days in every week for a month.

On the morning when the Colonel and his small daughter rode old Bob for the first trip to the Morris home where she'd be left, he said, "Now Alice, if you learn ten pieces in these four weeks, I'll buy you an organ!" She took his words literally and in good faith with no reservations. She knew if she learned ten pieces, the organ would emerge from somewhere.

She learned those ten pieces, to be sure. They were mostly hymns, but there was one, "Annie Laurie," in waltz time and the favorite, "Old Folks at Home," set to chords. She learned to play *and sing* both of these great classics. Not surprisingly, the organ arrived, and Alice developed her abilities.

Not too long after that, when the Colonel was to perform a wedding ceremony, he took Alice with him. The country road was rough, and her mother didn't want to go. Martha Jane had never regained her normal strength after the birth of her first child—country doctors were wretchedly ignorant about lacerations and what to do about them in those days. So Alice happily jolted over many a country road on trips with her father that her mother would have suffered on miserably had she been the one to go. Martha Jane felt much more comfortable at home.

When the ceremony of the wedding was over, and the bride had been kissed and blessed, and the groom congratulated by all and kissed by a few, there was, as always, that painful lull typical at a home wedding in the country. In the desperation of the situation, somebody had the sense of humor to ask the preacher's small daughter to play and sing, little supposing, no doubt, that she would respond. How startled must the guests have been when she promptly consented and, playing her own accompaniment and in the high, thin voice of a child, broke out in a hymn:

> Oh sometimes the shadows are deep
> And sometimes how long seems the day.
> And sometimes how weary my feet
> While toiling through life's dusty way.

And then the chorus:

> *Oh then to the rock let me fly,*
> *To the rock that is higher than I.*

There were four stanzas, and she sang all of them, and even more amazing, nobody stopped her! Miss Adelia must have been quite unstrung by the ceremony, or she might have chosen something more appropriate for her pupil to perform—if not suppressing her altogether! The Colonel's eyes were a study, full of sparks and doubts.

When he and Alice got home from the wedding and Martha Jane had sent Alice to change into her play clothes, she asked the Colonel, "How was the wedding?"

"'Bout like every other country wedding," he countered.

"Many people there?"

"A dozen—maybe a few more."

"What did the bride have on?"

"Some kind of a sort of blue dress, I think."

"Mr. Shepard, don't you ever look at the bride?"

He grinned and shuffled. "Yes, if she's purty."

"Did her mother cry?"

"Didn't notice—think her pa did though."

"My goodness! I never heard of such a thing. What was the matter with him?"

"Same thing that makes most cry, I reckon."

"Did they have anything to eat, any music? I thought it would be a real stylish wedding."

The Colonel got a broad grin on his face. Martha Jane got suspicious.

"Now what is the matter? What happened?" she asked.

"We had music."

"Huh? Did they have a fiddle and all of you dance? Or maybe all of you sang, 'Goodbye, My Lover, Goodbye.'"

"No. Alice played, and she sang, 'The Rock that is Higher than I.'"

"Mr. Shepard! No."

"Yes she did—did it very well, too."

"Why did she do it?"

"She was asked to play and sing."

"Why on earth did you let her?"

"How was I to stop her?"

"You could have ... you know you could have. What did the folks do?"

"They laughed and clapped when she finished."

"Did she sing all of it?"

"Every stanza."

"Mercy on us!"

"Don't say anything to her about it," he said. "They asked her to play. She didn't know any better. She'd be terribly hurt if you said anything about it. It wasn't so bad anyway. I think the folks really enjoyed it. They didn't have to talk while she sang. And they didn't have anything left to talk about—all talked out. That's why they asked her. It was time for the crowd to break up, by the time she got through. She was a real benefactor."

"Mr. Shepard, I never know what you and Alice will do next!"

The Colonel loved music though he couldn't carry a tune in a basket. He couldn't even whistle. But he had a deep love for melody and rhythm. From the day the organ was installed, Alice began to have him more or less under her thumb. She could tell by the way he walked from the front gate to the porch whether he was tired, bothered, or just all right. If she considered him tired, soon she would be pressing the ivories to his favorite hymn. If the day was warm, he responded by tilting his chair against the door. If the day was cold, he would come into the parlor and sit by the fire, half dozing. Either way, he was wholly contented.

He was particularly pleased when Sam got a harmonica—French harp, as it was called at the time. Sam could play "Home, Sweet Home," "Yankee Doodle," "Golden Slippers," and almost any tune or hymn he had ever heard. Alice's accompaniments couldn't be called works of art. She and Sam would entertain to the amusement of the family and sometimes for visiting friends.

It was spring, and that meant sewing time. Martha Jane had cut out dresses for Alice, shirts for Sam, and pants for Johnny. Mrs. Woodrum was the neighborhood seamstress. She was a widow with a family of children. The youngest, Bet, sometimes went with her from place to place where they would stay a day or two, as long as the sewing required.

They came walking in one morning early to do Martha Jane's sewing. The distance was not great. The only hindrance to their walking was a little wet-weather creek. There was a foot log for pedestrians, but if it rained very hard for any length of time, the foot log got submerged.

Miss Rebecca was also at the Colonel's for one of her frequent visits since the termination of her governess days there.

On the morning of Mrs. Woodrum's third day of sewing, it was raining. It had rained all the night. Mrs. Woodrum announced that her sewing would be finished by the afternoon and she would be leaving for the next neighbor's home, but she wanted Bet to go back home. Could the Colonel send her? George went to Martha Jane with his thoughts on how to get Bet home. Martha Jane said, "Mr. Shepard, I don't think you ought to make Sam take Bet Woodrum home. She could go on with her mother to Mrs. Sherrill's."

"Is her mother through with your sewing?"

"Yes, and she will spend tonight at the Sherrill's."

"Don't see how I'll manage any other way if Bet has to go home tonight. Sam couldn't cross that creek in the buggy. Water too high since the rain last night and this morning."

Bet was eight years old and very fat. She was a joke in the family. The day before at the dinner table, she had shocked Miss Rebecca almost out of her wits. There were whole buttered parsnips, and Bet scorned knife and fork. She would seize a parsnip by the big end, tilt her head back, and feed her mouth until the parsnip had disappeared. Miss Rebecca stopped eating and looked on in amazement. Bet paid no attention.

Under the circumstances, everybody was in favor of Bet's being restored to the bosom of her sisters and brothers. And the only—at least the best—way was for Sam to take her on old Bob, so the Colonel thought. But that was one time the Colonel reckoned without his proper gauge.

Sam and old Bob had a trick that nobody but they and Alice knew. There was a certain place on old Bob's belly, that if Sam touched it with the toe of his shoe, Bob would kick.

The time had come for Bet and Sam to go. The rain had stopped, the sun was shining, and the birds were singing. There was nothing in nature to indicate the seething on the inside of Sam's mind. He rode old Bob up to the horse block where Bet was waiting to mount behind him. Everything went smooth as butter until they rounded the corner of the yard fence and were opposite the woodpile. Then old Bob began reaching for the sky with his heels. Bet tumbled off. Sam slid off too and helped her to her feet. Alice was laughing fit to kill. The Colonel and all the rest stood astonished.

"What on earth was the matter with that horse?" said the Colonel. He got suspicious when Alice kept going off into fits of laughter. He turned to her, "Alice, do you know what the problem is?"

"Bet fell off," said Alice, when she could catch her breath.

"Yes. But what made her fall off?"

"Bob kicked up his heels," she said, and went off into another fit of laughing.

The Colonel said, "Humph!" and went to where Martha Jane was standing. "Mat, what does this mean?"

"I told you not to make Sam take that butterball home on old Bob. He's ashamed to be seen with her riding behind him with her arms around him—and I don't blame him," she said emphatically.

"Ought to be thrashed," said the Colonel.

"Now Mr. Shepard, don't you say a word to him."

The Colonel seemed puzzled, chagrined, and at a loss as to his next move. Martha Jane, watching him, grew more sympathetic with him in his predicament. She said, "Couldn't Sam take Bet home in the cart? That would be as safe as horseback, wouldn't it? I think he could get the cart across the creek."

The Colonel's face lit up. He lifted his shoulders and chin and started in Sam's direction. Sam was still holding Bob in the road, looking like he didn't know exactly what to expect next. Bet was sitting on a log, chewing cedar wax, and looking unconcerned. Sam's manner as his father approached was a mixture of defiance and apprehension.

"Sam," said the Colonel, "Hitch Joe to the cart. You can take her home in that."

"Yes, sir," said Sam, relaxing and feeling a little relieved, if not downright smug.

Later, the Colonel laid his paper down and announced, "Mat, the Cyclorama of Gettysburg is on exhibition in Nashville now." He took off his glasses and polished them on his shirtsleeve. "Would you like to see it?" he asked, as he settled further down in his chair and crossed his legs. Martha Jane was surprised. They never talked about the war. There was no tension about it, no studied evasion of the subject, just a mutual silence on the war as a topic of conversation.

When the children had asked him questions about the war, as they had been doing since they had begun studying the primary history of the United States at school, he had replied with a funny story of how some soldier had lost his gun or how one fellow got so tired on a retreat he lay down by a log and went to sleep.

"Did the Yankees get him, Papa?"

"No—not quite. Pretty soon, he found out by the bullets coming over that he was on the wrong side of the log."

"What did he do, Papa? Did a bullet hit him?"

"No. He just rolled over on the other side of the log and went back to sleep."

"The Yankees were coming, weren't they? Wouldn't they get him?"

"It would be a long time before they got there. He got him a nap and had time to outrun the Yankees."

That was as near as he would ever come to talking about the war. He had no notion of putting hatred into the minds of his children about the conflict. Mat knew that, but now he wanted to show them that awful Battle of Gettysburg.

"Mr. Shepard, surely you don't want to see that awful battle again, do you?"

"That's for you to say. I have some curiosity to see how it's done. The children should see it."

Martha Jane relaxed and picked up her sewing. She saw that he wanted to go. "I think it's too much of a trip for me," she said. "You take Sam and Alice. Johnny and I will be better off at home."

So off they went to Nashville. The cyclorama was a huge canvas encircling the spectators with graphic pictorials of the battle George remembered all too well. As the three stood in the center of it, the Colonel pointed out to his children the board fence, the Seventh Tennessee Regiment of Archer's Brigade alongside of Pickett's famous division, and the rock wall over which some of Archer's men had gone to fight hand-to-hand with the Federals. The children were amazed that their father could have known so much about one battle. He must have studied a different history than theirs, they thought. Why that battle was hardly mentioned in their history. Anyhow, they had no intention of ever studying that hard as he had on an old war. Alice viewed the canvas casually. She studied her father intently. She wondered why he was so tense, yet so smart. If only he had said, *I was in Archer's Brigade; I was lieutenant colonel in the Seventh Tennessee Regiment; Fry, the colonel, who was head of Archer's Brigade, was wounded and captured the third day, and I took his place. I was one of the men who went over that stone wall and fought hand-to-hand with the Federals that July third. I was close enough to Archer when he was captured on the first to see how tired his face looked.*

If he had only put in some *I*'s, that canvas would have sprung alive for his children. But he didn't say the *I*'s. Really, he couldn't have. It would have violated the foundations of his sensibilities. He was possessed of a delicate, ingrained modesty concerning his mental performances and physical activities, a modesty that he kept to the end of his life. His children would not learn these and other facts concerning his war record until twenty years after their father's death.

Very early one Saturday morning, Alice was awakened suddenly to see her father standing by her bed saying, "Want to go with me to Lascassas today?"

Did she! She was a big girl now, all of ten years, and feeling her grown-up-ness. Lascassas was eighteen miles away. She had never been so far from home in her life, except once or twice to Nashville. She was out of bed on the jump and calling to her mother, "Mama, can I wear my new, red dress?"

"Yes. Did you get a good bath last night like I told you to?"

"Yessum. Was that why you made me take my bath last night? Did you know I was going with Papa today?"

"Yes—if it wasn't raining."

"Does Sam want to go?"

"No. He'd rather stay at home. Besides, I need him. He'll go sometime."

"Mama, can I wear my new shoes?"

"Of course. What stockings have you got on?"

"The ones Aunt Mandy knit for me. All right?"

"Yes."

"Mat," came from across the hall, "do you know where my collar button is?"

Alice giggled. "Papa never does know where his collar button is," she said. "When I get married, I'm not going to know where my husband's collar button is." Her mother didn't hear all of her child's speech but enough to get the drift.

"Good idea," she said, as she came back from getting George's collar button for him. "Your papa is pitifully helpless when I'm sick in bed. I've spoiled him about that, I guess. Have you washed your face and hands?" she asked, taking Alice by the shoulders and looking at her face.

"Yes."

"Let's see if your neck and ears are clean. All right. Lace your shoes now and tie them; then come and let me comb your hair."

"Who'll comb my hair in the morning, Mama?"

"You can, can't you? You can comb it very nicely sometimes. You'll have to because your papa couldn't. At least he never has. I suppose he could if he had to. But you can do it. Stand still and let me get the plaits done well now, and they won't be so much trouble in the morning."

At the breakfast table, Alice was too excited to eat. Sam smiled and smirked. "Think you are powerful grown up, don't you?"

Becky brought in a plate of hot biscuits. "Here honey, you eat one of Becky's hot biscuits with lots of butter and soggum on it. You going on a long trip today. Um-uh! Ain't that a purty dress? Now don't you go get nothing down the front."

The Colonel had his bag in his hand and his hat on his head, ready to go. Taylor had brought old Joe and the buggy to the front, while breakfast was in progress.

"Got your hat on, Alice?" he called. "Time to go."

"She's already in the buggy, Colonel. Take care of her. She's too excited to do very well. Goodbye!"

"She'll be all right. We'll be back for supper tomorrow night."

When they were in the buggy, Alice said, "May I drive, Papa?" She knew and loved horses, thanks to Sam. She had been riding them bareback since she was big enough to walk. She and Sam were dependent on each other for companionship because there weren't other boys his age or girls her age close by to be pals and playmates. Hence, Alice did the things Sam did. He was an awful tease and was merciless toward her at times. But he was good to her, too, in that he was willing for her to follow him around, to ride the horses and mules he rode, and to be a tomboy with him. She'd been driving old Joe and the buggy to the Glade for nearly a year, but the Colonel wasn't sure at this time that she wasn't too excited to be allowed to drive. Nevertheless, he decided to let her have the lines.

"All right," he said. "Keep in the middle of the road. Give the other folks plenty of room if you meet anybody. Don't go too fast—got plenty of time."

"Where are we going to stay tonight, Papa?"

"At Sister Jones's."

"Who's she?"

"Brother Jones's wife."

"Who's he?"

The Colonel shuffled, got out his old cob pipe, packed in the tobacco, struck a match, lit up, and took a draw or two. He didn't want to have a conversation with anybody right now, so his answers were short. "He's a deacon," he said.

"What's a deacon?" He didn't want to be rude to his little girl, but he wanted to think about his sermon. "You know what a deacon is."

"You mean like Mr. Lannom and Mr. Pafford in our church?"

"Uh-huh." Then he settled himself against the back of the buggy seat and closed his eyes. Alice did not know then, but she learned later that when his old cob pipe was lit and he had settled back, he was off on a mental journey. He was reviewing his sermon or settling some church problem or praying for some sinner, old or young. That meant she and Joe must rattle on down the road and leave him to his uninterrupted meditation.

Sam took a trip with his father once. But one such trip was enough for him. Having old ladies, deacons' wives, make all over him while he had to sit still in some parlor and listen to talk he wasn't interested in was not his idea of a good time. But Alice loved it and went with her father many times. These occasions gave her a close, intimate, and priceless association with her father and a knowledge and acquaintance with the best people in many neighborhoods.

For food on these trips, they usually took a lunch from home. Sometimes they bought cheese and crackers at some crossroads store. Once in a great while, they would accept an invitation to stop at some friend's house for lunch. They had many such invitations because the Colonel knew everybody for miles around. He knew all the tollgate keepers. If he didn't remember the names, his cheery, "Good morning!" or "Good evening!" left them feeling that he was "powerful glad" to see them, as indeed he was. He loved folks.

Once, when on their way to Woodbury, a town some forty miles away, they accepted an invitation to stop and dine at a tollgate keeper's house. The keeper's invitation was cordial, "Light, Colonel, and have a snack with us. I think the old woman is bilin' some greens." The day was warm. It was time for lunch, and they were hungry. So they "lit." And right there was where they "lit" to their undoing. For greens it was, with sorghum molasses, buttermilk, and corn pone. But the greens were all pokeweed stalks—and they can be fairly poisonous! There was death in the pot and time for action. Where was Elisha and the handful of meal? "Light and have a snack" sounded good, but the sight of that table, with its soiled, red-checkered table cloth, muddy glassware, too sour buttermilk, and stick greens, looked bad.

The Colonel was close to his wit's end. He thought fast and furiously. He stirred his food, twisted in his chair, started asking questions, and did everything he could think to divert his host and hostess from wanting him and Alice to eat that food. So he saved the day. At least he and Alice got off without eating much of the poisonous stuff. They hurried to be on their way, leaving the host and hostess smiling in good humor and seeming to have had great pleasure in the visit.

"Mat, has Alice got a dress she could wear to a wedding?"

"She's got the dress I made for her to wear at Bettie's wedding. It's a year old, but it still fits her and looks nice. Why?"

"I want to take her with me to Jo Rushing's wedding next week. It will be a sort a stylish wedding."

"You mean the Rushings up near Lebanon?"

"Yes. They used to live near Powell's Chapel. Alice went with me to their home when they lived there. Jo's a Mary Sharp graduate now and a powerfully nice girl."

"Who's she going to marry?"

"Cog Robertson, son of one of the deacons at Powell's Chapel."

"Any bridesmaids or attendants?"

"Her brother, Bob, and Sophia Markham will stand up with them. The Rushings will put the big pot in the little 'un. Jo is the first of the children to get married."

"I'll show Alice's dress to you. You can decide." Martha Jane brought the brown, brocaded, woolen dress that had the wide, red, twilled silk sash. "Here it is," she said.

"Fine. That's all right. We'll be gone one night. The wedding's in the evening in their home."

On the way to the wedding, the Colonel tried to answer Alice's questions and coach her as to how to act at a stylish wedding.

"When the ceremony is over," he was saying, "there will be a lot of talking. Pay attention to what folks are saying and answer up when anybody speaks to you."

"Will there be any children there my size?"

"Jo has some brothers and sisters, some older and some younger than you. You'll meet other young folks, too, all older than you, but don't let that bother you—talk when you are talked to."

"Do you always say the same things to brides and grooms, Papa?"

"'Bout the same. Depends on the couple."

"What makes the difference?"

"Well, all boys are not alike. Neither are the gals."

"You said to Miss Delia's man, awful hard, to be 'good to her in sickness and in health.' Don't all husbands do that?"

The Colonel shuffled and clicked in his throat. "Some are better than others," he said. "And," he added, "some women are better than others."

"Can you tell what they are going to do after they are married?"

The Colonel felt himself getting into deep water. He twitched a shoulder and sighed. "Well, you can't," he said. "Folks change sometimes after they marry. Men and women both ought to try to change in the right direction. Takes both of them to make a home."

"When I get married, I hope I get as good a husband as you are, Papa."

The Colonel had a surge of emotions, surprise, gratitude, and some embarrassment. He didn't notice his reticence. She prattled on. His mind ran off into the future, wondering what sort of man he'd have to give her to someday. It was a disturbing thought. He was glad when they turned onto the lawn in front of the Rushings' house.

In the summer of 1885, a letter, the first from him in twenty-five years, came from Ben, the Colonel's older brother by about five to seven years. Ben was the brother who had gone to California in 1847.

During all these years, Fanny had written to Ben regularly, believing that he was still alive and that someday she would hear from him again.

In this long-delayed letter, Ben told of terrible hardships and of an accident years before that had left him a cripple. His letters, he said, during these twenty-five years after his accident had been intercepted by his partner, both letters to his brother and sisters and theirs to him. But when his gold was gone, the perfidious partner, with no prospect of gain at Ben's death, had departed for parts unknown. Now Ben wanted to return to Tennessee.

The Colonel bought a railroad ticket and sent it to him, not daring to send money for fear Ben would never get it. He got the ticket and came to the Colonel's an old, old man. He walked with great difficulty, aided by two canes. Other than that, he looked so much like the Colonel that people were constantly calling to him as they rode by the house, "Morning, Colonel," or "Evening, Colonel." It pleased Ben to be mistaken for his brother.

On account of much suffering from a badly injured spine, Ben had become a morphine addict. The Colonel did not believe the morphine helped him any. He consulted a doctor. The doctor agreed that the morphine was not much help and probably very bad for his stomach. The Colonel got permission from the doctor to dilute the morphine with quinine. When Ben would give his empty morphine bottle to his brother, there would always be a full bottle for him, a bottle that at first had only a little quinine mixed in the morphine. But as the weeks went by, the quinine grew in quantity, and the morphine diminished, till one day the Colonel said, "Ben, you haven't had any morphine now for three weeks. What about it?" Ben laid his morphine bottle aside and never asked for it again.

The Colonel's influence over his children was an extraordinarily unusual thing. He controlled them by a look, a gesture, a lift of his head, or a shrug of his shoulder. Of course, the lifting of an eyebrow was not always sufficient. There were times, very rare times, when he used sterner measures, and sad was that time for the culprit. Disobedience, George could not abide.

His patience with his children was equal to his influence over them. His characteristically quick, often abrupt, movements were never used in anger or impatience with them. "Take care" was his "don't" word.

While chopping stove wood, which he sometimes did, he would say, "Take care," if a child got in his way. He must have had to say it to Alice many times while he was building the new yard fence that she remembered with so much pleasure helping him to do. He never raised his voice or had a note of scolding or impatience in the words to his children. His "take care" sounded almost like a joke, but a joke to be heeded, not ignored.

Once when John was sick in bed with a cold and sore throat, a doctor was called in. When his mother went to the door to meet the doctor, John went out of bed and under it. He had no faith in doctors and, at his tender age of six, didn't want to be bothered with one. He was dragged from under the bed and put back into it. The doctor felt his pulse, looked down his throat and at his tongue, put a few pills on a plate, gave instructions for castor oil, and left.

When castor oil time came, it took both his parents to administer it. Alice stood breathless outside the door, listening to the struggle, and terribly afraid of hearing what she felt was needed, a spanking.

When John was settled and the Colonel came out of the room brushing his hands on his trousers, she timidly asked, "Didn't he need a spanking?"

Her father grinned at her, made the little sound in his throat, and said, "No, John's all right."

Alice's first, deep impression and memory of her father dates from the night John was born. She was nearly four years old and had been put to bed every night of her life by her mother. But on this night, she was so pleased to have her father put her to bed that she didn't think to ask where her mother was—ungrateful little beast—when she was "tucked in." He lay down on the bed beside her. She slipped out from under the cover on this cold January night, far enough to get her head onto his white shirt front, the old kind of shirt he forever wore. She was off to sleep in a twinkling, resting firmly on a solid foundation of contentment. It was a feeling toward him that grew stronger with her as the years went by. All of his children felt sure of his principles, his religion, and his honesty. They trusted his judgment, generosity, and good will. With him, they felt secure.

19 · Life with the Shepard Family

Books held an important place in the Shepard home. However, there was no extensive library. Fifty, perhaps a hundred, volumes occupied the shelves in the top of an old press with quilts and blankets behind the doors in the bottom part. A few histories and biographies were among the number and a mystery story by Edgar Allen Poe that Alice got hold of much too early in life and devoured with horrified delight. An edition of *Aesop's Fables* that had a second part in rhyme was another much-loved book. Then there was an encyclopedia that, to his children, seemed huge. They thought it contained all the knowledge in existence about all lands and all peoples. But the most important set in the whole collection was Matthew Henry's *Commentary on the Bible.* Next to the Bible itself, that collection of four volumes was the Colonel's meat and drink. On his retirement from the ministry, he sent these volumes to his grandson, Dr. George Alexander Carver, who used them in preparing his own first sermon.

The Colonel had an alert interest in what his children were reading. "Dime novels" were taboo, and none were found on his bookshelves. Martha Jane was a subscriber to the *Ladies Home Journal,* which furnished the light reading for the family. The Colonel had the *Home and Farm* magazine, which he read to help him in his farming. He also read the weekly religious paper from the front page to the last, as he did the weekly newspaper.

When Sam and Alice were very young, Joe Chandler Harris published "Aaron in the Wildwoods" and "The Story of Aaron" as serials in the weekly newspaper. The paper came on Friday afternoons, and the Colonel spent the next hour reading the current installment to his children. The fact that Alice always sat on her father's lap during the reading was as important to her as the story itself.

The Colonel had a rare supply of "folktales" he would tell his children and grandchildren as compensation for getting his head scratched. His tales had an *Uncle Remus* flavor, but he didn't use the same words as in Joel Chandler Harris's stories. After all, these were classic African-American tales that many people knew. The characters included Brer Rabbit, Brer Fox, the old red rooster, the hen, Brer Possum, Brer Bar, and various fouls. At times, he'd be sitting in his chair, his head bent over and his eyes closed, as the tiny "scratcher" stood by with a hand on his head and eyes and ears wide open to know what the old red rooster would do next.

One day, he was lying across the foot of Martha Jane's bed, his feet propped on a chair. Agnes was curled up on the bed by him in rapt attention. "And the old hen went out to find her a good nest. She went on down the lane, down lane till she came … came to … a fence … with… with a … a … stump in it. She made her a good nest behind the stump, and … and every day … every day … she would go there and lay … lay an egg … every day … lay … lay an egg … every day …"

Agnes was by that time completely exasperated. She slipped off the bed, snorting, "That old hen's laid two or three baskets full of eggs already!" The Colonel was fast asleep. Alice Carver Cramer, Alice's daughter and the Colonel's granddaughter, related a similar story when the Colonel was telling his grandchildren the "folktales," as he called them, and started to tell it slower and slower because he was falling asleep. "Cousin Ida, daughter of John Watson Shepard, threatened to spit on the Colonel's bald spot," related Alice. "Well, the Colonel gave them all full attention, and everyone had a good laugh, including the Colonel."

The Colonel was very pleased to see Alice not playing as much with Sam but becoming more interested in John's activities as he grew older. Thus, she stayed closer to the house and yard than when she was running farther afield with Sam. The big Shepard dog—"Shep"—made a third party in their games. Johnny rode the dog while Alice led him by a string tied around his neck for a bridle. That was a fine game to her, and Johnny liked nothing better. When Shep decided that he'd had enough of being a horse, he would lie down and tumble into the grass. The children would laugh and squeal and tumble in the grass with him.

Now Sam could divide his teasing between Alice and John. It was a real grief to Alice when he teased their little brother. But by the time he was seven years old, Johnny had learned how to take care of himself. He and Alice hadn't thrown rocks at cedar trees and gateposts so often and long for nothing. His aim was good, his eye accurate, and his arm surprisingly strong for a youngster his age. Sam learned that if he wanted to crook his finger at Johnny and say, "goodie, goodie," which at that time was highly provocative, he'd better be near a tree or the corner of the house where he could dodge and hide from the rock that was sure to come. John hadn't yet learned that he must aim below the neck. Sam, nearly seven years older than John, had to learn to use his head for better things than a target for rocks.

Alice, who had been almost a godmother to John since the night he was born, was sometimes almost overwhelmed with such a heavy responsibility. Since she had read *The Life of Daniel Boone* a few months before, the weight of the burden had increased. Her mind had become saturated with Indians, tomahawks, running gauntlets, and violent deaths of every variety, and she worried about them by day and dreamed about them by night. Her greatest worry was that she would never get John properly hidden if need be. If she succeeded in cramming him under the bed by the time the "war whoopers" reached the yard, in her violent imagination, he was sure to poke his head out at the most inopportune time.

And now that he was seven and his parents had decided to send him to school in August instead of waiting until January when he would be eight, she felt her burden heavy indeed. *What if the big boys tease him?* He was almost as big as she, but she felt years older.

The morning set for John's first day in school arrived. The Colonel said to Alice, "Keep an eye on him. Introduce him to his teacher. See that

COLONEL S. G. SHEPARD

he gets into the right place. He'll be all right—a little scared this first day. But he'll soon get acquainted."

When they got to the schoolhouse, John had no notion of going into the room for the first- and second-graders. He would sit with Alice. Minnie Harralson, her deskmate, was very obliging—giving all the room she could to make space for Alice's little brother.

The second was a repetition of the first day. Nobody, not even the teachers, noticed anything unusual. Sam was the only one who took notice and then only as they walked the mile and a half home. "Sissy," he called John, till John got a rock and Alice intervened. "Sam, will you please behave and leave him alone? He'll be all right tomorrow."

"How are things going, Alice?" asked her father on the second day after the boys were out of hearing range.

"He won't go to Professor Leming's room, Papa. He still wants to sit with me."

"Has Professor Leming said anything to him?"

"No. Nobody has. He just sits with me and watches the children write or work arithmetic on the board. Looks like he knows all about what they're doing."

"Well, he can read and figure some. Reckon he does know what some of them are doing. What does he do when you go to class?"

"Goes with me."

The Colonel laughed and walked away.

The next day, Alice was sure something would happen. She felt the teachers would act. She dreaded it.

In the middle of the morning, Professor Leming from the primary room came in and headed for Alice's desk. She stiffened. She knew the time had come. When he was close to her desk, he said, "Does your father want this boy to be in school?"

"Yes, sir," said Alice, almost choking. Professor Leming stepped behind him, slipped his hands under John's arms, picked him up, and walked out with him like he was an infant. Nobody spoke or laughed. John did not cry or say anything, but he kicked his heels against Professor Leming's legs all the way out of the room.

On the afternoon of that third day, George and Martha Jane sat on the porch watching for the children's homecoming. The Colonel was trying to read but not succeeding very well. Martha Jane was making her knitting needles fly with her eyes never off the road.

"There they are, Mr. Shepard," she said, as the children came strolling through the cedar-bordered lane. When they came onto the porch, the boys threw their school satchels and hats down and made for the backyard where a peach tree was loaded with ripe peaches. Alice stopped for a drink of water. Her mother called to her.

"Was Johnny good today?"

"Yessum," said Alice, "he was all right."

"Did he go to his room and do what the teacher told him to?" asked her father.

"Yes, sir. Professor Leming took him."

"Oh? How'd he take him? What happened?"

"Nothing, 'cept Johnny kicked on Professor Leming's legs all the way out the room. He didn't cry though—Johnny didn't."

"What did Professor Leming say?"

"He didn't say anything. He asked me if you wanted John in school is all. I was awful afraid he'd whip him, but he didn't." The Colonel nodded and picked his book up. Now, he could read.

There was no more trouble about John always being in his place in his room nor was it long before he was writing on the board in the older children's room and reading with the eight-year-olds.

Alice's fear about the big boys teasing John was soon realized, however. One day during morning recess as she went to the vestibule to get her bonnet, she saw three or four big boys outside the door in the yard teasing her little brother. He was on the verge of tears. She flung herself out that door, landing with her fists in the back of the nearest boy. It was her beau! She grabbed the top edge of his vest, a favorite vest of his *and* hers, and it came apart from top to bottom. They were all so startled that everything stopped. She fled back through the door and out another door onto the girls' playground. But there was no more teasing of John from that bunch of boys.

Another episode caused her much trouble. Mr. Castleman was the village storekeeper and postmaster. He had a big fat sow that roamed all the open spaces in the Glade and especially the grounds around the schoolhouse. She had, on several occasions, gotten into the vestibule of the schoolhouse where the children kept their lunch baskets or boxes and helped herself to ham, biscuits, and eggs. One day, when the pupils had been dismissed for lunch, John came in just in time to see the big fat sow ambling out the door with his lunch basket! He went after her, stopping only to find a suitable rock. He was as careful about his rock as David was in selecting his stone for Goliath. The children gathered around, some saying, "Why don't you stop her?" John found his rock. The sow ambled on her way some twenty feet down the gentle slope of the hill. John let his rock fly. It went *zip* like a bullet and *crack* against the old sow's leg, like the crack of a bat on a baseball. The old sow screamed and sat down on her haunches. The children jumped about and yelled, "Guess she won't bother us any more! That got her, all right!" Some went even so far as to pat John on the back with, "Good boy!" Alice heard behind her, "Good shot, John! But I guess your pa will have to pay for it!" She looked around to see Professor Leming, grinning from ear to ear.

This was not one of Alice's happiest afternoons. But what would Mr. Castleman do? What would Papa think? These were questions that loomed big in her mind. As soon as she got home, she hurried to get it over with. "Papa, something happened today—something awful bad." She looked so distraught that the Colonel was alarmed for a second. He put his paper down in his lap, took his spectacles off, and gave her his full attention.

"What?" he said. "What happened?"

"Johnny broke Mr. Castleman's old sow's leg."

"Mr. Castleman's old sow's leg? How?"

"With a rock."

"Was she stealing his lunch?"

"Yes, sir."

The Colonel relaxed, put his spectacles back on, and picked up his paper. "Good thing," he said, and started reading.

A few days later, he saw Mr. Castleman and offered to pay for damages done, but Mr. Castleman wouldn't let him. Mr. Castleman said, "Didn't hurt the old sow much—splinted her leg a few days, and she was all right. Professor Leming told me she'd been bothering the children's lunches for quite a spell. I'll keep her up now."

"Hey Sam, come here a minute," Alice called one day as Sam was hurrying out of the yard.

"What you want? I'm in a hurry." But he came back to where she stood halfway between the porch and the gate. He always wanted to know what Alice was up to.

"Mama needs a pit."

"A what?"

"A pit—a flower pit."

"What's the matter with her stand? It holds everything she's got, don't it?"

"Course, silly. But it's going to frost soon, and the frost will kill all her geraniums and begonias except the few she puts in the cellar. She has to begin all over again every spring."

"What's the matter with that?"

"Don't be a goose. She wants a pit."

"Why don't she get Pop to get her one made?"

"Aw, you know Mama—always saying 'Mr. Shepard's too busy to do this or that'—never asks him. Now when I get married, my husband's going to do things I want done."

Sam laughed uproariously. "You ain't going to get no husband! Not with that nose! Ha! Ha!"

Alice was pretty mad, but she knew that was what Sam wanted, so she held her temper.

"Plenty of women get married that ain't pretty. Look at Mrs. Bet Brown. She's cross-eyed and got a wart on her nose. Anyhow, I bet I get married before you do."

"Who? Me? Not on your life. I don't want no woman bossing me around—and a passel o' kids? No, sir." He started away.

"Sam, please. I think Mama ought to have a pit."

"Well, how's she going to get it if she won't ask Pap? Huh?" He was disgusted and minced in a falsetto voice, "Papa, Papa. Not me! No, sir!"

"We could get Taylor and Will to dig the pit, couldn't we?" Alice said, ignoring his effort to change the subject.

"They are gathering corn, and you know Pap would be mad as a hen if that corn ain't in when he gets home. You won't catch me making Pap mad. Not if I can help it."

Alice remembered something that had happened nearly a year ago but had never dared ask Sam about it. Now she dared. "Sam, did Papa whip you that time we were in the garden gathering grapes for Mama to can and Papa came while you were telling me some words you heard the horseshow men say? Did he?"

Sam grinned. "You mean that time you fell over three fences getting away and stayed out behind the barn all day?"

"Uh-huh."

"No, he didn't—'course not," he said pompously. "But," he added, "I had to do some powerful purty talking though."

"You didn't talk him out of it that time you didn't plow the garden while he was away like he told you to." Alice couldn't help saying that. But she knew immediately she had made a mistake.

Sam started away, saying, "Aw shucks."

Alice called to him. "Sam, please. Ask Taylor to dig the pit. I'll help get the corn gathered. Honest, I will!"

Sam turned around and grimaced at her. "You gather corn?"

"I bet I can gather corn as fast as you can. Sam, please!"

"All right! But if Pap gets mad, you'll have to take the blame."

"Of course, now hurry. Papa won't get mad," she added to herself as Sam hurried away.

Taylor and Will dug the pit. It took all of two days to get it fixed for use. Sam was uneasy before the second day was over. Alice wasn't quite easy in her mind either. Taking hands out of the cornfield might prove no slight offense. She hadn't supposed it would take so long. It might rain. That would be a tragedy. She prayed that the rain would stay away and helped all she could, she and Sam both. It didn't rain. She went with Sam to the cornfield and worked side by side with him for three days. Her mother wouldn't let her go in the afternoons. She thought the mornings were enough for a little girl to be gathering corn with a big brother three years her senior.

When the day for the Colonel to get home from his protracted meeting arrived, the corn was all in the barns and everything was moving along smoothly in the home. Soon, before he had noticed it, Martha Jane pointed out the pit to him. He was surprised.

"Who did it? Didn't know you wanted one."

"Taylor and Will. Sam and Alice got them to without asking me. But I knew what they were up to. I heard the conversation between them. Sam was doubtful, but Alice persuaded him. Now Mr. Shepard, if you are mad about it as Sam thought you would be, just blame me. Don't blame the children."

"Good pit, ain't it? Glad you've got it—if you wanted it. The corn is in. That's all I wanted Taylor and Will to do while I was away. Of course, if it had rained ..."

"But it didn't. And Alice went to the field and worked for three days to hurry the corn in for fear it might." The Colonel was very quiet, looking into the distance. Martha Jane thought she knew what he was thinking. She did not want him to be reproaching himself. She moved her hands, gave her skirt a little twist, and smiled brightly into his face.

"Glad you like the pit," she said. "It's wonderful. And now there's one other thing that happened while you were gone. Alice seems to get so many ideas. I wish she'd get them while you are at home."

The Colonel left the past and came to the present. "What's she done now?" he said.

"You know she's wanted bangs a long time."

"Silly nonsense."

"Yes, I know. But she got another spell of wanting her hair cut when she saw Maude's the other day. Maude's did look nice. Maude is a pretty girl. And Ben pleaded for Alice. He said it wasn't right not to let her have what other little girls had. You know Ben is quite partial to 'Allie,' as he calls her. Makes him mad as tucker for Sam to tease her. Well, I relented and cut her hair."

"Nothing for me to say, is there?" said the Colonel with the twinkle in his eyes and the grin that Martha Jane loved. Now she knew that he didn't object to the bangs—for if he did ... "But," added the Colonel, "no holes in her ears. That's pretty barbaric."

"Of course—no holes in her ears," said Martha Jane.

The Colonel was not demonstrative in his affections. But there was never a doubt in the minds of his children—or his wife—that he loved them. It just wasn't discussed nor demonstrated in any kissing or lovemaking words. It was a fact that needed no demonstration. But late in August of the same summer, Sam got another slant on his father.

Sam came through his mother's room late one afternoon on his way from the dining room to the front porch where Alice was sitting on a step enjoying the petunias, phlox, verbena, and asters that filled the borders from the porch to the front gate. He was excited and looked frightened. "Alice, is Mammy sick?" he asked.

"Why no. I don't reckon she is. She seemed all right a little while ago. Why?"

"Well, when I came through their room just now, Pap was holding her up in his arms and kissing her like he was telling her goodbye for the last time. I never saw Pap kiss Mammy before. She must be sick!"

"Silly! Don't you know men kiss their wives?"

"No, I don't, except that sissified cousin John Graves that comes out here from Nashville in the summers; him and his wife kiss. He's a regular slobber mouth. Looks like a cow that's been running in a clover field. Whew! Makes me sick at the stomach. 'Taint healthy! Won't ever catch me kissing any old woman."

"Bet you do when you get married."

"Ain't gonna get married."

"Well," said Alice, much wrought up. "If my husband doesn't kiss me, I'll ..."

"You'll what?" sneered Sam.

Alice ignored the sneer. "Did you see the new clock Pap gave Mama today when he got home from Lebanon?"

"Yes, sir, I saw it—on her mantel—purty, ain't it? Says 'Seth Thomas' down in the corner. But what's he given it to her now for? 'Taint Christmas."

"It's their anniversary day, August third."

"Their what?"

"The day they got married. They've been married eighteen years today, 3 August."

"How'd you know?"

"I heard Mama say so this morning when she and Papa were talking about him going to Lebanon."

"And him a kissing her! I never thought Papa was like that," Sam muttered as he started for the well to draw water for the stock.

The Colonel's habits were as dependable as was his character. For general good feeling and well-being in the home, his habit of punctuality was a real asset. He may have vexed Martha Jane about some things but never by being late for meals or starting to church or the post office or for the mail or coming home after the appointed time. She always knew just what he'd want at the table for any meal and how many biscuits, muffins, slices of bacon, ham, or apple dumplings he'd eat. She knew and the children knew that he'd keep his promises to them promptly.

His promptness however was not always as pleasant to all concerned as it sounds. One day, he was playing croquet with Sam and Alice, and at a crucial moment in the game, the supper bell rang. Alice was really vexed when he promptly laid his mallet across his ball and said, "We'll finish after supper." She wanted to know what that next stroke would do. But she didn't argue. She knew that he'd answer to no arguing. She and Sam put their mallets down and went promptly with him.

He had one habit of long standing that he abolished in middle life— tobacco. He decided that tobacco was bad for the young people in his churches. He couldn't give advice against its use since he was himself a user. When he came to that conclusion, he went out into a field near the house and to a thicket where there were some rocks. He took his pipe and tobacco out of his pocket, put them on a rock, and laid another rock on top of them. "And," interrupted the man to whom the Colonel's son-in-law was telling the story years later, "went back the next day and got them!"

"Ah," said the son-in-law, "if you knew the Colonel you wouldn't say that!"

Another bad habit, which he never broke himself of, was eating new Irish potatoes in the spring. He just couldn't resist, or didn't try to, the first mess of new potatoes. They usually made him sick—not very sick—but sick enough for a dose of castor oil and camphor or some other home remedy. One time, after he had reached the age of eighty, he made the mistake of taking paregoric, a pain medication made from camphorated opium, instead of castor oil. A doctor had to be called. Alice stood at the foot of the bed while Dr. Bate poked and listened and asked questions.

"How long have you had this trouble, Colonel?" referring to his hemorrhoids.

"He's never had such an attack before in his life," Alice spoke up promptly.

Already the Colonel's eyes were twinkling and his shoulders moving. "About forty years," he said in his brisk, optimistic voice. Dr. Bate laughed and wrote a prescription for a quart of oil to be administered as an enema. "The biggest dose of oil a man ever took," said the Colonel.

The Colonel had, in full measure, the "Southern hospitality" attitude toward folks. Martha Jane felt as he did. They were never able to turn anyone from their door. Everybody within a radius of five or more miles knew the Shepards' attitude, so travelers were directed to the Colonel's home. The "night-spenders" were many and varied. The Colonel had a quick mind and eye for character reading, so the family did not get imposed on by unworthy tramps.

One evening near sundown, a man rode up to the front gate and called to the Colonel, who was on the front porch reading.

"Hey, brother—be you Colonel Shepard?"

The Colonel laid his book down, took off his specs, wiped them on his sleeve, and hooked them back over his ears as he walked to the front gate. All the time, he was sizing up the man on the horse. "Evening, brother. What do you want?"

"Be you Colonel Shepard?"

"Yes."

"Well, sir, I'm looking for a place to sleep tonight. Couldn't find no place in that little town you got back up the road about two miles. Was told maybe you'd sleep me. Purty tired. Come all the way from t'other side of Nashville today, a purty fur piece, and hope to get into Rutherford County sometime tomorrow. My wife's got some folks there somewheres around Murfreesboro. Hope to find 'em." By the time the man had finished his speech, the Colonel had decided he was harmless so he asked him to light. He called Taylor to take his horse.

It so happened that Alice had a friend, a little girl her own age named Sallie, spending the night with her that evening. At the supper table, the guest told how skilled a dyer his wife was with "walnut hulls," only he pronounced it "wannit hulls." Every time he said it, the Colonel raised his eyebrows, flashed his eyes, twitched his shoulders, or lifted his head. When the traveler had finished the tale, saying "wannit hulls" several times, Alice and Sallie were about to burst out laughing. Sam choked and left the table. The Colonel passed the biscuit plate, asked Martha Jane if she'd have a glass of milk, buttered himself another biscuit, and then said in a serious and earnest manner, "What did you say she uses to make dye with?"

The guest, just as earnestly, said, "Wannit (walnut) hulls. I said wannit hulls." Alice and Sally asked to be excused and left the table.

The Colonel was in no sense of the word a comedian. He rarely set himself to be funny. On slight acquaintance with him, he impressed one as a very quiet, unobtrusive man, as indeed he was. His wit lay in the unusual phrase or the quick word that never changed his own expression or manner but would sometimes shock a listener into almost hysterical laughter. His regard for the feeling of others was kindly at all times. He wouldn't have embarrassed the "wannit-hull" guest for anything. And he didn't. He gave the children a good time with no harm done.

There was one time when the Colonel turned a weary traveler from his door. Mormon elders were occasional walking travelers through the country. The report had it that they were distributing propaganda to induce young women to go to Salt Lake City to become wives of Mormon men there. Whether there was any truth in the report or not, the

COLONEL S. G. SHEPARD

Colonel didn't stop to inquire when he saw two of these men turn through the gate into his yard. He dropped the paper he was reading and got to the gate by the time they did.

Nobody ever knew what he said to them, but from the way the elders turned and hurried, almost ran on their way, it was evident that he had said enough. He came back to his chair and paper with no word of explanation. Members of the family who saw it happen were very curious to know what he said, but all they ever got was, "No room."

The Colonel's house was a sort of home for itinerant preachers on their way to their appointments, for spinsters and bachelors to take on board for a week or two, and for widows and orphans. There was a dentist who lived in Lebanon who for years came every fall. He would put his various boxes of materials up at the Colonel's and go through the country "plugging" and pulling teeth and making false sets. He always got back in time for supper and bed for the night at the Colonel's. He played a violin, and when he had his violin among his boxes of materials, he was a very welcome visitor with the younger members of the family.

There was an old bachelor who wore a tall, silk hat and rode a handsome, bay horse named Toby. He came every fall for a week's rest. He was not a very welcome visitor with Sam and Alice because he didn't approve of children eating ham for supper. The Colonel never discussed the subject with the old gentleman.

When supper was served, they were seated, and thanks had been given, the *pièce de résistance* was a large platter of fried or broiled ham with plenty of red gravy. "Uncle Turner," as everybody called him, would begin in his mild, gentlemanly voice. "Children shouldn't eat ham for supper. Very bad for them." Then he'd look around the table for approval. The Colonel's eyes would twinkle and his shoulders twitch. He'd go right ahead serving the plates and agreeing with Uncle Turner. "Yes, yes—bad for anybody to eat too much." Sam's and Alice's plates would get the usual servings, with perhaps a little more, so they wouldn't pass back for a second helping.

One constant year-round visit was the family doctor. When he'd have a patient south of the Glade, he'd arrive at the Shepard home about noon, stop to pass the time of day, and remain to eat. He was very fond of sweet milk and had no use for buttermilk. On the days—and they were not a few—that he sat at the Shepard's dinner table, Sam and Alice would be deprived of a second glass of milk, which they usually wanted; they certainly did if the supply grew scanty. Martha Jane always saw that Johnny, who sat beside her, got his proper helping of milk. The doctor never stopped with less than three glasses.

The pitchers of milk and glasses were placed at the Colonel's end of the table. One day, he decided to put the doctor in his place on the milk question. As soon as glasses began to empty, he said to Sam briskly, "Milk, Sam?" Sam immediately passed his glass.

"Sweet milk or buttermilk?" asked the Colonel.

Sam promptly replied, "Sweet milk."

By then, Alice was on to her Papa's game and passed her glass too.

"Sweet milk or buttermilk?" asked the Colonel, with a twinkle in his eye and a shrug of the shoulder.

"Sweet milk," sang out Alice. The doctor got only one glass of milk that day.

One summer, some very interesting visitors came and by accident spent six weeks in the Shepard home. A young man in the neighborhood had moved to another state, gone into business there, and got married. In the course of time, he brought his wife and their nine-month-old baby to visit his brother's family.

When the Jersey wagon—a large wagon with a cloth top—with the trunk and passengers drove up to the brother's house, the young wife cast a calculating eye over the premises. She didn't see room in the small house of her brother-in-law for three extra people. She looked up the road through the cedars and saw a white house somewhat larger.

"Who lives there?" she asked.

"Cousin George," her husband said.

"Take my trunk there," she said to the driver.

Such a performance had all the makings for hard feelings. The fact that none were produced was due largely to what the two brothers thought of "Cousin George." There was no restraint in the visiting between the two families, and the visitors felt free to go in and out of the two homes as they pleased.

COLONEL S. G. SHEPARD

The passing years brought rapid changes to the Shepard home. Agnes was born on February 1, 1886, a lovely baby who immediately became the darling of the entire family. Ben had now been in Tennessee two years. He spent a part of each year with the Shepards, the Bradshaws, and the Robinsons. He didn't suffer so much pain any more, but he was rapidly growing more frail. He was not a professed Christian, which caused some concern in the minds of his brother and sisters. It caused so much concern in the mind of Miss Rebecca, the former governess who was visiting in the Shepard home at a time when Ben was there, that she did something about it. Nobody ever knew just what line of talk she used on him, but after she had spent an hour in his room one Sunday afternoon, Ben asked to be baptized. The deacons in his brother's church at the Glade came to the home and received him into the church. The baptism was set for the following Sunday afternoon.

During the week, the Colonel and Taylor made a baptistery, a huge box some nine feet long, five feet wide, and four feet deep. The board–heavy oak planks were an inch thick. Sheet iron covered the bottom and sides of the tank—a queer baptistery but an entirely adequate one.

On Sunday morning, Taylor filled the strange pool, which had been placed in the yard west of the house, with water from the well. Long before the hour had come for the great event to take place, neighbors and friends from far and near began filling the yard and all available spaces. They had seen baptisms in creeks, ponds, and rivers, but they had never seen a homemade baptistery or a baptism in a private yard.

There were some who thought it unnecessary and dangerous. But they wanted to see the Colonel baptize his frail, older brother, who was not strong enough to be taken to a creek or pond.

The day was perfect; the sun was shining. The shadows had begun to slant across the treetops, making patterns on the baptismal waters, when the Colonel came with his brother on his arm. Taylor had Ben by his other arm to take care of his canes and to help the Colonel lift him into the pool. Everybody had grown breathlessly quiet. Ben's face was shining. His usual death-like pallor had given way to a radiance—a shining that spoke of another world, proof of his conversion. When the simple ceremony was over, the people, with few words in muted tones, drifted quietly away.

Martha Jane had been in the kitchen telling Becky what to have for breakfast. It was a cool morning in April. The children were still in bed. Martha Jane came in her room to find Mr. Shepard sitting by the fire he had kindled—just a little blaze to take the chill off. Soon the sun would warm things up, but it was still very cool for April. She got her knitting to sit with him by the fire till it would be time to call the children. He put his paper down—yesterday's paper—took off his specs, and cleared his throat. Martha Jane could tell he had something important to say.

He began, "How would it do for me to take Alice with me to Woodbury in June? There's to be a special series of meetings at that time."

Martha Jane finished the needle, which was only half finished when he'd stopped talking. "Don't you think," she said, "that Alice is getting too old to go with you on these trips unless she has an invitation?"

"What do you mean?"

"I mean when a deacon asks you to dinner or to spend the night with him and his family, he hardly expects to entertain a big girl, too. At least *Mrs.* Deacon might not find it so convenient."

"Alice is not a big girl. She can sleep in the room with me, as she usually does when we are on a trip."

"Mr. Shepard, Alice is thirteen now, and girls that age don't sleep in the room with men—not even their own fathers—except in emergencies."

"Alice isn't thirteen yet, is she?"

Martha Jane sighed. One thing she had never been able to understand about her husband was his utter indifference, she thought, to birthdays or dates of any kind that were not connected with his work. He never forgot a meeting, even for months ahead, nor exactly when the corn was due to be in the ground. But he'd even forget their wedding anniversary. And as for knowing his children's ages ... well, he'd miss the time by months, and once in a while, he'd be a year off! Now, as she picked her knitting up and rolled it together to lay aside—she must get the children up—she said, "Thirteen, the last day of last month."

He seemed surprised, almost shocked. "A big girl ... soon to be off to college. Can't believe it."

When Martha Jane came back into the room, he said, "I'll manage an invitation for her when I go in May."

"Now Mr. Shepard, don't you go asking for an invitation for Alice. You'll wear her welcome out, and yours too, if you do that kind of thing."

"I won't," he said shuffling and grinning. "She'll be welcome. There will be a lot of young people for this meeting. If she's getting to be such a big girl, it's time she learned how to behave with big girls and boys."

Martha Jane smiled. "You seem to have changed your mind on some subjects. Are you set to teach her how to manage a beau?"

The Colonel looked uncomfortable. "Of course not!" he said. "But it won't hurt her, I reckon, to know the girls and boys at other places besides here at home."

"Mr. Shepard, do you remember, it's been nearly two years, how upset you were over that tale Johnny Strickland told you about Alice and Bill writing to each other, hiding notes under rocks and in fence corners, and using their schoolbooks as ... post offices?"

The Colonel shuffled, recrossed his legs, and laid his paper on his lap. "Johnny was always a sort of news carrier," he said. "Didn't know what he was talking about ... just guessing."

"No, he wasn't guessing."

The Colonel pricked up his attention, "What do you mean?"

"Well ... it was about that time that I found some notes on Alice's study table by her schoolbooks. Johnny's news had upset me too. So I read the notes."

"Why didn't you tell me?"

"Didn't think ... well, I guess I was ashamed of what I'd done in the first place, and then I didn't think I had any right to tell."

"Tell me now, not as it makes any difference."

"No hard or wrong in telling you now, I guess. I saw Bill's note that she was answering. It said, 'Dear Alice, I love you. I hope you love me too. I think you are the prettiest girl in school. Love, Bill.'"

The Colonel grunted and shuffled, "How old is he?" he asked.

"He's a year older than Alice."

"Did you read her answer?"

"Yes. She said, 'Dear Bill, We are too young to know anything about love. Love is for folks when they get grown and are ready to get married. Your *friend*, Alice.'"

"That all?"

"Yes—all I read. There were other notes, but I'd had enough."

"Nice boy, but she was too young—much too young."

"She's not much older now," said Martha Jane with solemn emphasis.

The Colonel made sounds in his throat, shuffled, and stood up. The breakfast bell was ringing.

The Colonel "managed" an invitation for Alice to go with him to Woodbury in June. Martha Jane made a new dress for her, a deep blue, soft muslin with narrow ecru lace at the neck, and sleeves and a ribbon for the waist. That would be her "dress-up" dress for special occasions. Alice had too much of her father's complexion to wear the pale blues, pinks, and greens that Martha Jane loved and wore herself when a young girl.

The trip to Woodbury was a success in every respect, so far as Alice was concerned, except for one incident: the buggy ride with a boy she hardly knew. She went to all the meetings, heard many preachers speak, including her father (who, for her, was the best speaker there), and then went to the party the teenagers had on Saturday night. It was called a "conversation party," but some games were played too.

Alice was a little puzzled by her father's attitude toward this party. Heretofore he had paid almost no attention to her party-goings, and she had been going to parties fairly frequently for several years, especially the past winter during the Christmas week. She and Sam usually went together, and she wore whatever her mother said to wear. She was sure he hadn't the slightest idea or concern about what she wore to the parties in and around the Glade. Now he was concerned.

"What are you going to wear to the party, Alice?" He was satisfied when she showed him the blue dress. "That's all right," he said. "Be friendly with the young folks and polite to the old folks. Try to get their names straight and play the games with them if they play any. You know the name of the boy who is to take you?"

She looked at him so hard he got fidgety. "Of course," she said. "All right. Don't forget it."

She wondered what on earth ailed him. She would have more to wonder about before they got home. A deacon from another of her father's churches had brought his family to attend these special meetings at Woodbury. They had driven through the country in a surrey.

When the meetings were over, the Colonel, Alice, the deacon, and his family were leaving from the same home at the same time for the homeward journey. Alice was in the buggy holding the lines, ready to start. Old Joe was as impatient to be on his way as she was. Her father was saying goodbye to the deacon and his family. There was a son in his party a few years older than Alice. His name was Bob. When the Colonel got through saying goodbye and came to the buggy, he said, "Alice, Bob wants me to swap driving places with him as far as" such and such a town. That was thirty miles away—a four-hour drive! She had no mind for such a long drive with a boy she hardly knew, even if the day was gorgeous and she was thirteen. She felt like yelling, "I won't!" but the twinkle in her father's eye restrained her, and she nodded a reluctant consent.

"You'd better let Bob drive," he said, as he started away. "He wouldn't like it if you drove."

That was the proverbial straw. What was her father trying to do to her anyway? She felt like weeping but managed a fairly decent smile as she turned the lines over to Bob and they started on their way. She didn't know what to say to him, but he didn't seem to notice that. He soon launched out enthusiastically on the story of his life, past and present, and his ambitions for the future. She found herself listening with one ear and wondering with the other side of her brain about her father and why this strange change in him.

The day went by somehow, and at long last, they reached the fork in the road where Bob climbed out of the buggy, and her father climbed in. Once more, the lines were in her hands.

As the Colonel tucked the robe around his knees, he cleared his throat, and she knew he had something to say. She had no mind to tell him much—not now. But she was intent to know his interest.

He said, tucking some more at the rug, "How'd you and Bob get on?"

She slapped old Joe with the lines, took a look at her father out of the corner of her eye, and replied, "He told me he is going to preach."

"Well now, that's interesting. What did you say?" Again, old Joe got an unneeded slap with the lines across the rump.

"I raised no objections," she said and firmly closed her mouth. The Colonel threw his head back, laughed, and at the same time reached for his pocket with the old cob pipe in it. Then Alice knew that there would be no more forced conversation, and she and old Joe could trot down the road at their own sweet pleasure.

It was August and hot. The Colonel lay sick with a fever. He and Martha Jane had been married for twenty-two years, and she had never before seen him sick in bed. When first married, she had been frightened by the headaches that wracked his body when he had been working hard too long and had gotten too tired and hot. She had quickly learned to be expert in fixing the poultices, made of brown paper folded several times and soaked in vinegar and black pepper that he always wanted. She bound these to his head with a towel. They seemed effective. The headaches had grown less severe and less frequent as the years went by. She had also gotten acquainted with his yearly tilt with new Irish potatoes. Two cups, each half-filled with black, hot coffee, the castor oil bottle, and a tablespoon fixed that ailment. He did his own measurement from the bottle. Many times, she had thought—and once said—as she saw him gulp that dose, "Mr. Shepard, I can't see for the life of me how you can ever like coffee after that dose."

"Can't taste the oil if the coffee's strong and hot enough," he said. The concoction gave him almost instant relief, so that by the next day, he'd be ready by dinner for a more modest helping of Irish potatoes if Becky had any on the table—which she usually didn't.

But this fever was a new experience. A doctor, looking very serious, coming every day, and staying sometimes an hour, filled Martha Jane with a terrible fear. If the doctor would only just say what the trouble was—but he probably didn't know, she thought. Just a "fever" was too vague, too mysterious. She wanted to know the name of the monster that seemed to be draining her husband's life away.

She followed the doctor to the gate. "Doctor, what is the matter with Mr. Shepard?"

"A sort of malaria fever, ma'am. I hope the worst is over."

"Where did he get malaria?"

"Malaria is everywhere, ma'am. It's queer, malaria is. He may have gotten it years ago, say in the swamps sleeping on the ground around the Chickahominy in Virginia."

"Why, Doctor Eskew! The war ended twenty-two years ago."

"Yes ma'am, but wars don't always end when the guns stop shooting. Just keep up the medicines, ma'am, and the hot poultices. I think you'll see a decided change in a few days. Good day, ma'am."

Dr. Eskew was noted for never having lost a typhoid patient. According to the Colonel's pension papers, Doctor Eskew was the family doctor and even signed the Colonel's pension papers. She prayerfully hoped he was as successful with malaria fever. He was careful and thoughtful. He always brought his medicine saddle pockets in and would dose the Colonel from some bottle and leave doses of some kind to be given during the day. Martha Jane got her own relief from giving the medicines and keeping the hot-bran poultices on his abdomen, as she did day and night for days that ran into weeks. There was also much quinine to be given—no such luxury as a capsule existed at that time. But old women had learned to make a sort of jelly from getting finger-length slivers of the inside bark from an elm tree and putting them in a glass of water. Soon a substance a little thicker than the white of an egg would form on the slivers, which could be raked off into a spoon and quinine wrapped up in it—a pretty fair substitute for a capsule. A glass of slippery elm bark stood on the Colonel's medicine table.

When he had been sick about three weeks, an infection appeared on one of his toes, which puzzled the doctor and distressed the family. One Sunday afternoon, Mr. and Mrs. Pafford, who lived about three miles from the Colonel's home, came to spend the night and to take complete charge of the Colonel, so that, they said, Mrs. Shepard could get a deep sleep. (According to Wylene Pafford, it was probably Settie and Byron Pafford.) After they came, Martha Jane was sitting alone on the front porch. August was nearly gone now, and the time for the whippoorwills to sing their mournful song had come. Tonight, they were singing in the huge hackberry tree just beyond the little schoolhouse. In the east, answering calls came from a faraway grove of trees. She loved their mournful, dreamy song before now, but not tonight. She went into her room and lay down on her bed ... perhaps she could shut out the song and get a little sleep.

During this trying period, Becky and Taylor had been priceless. They came early and stayed late. Every morning, the first thing Taylor wanted was to go into the Colonel's room to see if he looked any better and was well enough to speak to him. Sometimes, the Colonel wouldn't see him at all. And then he would speak again, "Well, Taylor, how's the stock and crops?"

"All right, Colonel. Got the wheat threshed last week. Big turn-out. Biggest in years."

"Fine. Keep things moving."

"Yes, sir, Colonel. We will sho' do that."

Becky was tireless in cooking for company that might be there at mealtime. "How many for dinner today, Miss Mat?"

"Don't know, Becky. Make it for three extra."

September came, and the days began to get cooler. Martha Jane was happier than she had been for weeks. The cause for the sudden happiness was an accident. She was giving the Colonel his dose of quinine. In trying to get the slippery elm bark jelly wrapped around the quinine, the whole mess slipped out of the spoon and onto the floor. The Colonel said, "Scoop it up. It's all nasty anyhow." He had something of the old twinkle and grin. She scooped it up off the floor, and he gulped it with a glass of water to wash it down.

On the afternoon of the same day, Joe Lannon, one of the Colonel's old war friends, was in to see him. He lived two miles away and came often. He was dressing the infected toe and said, "If we could just burn this toe right good, Colonel, I think we could cure it. They say any fool can cure a burn." They both laughed heartily.

Soon he wanted more to eat than just the fluids. He'd been living on only a few glasses a day for so long. It was music to Alice's ears when he said to her, in something of his old emphatic, brisk voice, "Get me a piece of corn bread about twice as big as that little piece you've got there."

Another week and he wanted to get out and see the fields of corn ready to be gathered and how the clover fields looked. It fell to Alice to take him out in the buggy. Sam was in the field working along with Taylor. The Colonel wanted to see the cornfield on the creek. There was no buggy road to that field, but there was a big gate for wagons once you got to it. Alice took him there, straddling big rocks and stumps that were quite enough for a farm wagon to get over and through. But when they got back to the house, only one stirrup had been dragged off the buggy by a too-high stump. The Colonel was very tired and very happy.

From the time the Colonel had a child, it was understood that each child would, when old enough, go to college. That was a big proposition for a farmer-preacher, not to mention that it was unusual for country children to go to college at all at that time.

In the fall of 1890, the Colonel moved his family to Murfreesboro where Sam was entered in the boys' college and Alice in Soule.[1] It was written in the Rutherford Historical Society publication that Soule College was tailored after Mary Sharp College of Winchester. There were others now in the 1890s as well, including Vassar, Wellesley, and Smith. Soule was a two- and four-year women's college that operated for about sixty-five years in Murfreesboro. It closed its doors in 1917 because of competition from public education. It was named after Methodist bishop Joshua Soule of Nashville. The years it operated, it tried to provide for women what men's colleges were providing for men.

In 1889, Z. C. Graves, founder of Mary Sharp College, was president until Ms. Virginia Wardlaw, who was a "charter graduate of Wellesley College," took over. Both of these individuals, according to the records, sought to forward the education of women. "During the Wardlaw administration, much emphasis was placed on concerts, lecturers, and visiting teachers. ... Piano, violin, organ, guitar, and voice were offered in music. There were offerings in expression and drama."

---

[1] Eugene H. Sloan, "Soule College Minutes," Rutherford County Historical Society, Publication No. 11, (Murfreesboro, TN, Summer 1978), 58–66, 69, 73, 74.

No graduates' names are listed from 1890 to 1893. Alice would have attended between 1890 and 1892. The school was closed during the Civil War and reopened in 1866 and was "described as having 'no school marms' from the North. The faculty members were all 'Southern Magnolias.'" Ms. Wardlaw introduced dressmaking, bookkeeping, typewriting, and commercial law into the curriculum. The sciences were taught with a well-equipped laboratory for performing experiments.

Taylor took complete charge of the Colonel's farm while the family was away. The Colonel continued to be pastor of his home church so he had a look in on things about his home once a month.

The move was not a wholly successful one. There was an epidemic of "la grippe" in Murfreesboro that winter. "Sis" (Amanda) took it and in a few days died. Martha Jane and the Colonel both had it.

Sam was not at all happy in college; he wanted to go home. In the spring, the Colonel moved his family back to the old home. Alice was left to board with some kinfolks for the rest of that term. She graduated from college two years later. But for Sam, his college days were over, which was a big disappointment to the Colonel. Nonetheless, the experience did not lessen his interest or confidence in Sam.

Alice wanted to continue her education in Nashville. She attended Boscobel College. According to the *Boscobel College Annual Catalogue for 1893–1894*, "Miss Alice Shepard of Partlow, Tennessee, received the Degree of B.A. 1893," with what we would now refer to as a major in music with concentrations in both piano and voice.[2] Alice Carver Cramer, her daughter, felt that if there were a major at that time, her mother would have majored in piano. The *Announcement from September 1912 to 1913* also lists under the third year for graduates, 1893, "Alice Shepard, B.A., (Mrs. W.O. Carver), Louisville, Ky." The college opened in 1890 and closed in 1914.[3] George Zepp claims that Boscobel became home to the National Baptist Seminary and Missionary

---

[2] *Boscobel College Annual Catalogue, 1893–1894*, (Nashville, TN, 1893), 9, 12.

[3] *Boscobel College Catalogue, Announcement from September 1912 to May 1913*, (Nashville, TN), 31.

Training School from 1918 until 1931, and in 1940, the buildings were demolished.[4]

During Alice's senior year in college at Boscobel College in Nashville, she got well-acquainted with a tall, handsome young man who attended the same church she did. During the summer following his graduation, he made a weekend visit to the Colonel's home. When time came for Alice to return for graduate work and to do some assistant teaching in college, her father said to her, "Alice, I wouldn't see too much of Mr. ——— this winter if I were you." She was very much surprised. She didn't ask why. She didn't say anything, but she did some fast thinking. The young man had seemed all right. Her father had made no criticism of him at all during his visit in the home, nor afterward. But in that "I wouldn't see too much of Mr. ——— if I were you," her interest had received a deathblow. In later years, the young man became a criminal.

Her father always had a sort of neutral attitude toward Alice's beaux. He neither condemned nor approved. He treated them cordially and politely when it was convenient but never went out of his way to notice them.

One evening when Martha Jane's younger sister Bettie had a beau, "the one who always stayed too long," the Colonel got vexed. He was having a bad time with a headache, and every time he dozed off, the young fellow's laugh would arouse him. At last, when Bettie was worn out and the Colonel on edge, he heard the young man in the hall, making his adieus. The Colonel, having put his clothes on, all hope of sleep gone, went out in the hall and spoke to the young man, "Morning, Mr. Brows! Won't you set a spell longer and have a cup of coffee with us?"

---

[4] George Zepp, *Boscobel College,* (Nashville, TN).

20 · A Marriage, A Death

During the summer of 1894, the Colonel met and got very well acquainted with a young theological student who was studying in the Baptist Seminary in Louisville, Kentucky. They happened to be in several meetings together. It was from the first meeting that a sort of Paul and Timothy friendship developed—though the Colonel would have been embarrassed to hear anybody say such a thing. The Colonel had great admiration for Dr. John A. Broadus and other members in the Seminary, but this young man studying there, a William Owen Carver, had such great potential, he thought. The Colonel felt it was expedient that he learn from his new friend and in no wise be his teacher.

The winter following their first acquaintance, Owen, as he was called, published an article in the *Seminary Magazine*. It was a paper he had written for class on an assigned subject. The subject required him to write about some person who had greatly influenced his life. He wrote about the Colonel.

He is to an extent, which I have never seen surpassed, a Holy Spirit preacher. I have been with him much in meetings and in his regular services, and have never known him to enter upon a service without a previous session of private prayer—I was about to write conference with God. This he does in a quiet, unostentatious way, and few, perhaps, know of his habit. His faith in God is as full and simple as that of a child. Once in a meeting at one of his churches, the evangelist was called away. The pastor heard a prominent sister remark: "Well, we might as well close the meeting. Brother ——— is gone. Brother Shepard has been here so long that everybody knows him. The meeting will do no good." His heart was heavy. He went to the woods and talked to God on this wise: "Now, Lord, you see the fix

*we are in. Brother —— is gone. These people think the meeting is a
failure ... Lord, we are greatly in need of a good meeting. I can't do
anything ... Lord, if anything is done, you must do it." He continued the
meeting, which resulted in some forty conversions and the greatest
revival the church had ever known. He talks of religion as a part of his
daily experience—of himself. It is an inspiration to higher and holier
living to be with him. He brings the personal God into the company.
There is no sickly sentiment, no affectation of piety, no forcing of
religious topics. He is even sportive and merry in season, a universal
favorite with young people ... his pastorates are long and successful.
He never leaves one but under protest of the church ... He is a man of
prayer ....*

The Colonel was indeed a man of prayer. He "went away" or he
"went up into the mountain" or he "went into the wilderness" are phrases
inseparable from the Man of Galilee. A man who has learned the secret
of "going apart" has learned the greatest lesson life has to teach. The
Colonel learned this lesson early in his ministry; indeed, he learned it
long before he began his public ministry. He had many bethels, many
places apart, where he could meet his God and get guidance for problems
and strength for duties and where he could worship in spirit.

He never imposed his religion on others, not even his own children.
He never "exhorted" them even when they went up to the "mourner's
bench," nor when they were converted, nor when they joined the church
and were baptized. His religion was such a matter-of-fact, everyday thing
that one never thought of it as religion.

While Alice was teaching at Bethel College in McKenzie,
Tennessee, the year following her postgraduate year at Boscobel College
in Nashville, she came up against a hard proposition. Records do not
show Alice obtaining a master's degree although Boscobel did have a
graduate program. Little Dan Cupid was messing things up pretty badly
for her. She had been seeing her dad's Timothy of two summers before
every two weeks. He was in the seminary at Louisville, Kentucky, but he
was also pastor of a church some ten miles from Hopkinsville, Kentucky.
There were also other beaux, and she was teaching full-time. She needed
her dad. She wrote him, saying, "Pray for me ..."

His answer came back promptly, "Prayed for you every day of your
life. Don't reckon I'll stop now." No questions were asked, and no

explanations were given then or at any later time. She was as sure of him then as a shelter, a firm foundation, as she was that night he put her to bed for the first and only time, as sure as she always was where he was concerned. His prayers provided the keystone in the foundation of her security.

At every church where the Colonel was a pastor, he had his bethel. One was a big tree at the turn of the road on his way to his church; another was a stump in a thicket hidden from but near his church. On this, he had placed some stones. He would go there before the service started and consult with his God. Another bethel was a fence hidden from his church by some trees. He'd go there half an hour before it was time for the service, sit on the fence watching the people go by, and pray for them individually and collectively until time to go in. Another was a little red ticket a railroad conductor had stuck in his hatband when he was on his way to preach in a meeting in Kentucky. When the train crossed the line into another state, he began looking for a bethel. He took the little red ticket out of his hatband and put it in his wallet, saying, "Now, Lord, I will always keep this to remind me of how you were with me in this strange place." That revival was a success, and he accepted an invitation to hold another meeting before leaving Kentucky.

As a preacher, the Colonel was no orator. His speech was quiet, brisk, and almost staccato with a note of finality. He had no marked idiosyncrasies, no pulpit mannerisms, no inferiority complexes, and no superiority complexes. He was humble without effort. He was a just man without peculiarities, but to his intimate friends, a great man who habitually did so many things just a little differently from the way other men did them that one could not help but be profoundly impressed and influenced. He had emphatic opinions and lived them. He was of no mind to shout either his acts or his beliefs from the housetops or in any way to bring himself before the public. But, neither was he the least bit hesitant to express his opinion when asked or the opportunity presented itself on questions involving principles in morals, ethics, or religion.

As he had been a self-made lawyer, so he was a self-made preacher. He did his own thinking and studying, getting help from all sources, scorning none. He had many friends in other denominations. He was not a religious isolationist. He was a thoroughgoing Baptist, but he did not believe Baptists had a monopoly on heaven or on truth. He had a legal mind, both by trend and training. His sermons had the expository form— a sort of running commentary as he interpreted the scriptures. He didn't spiritualize nor make demands on the emotions; rather, he challenged the intellect and the will. He told no deathbed stories. He was deeply in earnest and always had a message he wanted to give to his listeners. He used everyday facts and truths as illustrations. He had the gift of adaptability, himself to his people, and everyday life to eternal truth as found in the Bible. He emphasized strict obedience to God's commandments.

The date had been set for Alice's marriage to her dad's Timothy, W. Owen Carver, who had received his doctorate in theology in the seminary and had a few months before he was to become a member of the faculty. Dixon Merritt[1] wrote that William Owen Carver and Byron H. Dement, both of Wilson County and both in their boyhood, had memorized the entire New Testament. See Figure 20-1 for his accomplishments. He was being sent to Florida in January to represent the seminary at the state convention. He wanted to take his bride with him.

He arrived at the Colonel's home on the morning of December 28. The wedding was to be the next morning.

As the family and a few friends sat around the fire in the parlor making merry, the young man said to Alice's father, "Colonel, you know her better than I do. Got any advice to give?" Alice was standing by a little window at the end of the mantel. She faced her father. The young man's chair was between them, his back to her, so that she did not see his face as he asked this affectionately impertinent question. He loved the Colonel. She probably wouldn't have seen his face anyhow. She was gazing at her father, who was going through his casual shuffling when in a mental jam. He recrossed his legs, lifted his face to his future son-in-law, and said deliberately, with a slow emphasis on his silly pronunciation of "little." "She's a *leetle* hard-headed." Everybody

---

[1] Dixon Merritt, ed., *The History of Wilson County, Its Land and Its Life*, (Nashville: History Associates of Wilson County, 1961), 128.

laughed ... everybody but Alice. She saw the usual twinkle in his eyes, the same old grin on his face, but there was something more, something she had not seen before, something that kept her from laughing. She had just gotten a glimpse of the depth of her father's love. She left the room.

Next morning, Dr. William H. Whitsitt, president of the Southern Baptist Theological Seminary–Louisville, Kentucky since Dr. Broadus' death, arrived before breakfast. He was to make the prayer in the wedding. The Colonel, of course, was to say the ceremony. Neither Alice nor Owen would have had it any other way.

On this her wedding day (December 29, 1897), Alice was to have another surprise from her father. The surprise was that for the first time in all the wedding ceremonies he had said during the nearly thirty years of being a pastor, he left out the word "obey" in the ceremony he used for her.

There was much hurry and bustle after the ceremony. Many people were there, and the newlyweds had to catch a train. Alice avoided saying goodbye to her father—neither of them wanted to. Her mother followed the pair to the front gate. When they had said goodbye and gotten into the buggy, they waited a minute to take a last look at the surroundings and the many people surging through the halls onto the porch. Then they smiled another farewell to the little mother who was leaning with her elbows on the fence, her chin in her hands, and tears in her eyes. "Be good to each other," she said as they drove away. That "Be good to each other" followed that bride and groom down through the years. Figure 20-2 shows Dr. and Mrs. William Owen Carver on their wedding day or not long after they were married. Figure 20-3 shows the Colonel about the time of the marriage.

During the first eleven years of Alice's married life, she went back every summer to the old home for a visit of from six weeks to four months and with from one to four children. The union of Alice and Owen produced six children—three girls and three boys: Ruth Carver Gardner, born 1898; William Owen Carver, Jr., born 1900; Dr. James Edward Carver, born 1902; Dr. George Alexander Carver, born 1909; Dorothy Carver Garrott, born 1910; and Alice Carver Cramer, born 1912.

The old log house, with its huge rooms, big halls, and big, well-fenced-in yard, was an ideal place for city children to spend their summers—especially with grandparents who gave the children the full run of the place—everywhere except the kitchen. Alice gave the ultimatum on the kitchen question. They were not to invade the kitchen or bother the cook.

Her parents seemed to think Alice knew what to do and how to do it so far as the children were concerned. Only a very few times did Alice suspect that there was any worry about her control or proper management. One of the few times was when the three older children— two, four, and nearly six years old—were sleeping crosswise on a great big bed. The two-year-old was having fun sliding off onto the floor. Part of the fun was being picked up and put back on the bed by his mother. Presently, she heard her father say, "Come on in, Mat. Alice knows what to do. She won't spank him."

The nearest the Colonel ever came to a criticism was when one of the children was misbehaving, and Alice said, "I don't know what ails her. She never acts like this at Uncle Jim's."

The Colonel straightened up—he'd been dozing or meditating with his eyes closed—took his specs off, and, putting them away, said, "You ought to keep her there a right smart." He stood up and walked off down the path and out the front gate. His look and remark struck everybody as very funny but not Alice. She felt slapped as indeed she had been. He was a polite man, and he expected his children to be polite.

One summer, when Alice was going on her usual visit to her parents, she took the children's nurse, Mary Bell, with her. Mary Bell was a very attractive, light-skinned, young girl of mixed race. Becky gave a party for her in her home. Next morning, when Becky came, she was very excited and told Martha Jane about how some grown, white boys had chased Mary Bell home. Becky was sure these boys had meant to harm the girl. She stoutly repudiated Martha Jane's idea that they were perhaps just having a little fun scaring a city "mulatto" gal.

Martha Jane thought she'd better tell the Colonel. He was just getting out of bed when she went into his room. He made no comment as she talked. When she had finished, he put on his hat and then the rest of his clothes and was off down the path and out the gate. Martha Jane knew he was going to see the boys and their father. Everybody wanted very much to know what he said to them. But all anybody ever found out was that he called the father and his sons to their fence and made it clear to them what their future conduct must be toward Alice's children's nurse.

Two neighbor men were discussing the event and wondering how it would end. Said one, "They ain't going to bother that gal no more. Why I'd as soon go in a lion's den as try to go in the Colonel's house if he didn't want me to." He was right. There was no more trouble.

When Agnes finished college, and there is no record of where she went, it is assumed she studied music as did Alice. The Colonel and Martha Jane sold their farm in 1908 and bought a home in Lebanon on the south side of Gay Street. Records show he disposed of 339 acres from 1906 to 1908. Sam was already in the courthouse in Lebanon as the county registrar, Alice was living in Louisville with her family, and John was in the seminary in Louisville getting ready to go to South America as a missionary. The Colonel had been resigning from his churches since he turned seventy-five. But as fast as he would resign from one church, he'd be called to another. He continued to preach until he was well into his eighties. But he did not preach often after leaving his country home in 1908.

After they moved to Lebanon, he was involved in what might have been a very tragic affair. A black man made an unsuccessful attempt to assault a white girl who was very dear to the Colonel—a horrible experience, a miraculous escape. She was a well-known, much-loved, and an honored young woman in the town. Excitement was at white heat. A mob caught the black man and was ready to swing him. The man was crying and pleading that "he meant no harm—it was the whiskey." Somebody suggested that the Colonel be consulted. He was sent for and came. He urgently advised the excited and angry men to allow the law to take its course. Finally, the mob yielded to his advice.

At his trial, the black man was given a life sentence. His lawyer was ready to make an appeal to the higher court. The Colonel went to the lawyer and said, "I advised the men, as you know, when they were ready to hang this criminal, to let the law take its course. If you take an appeal, I shall withdraw such advice." No appeal was taken. The black man died in the penitentiary.

Agnes, the Shepards' idolized last child, had whooping cough when about two years old, which left something wrong with her throat, so that she was never very strong. But the harm did not reach her mind and spirit. She had her father's brisk optimism and her mother's silent and patient endurance of pain. Socially, she was as exhilarating as a breeze. She had a wholesome aversion toward anybody's sympathy for her bodily ailments. A neighbor told about seeing her on her way downtown on some errand. The neighbor saw her turn into an alley and, with her back to the street, have a hemorrhage from her throat. She then reported seeing her using her handkerchief and pocket mirror to fix her face before going back into the street and on her way downtown as planned.

She grew to womanhood, graduated from college, and got a diploma in music with a concentration in piano. She married law student George W. Bates. He was a splendid fellow whom her parents loved dearly.

When she and her George had been married nearly a year, she was stricken with typhoid-pneumonia and lay dying. They lived in Earlington, Kentucky. For three days, Agnes went to her neighbor's house at about four o'clock in the afternoon to take the daily chill that wracked her terribly. She was afraid to stay at home for fear she might become unconscious. She made the neighbor solemnly promise that she would not tell George, saying that she would soon be all right and she didn't want him to be bothered about it. The neighbor was conscience-stricken when she knew that Agnes would not "soon be all right."

It was pitiful to see her parents when they knew of her condition. They had hoped that she and George would live with them in Lebanon the next winter when George finished the work he was doing in Earlington. It was tragic how the Colonel held on to her, how he went "apart" so often. Days after the doctors and nurses had given her up, she kept on breathing. Her father's faith would not let her go—not yet. Then a day came early one morning when he went to his bethel down by a small lake on the edge of the town, a bent and tragic figure. Late in the morning, he returned, no longer bent and hopeless, but with a firm step and a light on his face. That afternoon, his child smiled him a radiant goodbye.

She was taken to Lebanon for burial. Just before her body was taken from the house to the church for the funeral services, her father the Colonel, her husband George, and other members of the family were in Martha Jane's room. The Colonel was talking. His face shone with a look of otherworldliness that seemed to envelop him. He said, "I never realized until now the greatness of God's goodness and mercy."

Agnes Shepard Bates died on October 30, 1912, in Earlington, Kentucky. She was buried in Cedar Grove Cemetery, Lebanon, on November 3, 1912. She was twenty-six years old. According to the death certificate, Agnes was ill or saw a doctor starting October 5. She died of "typhoid fever and pneumonia in both lungs." The Colonel must have been devastated in more ways than one, for he knew a doctor in Wilson County who had "never lost a typhoid fever patient," but the Colonel didn't know his daughter was ill until it was too late. Alice Carver Cramer, the Colonel's granddaughter by Alice Shepard Carver, said she never remembered meeting Agnes, but that George, Agnes' husband and a lawyer, was a frequent visitor of the Carver family in Louisville and once came with the Colonel. Alice says her memories of "Aunt Aggie" were of stories told about her. She said, "Aunt Aggie was a music teacher. She supposedly was beautiful, and the family looked upon her with great admiration. She used to drive in a surrey throughout the area to give her music lessons. I think she graduated from Boscobel College where my mother, her sister, went." Boscobel does not list her as a graduate.

Carver, William Owen 236

CARVER, WILLIAM OWEN (b. Wilson County, Tenn., Apr. 10, 1868; d. Louisville, Ky., May 24, 1954). Minister, educator, author, and missionary statesman. Son of Alexander Jefferson and Almeda Adaline (Binkley) Carver, he was the second of 11 children. When Carver was 19 his mother died, after which his father remarried and had nine children by his second wife. Carver's father, a farmer and mill operator, was a Baptist deacon; and his mother, a devout Christian, had a profound influence upon her son's life. Before going away to college Carver told his mother that he felt called to the ministry, after which he secured the sanction of his church, New Hope, at Hermitage, Tenn., in his call.

During his final years as a student at Richmond College, Richmond, Va., Carver held his first pastorate at Concord Church, Caroline County, from 1889 to 1891. He also served at the same time as supply pastor for Mount Horeb Church in a near-by community. After receiving the M.A. degree from Richmond College in 1891, Carver returned to his Tennessee home expecting to spend the next year paying off college debts. He became pastor of his home church where he was ordained Dec. 25, 1891, and also began his studies in Southern Baptist Theological Seminary. After leaving the seminary in 1893 Carver became professor of philosophy and ancient languages in Boscobel College, Nashville, Tenn., and pastor of South Union Church, Church Hill, Ky. In Jan., 1895, he resumed his studies in Southern Seminary, receiving the Th.M. degree that year and the Th.D. in 1896.

Carver became instructor in New Testament at Southern Seminary in 1896 and also taught some courses in homiletics and theology. In 1899 he introduced a course in comparative religion and missions, and the following year became head of the missions department, the position in which he served until his retirement in 1943. In 1900 and again in 1907-08 Carver visited and studied missions in Europe. In 1922-23 he toured mission fields in South America and the Orient. Carver's advice on missionary problems was sought by both missionaries and board secretaries. From 1936 to 1944, he represented the seminary as a member of the executive committee of the American Association of Theological Schools. From its organization in 1939, he was a member of the American Theological Committee, a subsidiary of the World Conference on Faith and Order, and in this connection wrote the paper on Baptist churches which appeared in *The Nature of the Church*, published in 1952.

Instrumental in founding the Woman's Missionary Union Training School at Southern Seminary in 1907, Carver taught there for many years while also teaching in the seminary. The name of the school was changed to The Carver School of Missions and Social Work in 1953. Charter member and for a long time president of the Southern Baptist Historical Society,

Carver was largely responsible for the founding of the Historical Commission of the Southern Baptist Convention. In recognition of his contribution to the preservation of Baptist history, the library of the Historical Commission in Nashville, Tenn., when merged with the Dargan Memorial Library of the Sunday School Board in 1953, was named The Dargan-Carver Library. He was also a member of the Kentucky Baptist Historical Society and the Baptist Historical Society of Great Britain and Ireland.

Carver was managing editor of the *Review and Expositor* from 1920 to 1942, contributing editor of the *Commission* for 12 years, and frequent contributor to other journals. Carver's 19 published books include *History of the New Salem Baptist Church, Nelson County, Ky.* (1901); *Baptist Opportunity* (1907); *Missions in the Plan of the Ages* (1909); *Missions and Modern Thought* (1910); *The Acts of the Apostles* (1916); *All the World in All the Word* (1918); *The Bible a Missionary Message* (1921); *The Self Interpretation of Jesus* (1926); *Thou When Thou Prayest* (1928); *The Course of Christian Missions* (1932); *How the New Testament Came to Be Written* (1933); *The Rediscovery of the Spirit* (1934); *The Furtherance of the Gospel* (1935); *Sabbath Observance* (1940); *Christian Missions in Today's World* (1942); *God and Man in Missions* (1944); *Why They Wrote the New Testament* (1946); *The Glory of God in the Christian Calling* (1949); *Out of His Treasure* (unfinished memoirs, published posthumously in 1956).

He married Alice Hughes Shepard in 1897, and they had six children, two of whom became foreign missionaries.

GEORGE A. CARVER ~~and S. O. BOYKIN~~

CARVER SCHOOL OF MISSIONS AND SOCIAL WORK. Located at 2801 Lexington Road, Louisville, Ky., operated from 1907 to 1953 as Woman's Missionary Union Training School for Christian Workers, under the auspices of Woman's Missionary Union, Auxiliary to the Southern Baptist Convention; in 1953 the trustees adopted and the Woman's Missionary Union approved the present name, better describing the enlarged program of the school and honoring William Owen Carver (q.v.), who had been largely instrumental in the establishment of the W.M.U. Training School, had been its first professor, and had continued as faculty member and counselor throughout the school's history. In May, 1956, at the annual sessions of Woman's Missionary Union and the Convention, actions were taken by which the Convention would assume responsibility for and control of the school.

The W.M.U. Training School was formally inaugurated on Wednesday, Oct. 2, 1907, at exercises in the Broadway Baptist Church, Louisville, Ky., as the culmination of developments reaching back into the 19th century. Ezekias Z. Simmons (q.v.), missionary to China since 1870,

Figure 20-1. This is the biographical sketch of Dr. William Owen Carver as it appeared in the 1958 edition of *Encyclopedia of Southern Baptists*. (It is used by permission from LifeWay Christian Resources of the Southern Baptist Convention, 127 Ninth Avenue, Nashville, TN 37234.)

Figure 20-2. Dr. and Mrs. William Owen Carver—better known as Owen and Alice—taken the day they were married. (Courtesy of the Carver family.)

Figure 20-3. The Colonel. Taken when he was sixty-five, a couple of years before the wedding. (Courtesy of Wilson County Archives.)

21 • Final Days

An example of the Colonel's persona was his ability to "reconstruct" himself as he did, even before the Civil War was over. When he was in his eighties, had retired from being a pastor, and was living in Lebanon, some of his soldier friends came to see him. They wanted to know if he was getting a pension.

"No," he said. "I've never had a pension."

"Why?" they wanted to know.

"Well, I've never considered that the state owed me anything for fighting against the Union." But his friends would not accept his words on the subject. They thought he needed and deserved a pension, which they subsequently managed to get for him. The pension was for $15 per month, paid in quarterly checks for $45.[1] He, along with his friends helping, applied for the pension in August 25, 1914, and it was granted on 13 October. His long-time physician, Dr. A. O. Eshew, claimed on the papers that his condition was mainly old age. His attorney, R. P. McClain, and long-time friend, A. K. Miller, signed as witnesses.

These same friends, along with others, also came with plans and funds ready to erect the monument that now stands in the square of Lebanon. The statue is a life-size replica of Brigadier General Robert Hopkins Hatton, who was commander of the Seventh Tennessee Infantry Regiment from the time it was organized at Camp Trousdale until his death. He was the highest-ranking Confederate soldier from Wilson County. Originally, he was from Ohio, but he settled in Lebanon. He got

---

[1] *Military Records,* Civil War (1861–1865), S. G. Shepard, Pension No. 14493, Nashville, TN, Tennessee State Library and Archives.

a B.A. from Cumberland in 1847 and received his law degree from Cumberland in 1851,[2] was a licensed lawyer, was elected to both the Tennessee House of Representatives and the United States House of Representatives, and made an unsuccessful bid for governor of Tennessee—all before 1861.

In 1862, a brigade, which consisted of the First, Seventh, and Fourteenth Tennessee Infantry Regiments, was formed. It was called the Tennessee Brigade, and Hatton was promoted to Brigadier General to command such. He was killed eight days after his promotion on May 31, 1962, at the Battle of Seven Pines (Fair Oaks)—the first major battle of the war for the Tennessee Brigade, and of course, the Seventh Infantry Regiment. Colonel S. G. Shepard was already the commander of the Seventh Infantry Regiment. According to Alice Hughes Shepard Carver, her father was the one who, under fire, put the general's body on his own horse, carried him to the rear, and then returned to fight.

The monument was dedicated on May 20, 1912, the fifty-first anniversary of the day six companies of soldiers left Wilson County. Rev. S. G. Shepard offered prayers. See Figures 21-1 and 21-2. It was erected by the S. G. Shepard Camp, No. 941, United Confederate Veterans (U.C.V.), which is now Sons of Confederate Veterans (S.C.V.), Robert H. Hatton Camp 723.

The U.C.V. camp was originally named for the general but became inactive. Dixon Merritt in his *History of Wilson County* stated that, "in 1889, Robert Hatton Bivouac No. 23, U.C.V., was formed. Dr. J. R. Lester was president; W. P. Brandy, vice-president; A. K. Miller, second vice-president. This became inactive. In 1897, the S. G. Shepard Camp, U.C.V., named to honor the final commander of the Seventh Tennessee

---

[2] Frank Burns, local historian from Wilson County and Cumberland University archivist, unveiled General Hatton earning the law degree. Frank Burns wrote April 23, 2001 in a letter containing the following statement: "Also I can now tell you something I have just discovered. General Robert H. Hatton did receive the B.A. degree from Cumberland in 1847 and also the M.A., but I have read in his biography and other sources that he never completed the law course but began practice after additional reading in an attorney's office, a common practice at that time. Apparently this is not true. I find in the 1852 catalog him listed in the graduating law class of 1851. I cannot explain this."

Infantry, was formed." Colonel Shepard was elected the commander, and a motion to organize into a Wilson County Confederate Veterans Association was adopted. See Figure 21-3 from the *Lebanon Democrat* dated October 14, 1897.

Thomas Partlow's book of the minutes of the U.C.V. states the Colonel was the commander until 1901, at which time he was made chaplain—an office he held until his death. He apparently was seldom able to attend because of his schedule, but would when he could. One time, Colonel John A. Fite gave a "speech and responded in some pleasant remembrances of the war. One which told tales on the man after whom this camp is named, but nothing to the detriment of his honor." The Colonel was once asked to give a talk on any subject. He talked about the Seventh regiment at Gettysburg and demonstrated the positions of the troops on the blackboard. His son Sam became a member after his father's death.

These camps were an outgrowth of soldiers wanting to get together and talk about their exploits, their memories, and the close friendships they formed. Only another soldier would understand. Until the U.C.V. camps were organized, these meets were called reunions. One such reunion that started in the square of Lebanon rocked the North. Dixon Merritt in his *History of Wilson County* wrote:

> On a quiet evening in 1871 or 1872, Capt. F. S. Harris and W. M. McCorkle were chatting, in front of a Lebanon store. As a result of the chat, 7,000 people attended a reunion of the old 7th. It created quite a sensation over the country, Northern newspapers proclaiming in flaming headlines—An Uprising of the Rebels at Lebanon, Tennessee. Another was held in Lindsley's Bottom at Greenwood on August 20, 1889, to which 8,000 came to enjoy feasting, speech making, and memories. The "two Fourths" and the 7th were well represented.

During the winter of the Colonel's eighty-fourth year in 1914, a trouble developed in his throat. After taking examinations and tests, the doctor advised an operation. The Colonel replied, "I'll let you know in the morning." When the doctor came next morning, the Colonel said, "No operation. Trouble in throat won't shorten my numbered days much, if any." The doctor was content. The throat got well for the time being.

COLONEL S. G. SHEPARD

Martha Jane, in telling the story, said, "I knew Mr. Shepard wasn't going to die." After a pause, she added quietly, "I couldn't do without him." And she couldn't have. She was in bed herself nearly all the remaining months of her life. He was with her almost every hour until the end. She had had much suffering during the fifty years of her married life—a semi-invalid since the birth of her first child, who also later died. But the tender care her husband gave her during the last years of her increased inactivity repaid her for every ache and pain she had suffered.

When a full-time nurse had to be obtained, Martha Jane still wanted George to lift her into her chair for her evening hour of rest from the bed. She wanted him to smooth out the covers, no matter how clumsily he did it. He grew more skillful as the weeks went by. His remarks as he smoothed out a sheet here and there, such as "nary a knot left" or "smooth as a peeled onion," always amused her. When he lifted her back into the bed and had given her the sleeping pill, he always sat down by her until she was asleep. He slept in the room with her. She was conscious that he was where she could get him at any hour. When she awakened in the morning or at any time in the night needing a glass of water or a dose of medicine, she knew that she could get him with the slightest noise.

Martha Jane Major Shepard died on June 20, 1915, and according to the death certificate, File No. 623,[3] died of longstanding chronic bronchitis. See Figure 21-4 for newspaper obituaries from the *Lebanon Democrat* and the *Nashville Banner*. She was less than two months from her fiftieth anniversary with the Colonel. Figure 21-5 shows them together. It is believed it was an anniversary picture taken not long before she died. Her two sons, Samuel George Shepard, Jr. and Rev. Dr. John Watson Shepard, her daughter, Alice Hughes Shepard Carver, and her devoted husband, the Colonel, all survived her.

The Colonel would indeed have been a very lonely old man after Martha Jane left him if the habit of many years had not remained with him. It was his habit of always keeping his face to the front. "Every day is a new day to me," he said, "something more to do, something to look forward to."

---

[3] Martha Jane Major Shepard died on June 20, 1915, File No. 623.

Sam had long lived up to his declaration that he "wanted no wife, nor a passel o' kids." But at the advanced age of thirty-five, in 1906, he tumbled to the little god of love and married a lovely girl, Moncye Bond. They had their home near the Colonel's. The Colonel loved Mon, as he called her, as his own child and got great pleasure out of Sam's and Mon's little girls, Agieray and Tommye.

When his beloved Mat died, the Colonel went to live with Sam and his family. Sam was the Wilson County Deputy Trustee, according to the *City Directory,* and they lived on Main Street. The Colonel was intensely interested in Tommye's and Agieray's schoolwork and music lessons. He had the rare quality of being interested without being meddlesome. Not once during the two years he lived with them did Sam or Mon feel that he was trying to "boss" them in raising their children.

During the winter of 1915, following Martha Jane's death, he went to Louisville to visit Alice and her family. He was very tired when he arrived—not tired from so long a journey but more from the meetings, which were a series of sermons he had preached in a little church near Sam's the week before. He never really got rested and was very sick soon after he got to Louisville. But his good spirits never wavered. His egg, coffee, and toast for breakfast were always "just right."

Sam and Mon missed him. They kept writing for him to hurry with his visit and come back home. Alice's husband, Owen, accompanied him home on his eighty-sixth birthday, January 28, 1916.

Mon has many rare stories to tell of the doings of those two years he lived with them from 1915 to 1917.

Mon was asked if she had trouble getting her girls to the breakfast table. She replied "Yes, but not when Granddad was here. He raced them to breakfast. They always came in laughing and in a good humor. It certainly helped me a whole lot. Sometimes he'd come in with his shoelaces not yet tied just to beat them. He was their biggest inspiration to practice the piano," she said. "It never bothered him when they practiced. Oh, no—he loved it! He was always pleased no matter what they played.

"He ate whatever was on the table and never complained. I never did anything for Granddad that wasn't 'just right.' That was a great set of words for him—'just right.' Old folks are so much trouble, hard to please, and have to be waited on so much—but not Granddad. He was always cheerful and good company. I loved him as my own father."

In his eighty-seventh year (1917), the old trouble in his throat returned in a developed stage and held him in and down for three weeks until he died. He may have been conscious of the throat trouble many times during the three years since the first bad attack, but if so, his family never knew. He never mentioned it.[4]

During the last three weeks of his life, his beloved son John was in the United States on furlough from Rio de Janeiro, Brazil, where he was president of the Rio Baptist College and Seminary. According to the 1958 edition of *Encyclopedia of Southern Baptists,* Rio Baptist College and Seminary was later named the John W. Shepard Memorial College.[5] See Figure 21-6 for a biography of John Watson Shepard.

John was able to spend some days with his father. John left his wife, Rena, with her mother in Georgia and a young baby. John married Rena Groover on June 6, 1909. They had six children—Ida, Alice, Mary Gertrude, Evelyn Rena, Samuel Groover, and John Watson Shepard, Jr.

John told his sister, Alice, "In our family worship one evening with my father, I read the ninetieth Psalm. When I came to the tenth verse and read, 'we fly away,' he stopped me with 'There it is! That's it! We fly away!' He said it in his brisk, optimistic voice. He talked about his death as though he was preparing to go away for a preaching engagement or on a visit to a beloved child in another state. His cheerful optimism was contagious."

The time came for John to do some denominational work in the South and leave his father. Both John and his father knew that death

---

[4] His death certificate, File No. 612, states that the doctor started seeing him the March preceding his death.

[5] *Encyclopedia of Southern Baptists*, 1958 edition, vol. II, (Nashville: Broadman Press), 1199.

might come at any time. The dread disease had destroyed some of the blood vessels in his throat and might sever the jugular vein at any hour. John proposed breaking the engagement, but his father would have none of it. "No, John, you go on to your work," the Colonel said firmly. "It's the Lord's work."

John said, "Never will I forget the look of him as he sat up in his bed the morning I told him goodbye nor forget his last words to me. He said, 'It's great to be a servant of the Lord,' and then he repeated, 'It's great to be a servant of the Lord.' Not for anything would I have missed seeing and being with my father when he was making his last preparations to set sail for another world."

One item on his list of final preparations was to write a note to each of his grandchildren, not to say goodbye, but to remind each that life was good, if well spent. He also wrote a note to Owen, his son-in-law, saying that he, the Colonel, now stood "on the edge of two worlds." Both looked good to him, he wrote. However, he would "like to stay on this side long enough to see the end of the war" and made the comment that the "Allies ought to go on to Berlin." (This country's involvement in World War I was declared on April 6, 1917, and ended when the armistice was signed on November 11, 1918.)

In his letter, he again expressed the belief in Owen's ability to inform him on any theological subject or questions of interpretation of the Bible. The Colonel wrote, "Write me what you think I'll be doing over there. I don't want to be idle. I want to be busy—something to do."

Alice undertook to answer his words about seeing the end of the war. "You'll be on the battlefields of Europe," she wrote. "You'll see the end of the war. And if your grandson, William, is there, keep an eye on him. He's too young to go now, but he's in training. If this terrible slaughter goes on, he may be there. If he is, keep an eye on him and help him." (William Owen Carver, Jr., son of Alice Shepard and William Owen Carver, was born in April 1900. He missed World War I but was on the news staff of General Douglas MacArthur in Japan during World War II, according to Alice Carver Cramer.)

In his letter to Owen, George requested that Owen preside at his funeral and to speak on the text, "By the grace of God, I am what I am."

One day, a week before the end, when Sam went into the Colonel's room, the Colonel handed Sam money and a slip of paper with a list of things to get for him "sometime when he was downtown." When Sam saw the list, he knew his father was getting his burial clothes ready. Sam couldn't stand it. He turned the money and list over to George Bates, the husband of his sister, Agnes. George had remained in Lebanon after Agnes's death. He was a daily visitor to see the Colonel during his last illness.

When George got the clothes, he gave them, all wrapped and tied up, to the Colonel, who handed the package to Mon, saying with a twinkle in his eye and the old grin, "Here Mon, it's all there, but the 'biled' shirt [referring to starching shirts by boiling them in water and starch]. Put it up somewhere and forget it till it's needed."

The Colonel died on June 6, 1917, of throat cancer, according to his death certificate, File No. 612—a condition he had had for three years. See Figure 21-7 for the obituary in the *Nashville Banner*. The local newspaper for that period is nonexistent. He didn't have a military funeral for the United States Confederate Veterans (U.C.V.) regulations did not approve of such.

He was buried next to his wife in Cedar Grove Cemetery, Lebanon. The Dixon Merritt, *History of Wilson County,* states that, "No military honors marked the funerals of any Confederate veteran. The U.C.V. regulations forbade the sound of bugle or drum upon such occasions." It wasn't until 1912 that graves could be decorated. Veterans from his camp were pallbearers, according to the obituary in the *Nashville Banner.*

His beloved son-in-law, Dr. William Owen Carver, officiated as the Colonel requested. He was laid to rest next to his wife, Martha Jane "Mattie." Martha Jane was next to their daughter, Agnes Shepard Bates, who had preceded them both. Next to Agnes was to follow Sam, Jr. and his wife, Moncye.

In later years, the Sons of the Confederate Veterans placed a marker at the Colonel's feet. The maker listed his rank, name, birth and death dates, and the CSA designation, company, and Seventh Tennessee Infantry Regiment. The marker shows the company as "S," which is incorrect. See Figure 21-8. The Colonel's company was "G."

Until now, Colonel Samuel George Shepard was but a page of Civil War history yet to be written.

Ço̧federate̜ Veteraŋ. 309

GATHERING IN LEBANON, TENN., TO DEDICATE MONUMENT TO GEN. ROBERT HATTON.

A most worthy tribute to Gen. Robert Hatton and thousands of other Confederates in Wilson County, Tenn., has been paid in the recent erection of a monument at Lebanon. While it was undertaken as a monument to the Confederate soldiers of the county, it was most fitting to place upon it the figure of the distinguished citizen who after opposing the war was one of its early soldiers and one of the first generals killed. The four tablets bear the following inscriptions:

North side: "Erected by S. G. Shepard Camp, No. 941, U. C. V., with contributions from true friends of the Southern soldier. A. J. Casey, Chairman; A. W. Page, W. M. Harkreader, Committee."

East side: "To the heroes of 1861-65; not dead, but living in deeds such lives inspire."

South side: "As long as honor or courage is cherished the deeds of these heroes will live.

'Whether on the scaffold high or in the battle's van,
The fittest place where man can die is where he dies for man.'"

West side: "Erected in honor of Confederate veterans of Wilson County and all other true Southern soldiers, 1861-65."

Miss Manie Hatton, of Nashville, General Hatton's daughter, and Miss Manie Hatton Towson, a granddaughter of General Hatton, and Rev. W. E. Towson were present.

Mrs. Robert Hatton came from Georgia to Nashville, but was unable to attend. She is eighty-five and greatly beloved.

Capt. A. K. Miller, who was leader of the movement whereby a fine Confederate monument was erected in the cemetery at Lebanon some years ago, was master of ceremonies.

It is impracticable at present to give the addresses and reports of the proceedings in full that the enterprise merits.

PROMOTER OF THE MOVEMENT

In a letter as to how the movement was started to erect the monument its promoter, Mr. A. J. Casey, writes:

"I moved to Lebanon from Kentucky November 25, 1910, and leased the Lebanon Democrat until January 15, 1912. While publishing this newspaper I went before the S. G. Shepard Camp and asked them to grant me the privilege of erecting a monument to Confederate soldiers on the Public Square of Lebanon without asking any local veteran for a contribution. The Camp at my request appointed A. W. Page, W. M. Harkreader, and myself a building committee for the erection of a Confederate monument. I was elected chairman, secretary, and treasurer. I solicited the funds from citizens in Wilson County and throughout the State, and am in debt $196, for which I have no pledges.

"The contract was let for the erection of the monument by the building committee to the Oman Stone Company, of Nashville, Tenn. The contract for the concrete park, etc., was awarded to W. S. Page, son of A. W. Page. At the April (1911) term the county court granted the right to erect the monument in the Public Square, and the City Council, with Mayor J. T. Odum, later granted us the privilege.

"In September, 1911, I began soliciting money for the monument, and May 20, 1912, was selected as the day for the unveiling, it being the fifty-first anniversary of the day when General Hatton and six companies of soldiers left this county for the war. The day of the unveiling was ideal. One of the largest crowds ever seen in Lebanon was here that day. Commander Bennett H. Young, of Louisville, Ky., was the orator of the day. Rev. S. G. Shepard offered prayer. Judge Beard made the address of welcome, and I as chairman and treasurer of the building committee turned over the monument to the S. G. Shepard Camp. Capt. Rufus McClain accepted the monument for the Camp, and at this point the unveiling took place by Miss Manie C. Towson, of Ashburn, Ga., a granddaughter of General Hatton, assisted by W. S. Page's little daughter and W. M. Harkreader's grandson.

"A crowd of grandchildren of veterans stood in front of the monument and sang 'Dixie.' As the curtain fell a detail of the Tennessee State Guard (Captain Boyle) fired a salute.

"A. W. Page on behalf of the S. G. Shepard Camp turned over the premises to the Daughters of the Confederacy.

"Mrs. A. B. Martin, wife of Dr. M. B. Martin, who is at the head of the Law Department of the Cumberland University, being President, accepted the care of the monument and park."

[The father of the promoter, A. W. Casey, was color bearer in Col. John W. Caldwell's regiment from Russellville, Ky., and was killed in the battle of Shiloh on Sunday morning.]

Figure 21-1. Picture shows the crowd gathered to unveil the statue of Brigadier General Robert Hopkins Hatton. The monument was dedicated May 20, 1912, the 51st anniversary of the day General Hatton and six companies of soldiers left Wilson County for Camp Trousdale. Rev. S. G. Shepard offered the prayer. On the north side of the statute is a plaque stating it was erected by S. G. Shepard Camp, No. 941, U.C.V. This article appeared in the *Confederate Veteran* July 1912, page 309. Added since is a monument plaque about General Hatton. The plaque was added by General Robert H. Hatton Camp #723, Sons of Confederate Veterans, December 28, 1996.

Figure 21-2. Statue of Brigadier General Robert H. Hatton today in square at Lebanon. General Hatton was the highest-ranking officer from Wilson County. He was also the first commander of the Seventh Tennessee Infantry Regiment. A Tennessee Brigade, consisting of the First, Seventh, and Fourteenth Tennessee Infantry Regiments, was formed, and Hatton was promoted to brigadier general to command it. Eight days later, General Hatton was killed at the Battle of Seven Pines, 31 May 1862, in the first few minutes of the first major engagement for the Tennessee Brigade. Colonel Shepard carried his body off the battlefield. After Hatton's death, General James J. Archer took over, and the Fifth Alabama Battalion and the Thirteenth Alabama Infantry Regiment were later added. This new brigade was dubbed Archer's Light Brigade.

THE BOYS IN GRAY

S. G. Shepherd Camp of Confederate Veterans

HOLD AN EXCELLENT MEETING

A Committee Appointed to Secure the Names of all Old Soldiers in the County.

S. G. Shepherd Camp, United Confederate Veterans, met at the court house Saturday, Oct. 9, 1897, persuant to a call previously published by Commander Shepherd. The commander being absent, comrade A. K. Miller was called to the chair, when the following business was transacted:

The commander pro tem. stated that the object of the meeting was to effect a more permanent organization of the ex-Confederates of the county, and to devise a plan, if possible, by which the name of every soldier in the county might be obtained, and a complete roster arranged. To effect this purpose a committee of seven from different parts of the county, whose duty it was to select a suitable ex-soldier from each civil district, and two from the 10th to act as an enrolling committee to obtain and report the name of every ex-Confederate in his district, together with the name of his company, regiment and branch of service to which he belonged.

The selecting committee was composed of comrades B. F. Sullivan, J. H. Martin, W. H. Barrow, B. L. Swaffer, Spencer Jennings, Z. B. Ramsey, and W. M. Harkreader.

The following enrolling committee was selected and reported according to their districts:

Jo. B. Scobey, 1st district; W. A. McClain, 2d district; R. Q. Word, 3d district; W. H. Barrow, 4th district; R. C. Morris, 5th district; Thos. Petway, 6th district; S. W. Bell, 7th district; A. J. Sherrill, 8th district;
James Nelson, 9th district; A. McGregor and R. P. McClain, 10th district; Matt J. Turner, 11th district; John Johnson, 12th district; J. D. Wheeler, 13th district; J. M. Davis, 14th district; John A. Jennings, 15th district; Alex. Young, 16th district; J. R. Mathes, 17th district; J. H. Williams, 18th district; John Cox, 19th district; S. P. Christian, 20th district; J. W. Hewgley, 21st district; Thomas Eddins, 22d district; J. C. Ingram, 23d district; W. B. Sullivan, 24th district; James Wright, 25th district.

The name of S. G. Shepherd, which was selected for the Wilson county county camp at the reunion in Nashville, June 22, 1897, was unanimously ratified at this meeting.

The committee on enrollment was constituted a permanent obituary committee.

Comrades present were A. K. Miller, Z. B. Ramsey, S. L. Phillips, R. P. McClain, A. McGregor, Alex. Graves, D. T. Williams, J. W. Hewgley, S. D. Wright, B. F. Sullivan, Ben Terrell, J. H. Martin, R. Q. Word, R. C. Morris, J. H. Taylor, W. H. Barrow, L. W. Raulston, R. M. Whitecarver, W. M. Harkreader, James Johnson, Abe Britton, T. H. Eddins, Ben Swafford, A. C. Lea, B. P. Martin and Al Hankins.

A motion carried that the camp meet once a month; and the second Saturday in each month, at 11 o'clock, was adopted as the time of meeting.

The camp then adjourned until the next meeting.

A. K. MILLER. Com. Pro Tem.
W. M. Harkreader. Adjutant.

TO CURE A COLD IN ONE DAY
Take Laxative Bromo Quinine Tablets. All Druggists refund the money if it fails to Cure. 25c.

Figure 21-3. This article, "Boys in Gray," is from the *Lebanon Democrat*, 14 October 1897, and describes part of the story of the beginning of the S. G. Shepard Camp No. 941.

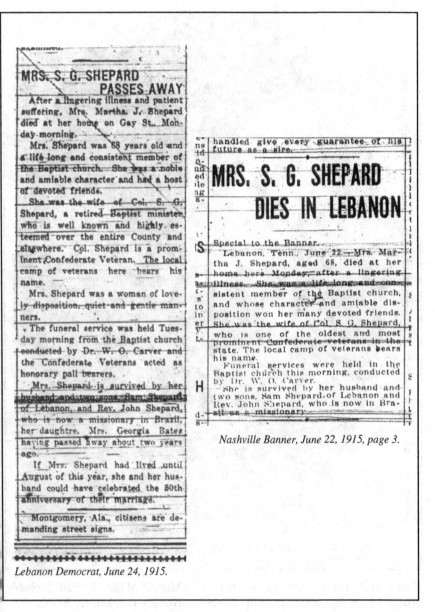

MRS. S. G. SHEPARD PASSES AWAY

After a lingering illness and patient suffering, Mrs. Martha J. Shepard died at her home on Gay St. Monday morning.

Mrs. Shepard was 68 years old and a life long and consistent member of the Baptist church. She was a noble and amiable character and had a host of devoted friends.

She was the wife of Col. S. G. Shepard, a retired Baptist minister who is well known and highly esteemed over the entire County and elsewhere. Col. Shepard is a prominent Confederate Veteran. The local camp of veterans here bears his name.

Mrs. Shepard was a woman of lovely disposition, quiet and gentle manners.

The funeral service was held Tuesday morning from the Baptist church conducted by Dr. W. O. Carver and the Confederate Veterans acted as honorary pall bearers.

Mrs. Shepard is survived by her husband and two sons, Sam Shepard of Lebanon, and Rev. John Shepard, who is now a missionary in Brazil, her daughter, Mrs. Georgia Bates having passed away about two years ago.

If Mrs. Shepard had lived until August of this year, she and her husband could have celebrated the 50th anniversary of their marriage.

Montgomery, Ala., citizens are demanding street signs.

Lebanon Democrat, June 24, 1915.

MRS. S. G. SHEPARD DIES IN LEBANON

Special to the Banner.

Lebanon, Tenn., June 22.—Mrs. Martha J. Shepard, aged 68, died at her home here Monday, after a lingering illness. She was a life long and consistent member of the Baptist church, and whose character and amiable disposition won her many devoted friends. She was the wife of Col. S. G. Shepard, who is one of the oldest and most prominent Confederate veterans in the state. The local camp of veterans bears his name.

Funeral services were held in the Baptist church this morning, conducted by Dr. W. O. Carver.

She is survived by her husband and two sons, Sam Shepard of Lebanon and Rev. John Shepard, who is now in Brazil as a missionary.

Nashville Banner, June 22, 1915, page 3.

Figure 21-4. Two articles on the death of the Colonel's beloved Martha Jane.

LT. COL. SAMUEL G. SHEPHERD
1829-1917, 7TH TENN. CAL.,
WIFE MARTHA J. MAJOR,1845-
1915, PICTURE BELONGED TO
MARTHA V. TAYLOR BROWN b.1896

Figure 21-5. The Colonel and Martha Jane "Mattie" Major Shepard, probably posing for an anniversary portrait. Which anniversary is unknown. Martha Jane died a few months before their 50th. (Courtesy of Glendon Lannom.)

1199

SHEPARD, JOHN WATSON (b. Gladeville, Tenn., Jan. 28, 1878; d. Atlanta, Ga., Aug. 12, 1954). Missionary, educator, pastor, and author. He was ordained to the gospel ministry at Gladeville, Tenn., Dec. 11, 1900. His academic study included a year at Bethel College, Russellville, Ky., followed by four years in Richmond College, Virginia, where he received the A.B. and M.A. degrees (1900). In four years he graduated from the Southern Baptist Theological Seminary with Th.M. and Th.D. degrees (1906). In 1918 he earned the M.A. degree in education from Chicago University, and in 1926 he completed one year of residential credits toward the Ph.D. degree in George Peabody School for Teachers, Nashville. His pastoral ministries included student pastorates while in the seminary, interim pastor of First Baptist Church, Rio de Janeiro, Brazil; and pastor, First Baptist Church, Morgan City, La., 1930. He was appointed missionary to Brazil by the Foreign Mission Board on Apr. 4, 1906; he served until 1930. After language study in Recife, 1906, he was selected by the Brazilian Baptist Convention in Recife to found a college and seminary in Rio. Foundation work in 1907 led to the creation of Rio Baptist College and Seminary of Rio de Janeiro. An elementary school opened in Mar., 1908, with 12 pupils. Five years later a high school was opened. The furlough year of 1912-13 was devoted to raising funds for the campus in Rio, thus enabling the college to open. The school is now known as the John W. Shepard Memorial College. In 1913 the Girls' School and Normal School were founded. By 1918 the Rio Seminary included 10 professors and about 75 students, and the college included 70 teachers with 835 students. Shepard served as president for 24 years. Joining the faculty of Baptist Bible Institute, New Orleans, he was professor of missions and religious activities, 1930-35; professor of New Testament interpretation and missions, 1936-37; and professor of New Testament interpretation and Greek, 1937-47, serving as head of the department. From 1930 to 1943, he was director of religious activities, during which time more than a dozen churches were organized. As an author, he wrote exten-

sively in Portuguese and English. In Portuguese were published Os Atos dos Apostolos, O Preador, A Epistola de Thiago, and numerous leaflets and small books. Major English works were The Christ of the Gospels (1939) and The Life and Letters of the Apostle Paul (1950). Unpublished manuscripts include "Education on a Christian Basis" and "How Jesus Trains His Workers." He married Rena Groover on June 6, 1906, and to them were born six children: Ida (Shepard) MacRae, Alice (Shepard) Kimbrough, Mary Gertrude Shepard, Evelyn Rena Shepard, Samuel Groover Shepard, and John Watson Shepard, Jr.   FRANK STAGG

Figure 21-6. This is the biographical sketch of Dr. John Watson Shepard as it appeared in the *Encyclopedia of Southern Baptists*, 1958 edition, Nashville, TN: Broadman Press, vol. II, page 1199. (It is used by permission from LifeWay Christian Resources of the Southern Baptist Convention, 127 Ninth Avenue, Nashville, TN 37234.)

COLONEL S. G. SHEPARD

COL. SHEPARD DEAD IN LEBANON

Special to the Banner.

Lebanon, Tenn., June 7.—In the death of Lieut.-Col. S. G. Shepard, at the home of his son, Sam Shepard, here, Wednesday morning, the county loses one of its most prominent and influential citizens. Col. Shepard was 88 years old, and his long life has been one of usefulness, both to his country and his fellow-man.

He was born in Wilson county, near Gladeville, and when grown went to Mississippi and taught school; then returned home and began the study of law just before the civil war. He made up a company at Baird's Mill, near Lebanon, and he was elected captain of his company at Yorktown. After the death of Col. Goodman and Col. Hatton he was made lieutenant-colonel of the Seventh Tennessee, which he filled until the close of the war.

Since the death of Col. Shepard the only surviving colonel of a Southern regiment is Col. John A. Fite of Lebanon.

After the surrender at Appomattox under Gen. Lee he came home and began preaching in 1865, and up until his health failed him, about two years ago, was one of the ablest men in the councils of the Baptist church. He was selected as Wilson county's representative in the constitutional convention of 1870. There are now only seven members of this convention living.

Col. Shepard was a gallant soldier and a Christian gentlemen in its truest sense, and the loss of his influence will be felt in many ways in this county. He is survived by one daughter, Mrs. W. O. Carver, of Louisville, Ky., and two sons, Sam Shepard of Lebanon and Rev. John Shepard of Alabama, who is a returned missionary from Brazil.

Funeral services were held at the Baptist church this morning at 10 o'clock, conducted by the Rev. T. N. Compton, local pastor, and Dr. W. O. Carver of Louisville, Ky. Honorary pall-bearers were Confederate soldiers of the local camp, which was named for him, "S. G. Shepard Camp of Confederate Veterans." Interment was at Cedar Grove cemetery.

Figure 21-7. This is the only article on the death of Colonel Shepard. It was in the *Nashville Banner*, 7 June 1917, page 14.

Figure 21-8. Photos show the family headstones (rear of them). Left to right is Colonel Shepard with his wife, Martha Jane, Agnes Shepard Bates (his daughter), and Sam (his son) with Moncye (Sam's wife). The lower photo is the footstone at the foot of the Colonel's grave. Co. *S* should be Co. *G*.

Epilogue

The Colonel's ministry continued through his son, Dr. John Watson Shepard, through John Watson's two sons, Dr. John Watson Shepard, Jr. and Dr. Samuel Grover Shepard, and through his son-in-law, Dr. William Owen Carver. Dr. Carver and the Colonel's daughter, Alice Hughes Shepard, had two children who followed the ministry. Dorothy, their daughter, who in addition to being a foreign missionary, married Rev. Maxfield Garrott, who was a missionary and a student of Dr. Carver. The Carver's son, Dr. George Alexander Carver, was a teaching minister.

His love and respect of the academics continued even though he never had the opportunity to obtain a formal education. Four of his five grandsons obtained doctorates. Three were missionaries. Dr. James Edward Carver was a professor of English. William Owen Carver, Jr. was the only one who not only didn't receive a doctorate, he didn't receive an undergraduate degree. William Owen Carver, Jr. quit the University of Richmond six weeks before receiving his bachelor's degree to take the job of city editor of a Louisville daily newspaper. He was on the news staff of General Douglas MacArthur during World War II.

The daughters of Dr. William Owen Carver and Alice Hughes Shepard all obtained degrees. Ruth obtained degrees in both English and music (piano) from the West Hampton College, female section of the University of Richmond. She married Doctor of Theology Norfleet Gardner. Dorothy received a B.A. and an M.A. from the University of Richmond and taught in Fukuoka, Japan. Alice, the youngest of the Carvers, obtained a B.A. and an M.A. from Mount Holyoke in Massachusetts. She did advanced work at Radcliffe. Her majors were medieval history and English. She married Dr. Maurice Browning Cramer, professor of English.

It is unknown what happened to the daughters of John Watson and Samuel, Jr.

The Colonel's love of music continued with his two daughters, Alice and Agnes, and with his granddaughter, Ruth. According to his granddaughter, Alice, "Ruth was a child prodigy of music. She played the classics on the piano at eleven!" His granddaughter Alice's son, Browning, at the time of this writing was a violinist and in the first chair section of the Metropolitan Opera.

I was struck by the number of doctorates. Once, when talking with Carol Whitehead, great-granddaughter of the Colonel, I mentioned that. She said, "You should count the Phi Beta Kappa keys."

It is unfortunate I didn't find the offspring of Sam, Jr. or Dr. John Watson Shepard. After I found Alice, the last child of Dr. Carver and Alice Hughes Shepard, I stopped looking and started listening to her. Then Dr. Owen Cramer, son of granddaughter Alice and originator and head of the classics at Colorado College, sent me the manuscript about the Colonel written by his grandmother, Alice Hughes Shepard Carver. See the Shepard Family Tree.

When I view the offspring of the Colonel—and it is with great admiration and awe—the comment I have is this: How bright the Colonel's light continues to shine.

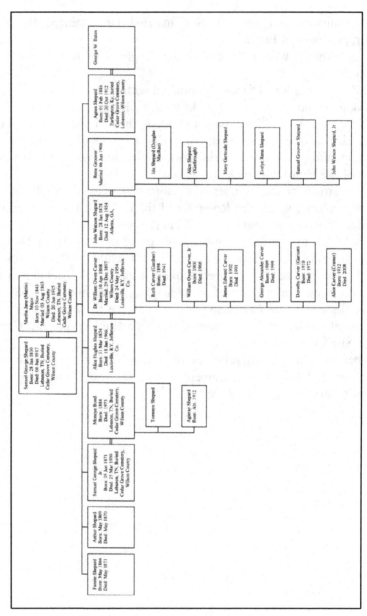

Epilogue. Descendants of Colonel and Martha Jane.

Appendix A

**Report of Lieutenant Colonel S. G. Shepard,
Seventh Tennessee Infantry of
Operations of Archer's Brigade
10 August 1863
The Battle of Gettysburg**

THE

WAR OF THE REBELLION:

A COMPILATION OF THE

OFFICIAL RECORDS

OF THE

UNION AND CONFEDERATE ARMIES.

———

PREPARED, UNDER THE DIRECTION OF THE SECRETARY OF WAR, BY

The late Lieut. Col. ROBERT N. SCOTT, Third U. S. Artillery,

PURSUANT TO ACTS OF CONGRESS.

———

SERIES I—VOLUME XXVII—IN THREE PARTS.

PART II—REPORTS.

———

WASHINGTON:

GOVERNMENT PRINTING OFFICE.

1889.

the wounded; hence the uncertainty of a good many being killed late yesterday evening. I must close.

Yours, truly,

J. J. YOUNG,
Captain, and Assistant Quartermaster.

His Excellency Gov. ZEBULON B. VANCE.

No. 552.

Report of Lieut. Col. S. G. Shepard, Seventh Tennessee Infantry, of operations of Archer's brigade.

AUGUST 10, 1863.

SIR: In compliance with General Orders, No. — (to report the part that Archer's brigade took in the recent engagements in Pennsylvania and Maryland), I beg leave to state that, although I was not in command of the brigade, yet I was in each of the engagements, and upon my own observation and the testimony of the officers of each of the regiments I predicate my statements.

We left our camp near Cashtown, Pa., early on the morning of July 1, and marched down the turnpike road leading to Gettysburg. We had advanced about 3 miles when we came upon the enemy's pickets, who gradually fell back before us for about 3 miles, which brought us in sight of the enemy, upon a slight eminence in our front and to the right of the road. General Archer halted for a short time while a section of a battery opened fire upon them. He then deployed the brigade in line, and advanced directly upon the enemy through an open field. At the extreme side of the field there was a small creek with a fence and undergrowth, which was some disadvantage to our line in crossing, but the brigade rushed across with a cheer, and met the enemy just beyond. We were not over 40 or 50 yards from the enemy's line when we opened fire. Our men fired with great coolness and deliberation, and with terrible effect, as I learned next day by visiting the ground.

We had encountered the enemy but a short time, when he made his appearance suddenly upon our right flank with a heavy force, and opened upon us a cross-fire. Our position was at once rendered untenable, and the right of our line was forced back. He made also a demonstration upon our left, and our lines commenced falling back, but owing to the obstructions in our rear (the creek, &c., above referred to), some 75 of the brigade were unable to make their escape, General Archer among the rest. I saw General Archer a short time before he surrendered, and he appeared to be very much exhausted with fatigue.

Being completely overpowered by numbers, and our support not being near enough to give us any assistance, we fell back across the field, and reformed just in rear of the brigade that had started in as our support. Colonel Fry took command of the brigade, and, after remaining in the woods for two or three hours, the whole line upon our left advanced. Archer's brigade advanced at the same time upon the extreme right of the line. While advancing, the enemy threw a body of cavalry around upon our right flank. Seeing this, Colonel Fry changed the direction of his front so as to protect our flank.

COLONEL S. G. SHEPARD

The cavalry did not advance upon us, but hung around during the entire engagement of the evening of July 1.

During the night of the 1st, and the 2d, we lay in position upon a road upon the right of our line. We were not in the engagement of July 2.

During the night of the 2d, we moved around, and took our position in front of the enemy's works, and remained there until the evening of July 3.

In the engagement of the 3d, the brigade was on the right of our division, in the following order : First Tennessee on the right; on its left, Thirteenth Alabama; next, Fourteenth Tennessee ; on its left, Seventh Tennessee, and, on the left, Fifth Alabama Battalion. There was a space of a few hundred yards between the right of Archer's brigade and the left of General Pickett's division when we advanced, but, owing to the position of the lines (they not being an exact continuation of each other), as we advanced, the right of our brigade and the left of General Pickett's division gradually approached each other, so that by the time we had advanced a little over half of the way, the right of Archer's touched and connected with Pickett's left.

The command was then passed down the line by the officers, "Guide right ;" and we advanced our right, guiding by General Pickett's left. The enemy held their fire until we were in fine range, and opened upon us a terrible and well-directed fire. Within 180 or 200 yards of his works, we came to a lane inclosed by two stout post and plank fences. This was a very great obstruction to us, but the men rushed over as rapidly as they could, and advanced directly upon the enemy's works, the first line of which was composed of rough stones. The enemy abandoned this, but just in rear was massed a heavy force. By the time we had reached this work, our lines all along, as far as I could see, had become very much weakened ; indeed, the line both right and left, as far as I could observe, seemed to melt away until there was but little of it left. Those who remained at the works saw that it was a hopeless case, and fell back. Archer's brigade remained at the works fighting as long as any other troops either on their right or left, so far as I could observe.

Every flag in the brigade excepting one was captured at or within the works of the enemy. The First Tennessee had 3 color-bearers shot down, the last of whom was at the works, and the flag captured. The Thirteenth Alabama lost 3 in the same way, the last of whom was shot down at the works. The Fourteenth Tennessee had 4 shot down, the last of whom was at the enemy's works. The Seventh Tennessee lost 3 color-bearers, the last of whom was at the enemy's works, and the flag was only saved by Captain [A. D.] Norris tearing it away from the staff and bringing it out beneath his coat. The Fifth Alabama Battalion also lost their flag at the enemy's works.

There were 7 field officers who went into the charge, only 2 of whom came out. The rest were all wounded and captured. The loss in company officers was nearly in the same proportion.

Our loss in men was also heavy. We went into the fight on the 1st with 1,048 men, 677 of whom were killed, wounded, and captured during these engagements.

I cannot particularize where so many officers and men did their whole duty. There are doubtless some, however, as is always the case, who did not do their duty, and richly deserve the severest punishment that can be inflicted.

After our unfortunate repulse, we reformed upon the ground from which we advanced, and waited for an advance of the enemy, which, however, they did not see proper to make, and so ended the conflict of the day.

We remained here until the night of the 4th, when we retired, and fell back beyond Hagerstown, Md. We next took position between Hagerstown and Williamsport, where we lay in line of battle two days, and retired on the night of the 13th instant. Owing to the darkness of the night and the impossibility of the artillery getting on, we found ourselves 5 miles from the river at daylight. We moved on to within 2 miles of the river, and formed a line of battle upon the crest of a hill, to protect our rear until the artillery and the column in advance of us could cross the river. While here, a small squadron of the enemy's cavalry, consisting of 75 or 100 men, made their appearance in our front. They were mistaken at first for our own cavalry until they had advanced close upon us. Their first charge was upon the First Tennessee Regiment, which was upon the right of the brigade. Our men, unfortunately, did not have their guns all loaded, and were forced to fight with clubbed guns. The enemy, finding they were making rather slow headway at this point, moved down the line upon the Thirteenth Alabama, Seventh and Fourteenth Tennessee Regiments, who by this time had succeeded in getting many of their guns loaded, and were but a short time in killing and wounding a majority of them. The rest made a desperate effort to escape back to the woods, but most of those were shot from their horses as they fled, so that not over a dozen or twenty made their escape. We lost in this encounter 1 man killed and 7 wounded.

It was our sad misfortune, too, in this affair, to lose General Pettigrew, who was in command of the brigade. No encomium that I might add could do justice to his memory. Both officers and men of the entire brigade feel that by his death the Confederacy has lost a model soldier and one of her most noble and gifted sons.

We received orders to retire toward the river, and we moved out, with General Pettigrew's brigade upon our left. Our route to the river was part of the way through a dense and tangled copse of undergrowth, with deep ravines running up from the river. We kept our line pretty well organized in passing through these obstructions, and passed beyond the river.

Not wishing to burden you with a report too lengthy, I have noted down in a brief style the facts deemed most important for your information.

All of which I respectfully beg leave to submit.

        S. G. SHEPARD,
   Lieutenant-Colonel Seventh Tennessee Regiment.

Capt. WILLIAM BROWN,
  Acting Assistant Adjutant and Inspector General.

No. 553.

Reports of Brig. Gen. Joseph R. Davis, C. S. Army, commanding brigade and Heth's division.

    HEADQUARTERS DAVIS' BRIGADE, *August 26, 1863.*

MAJOR : I have the honor to submit the following report of the part taken by my brigade in the battle of July 1, at Gettysburg :

Early on the morning of the 1st, I moved in rear of Archer's bri-

Appendix B

Roster of Original Company G, Seventh Tennessee Volunteer Infantry, CSA [1]

Commissioned Officers

S. G. SHEPARD, Captain | J. A. HOBBS, First Lieutenant
M. M. BOND, Second Lieutenant | W. F. GRAVES, Third Lieutenant

Privates

Allen, Wm. H.	Harrison, John	Oliver, W. L.
Aubrey, Henry H.	Harrison, John T.	Ozment, J.D.
Baird, Wm.T.	Harrison, Thos.	Ozment, R. B.
Balentine, F.Cannon	Harrison, W. H.	Patterson, Thos.
Baskin, R.A.	Hawks, John A.	Picket, J. B.
Blankenship, George	Hobbs, John H.	Pool, W.
Bond, J. H.	Huddleston, G. W.	Quesenbury, H.E.
Bradley, James	Hutchens, A.	Quesenbury, R. T.
Bradshaw, Hartwell	Hutchens, L.	Quesenbury, W.J.
Bright, Joe H.	Hide, Ed	Ray, J. K.
Cluck, Fount W.	Hide, Joe	Rice, J. Thos.
Curry, B. Frank	Ingram, J. C.	Richmond, L. Alex
Curry, James	Jackson, Tom R.B.	Richmond, J.P.
Curry, John S.	Jennings, N.A.	Robbins, W. H.
Daugherty, Nathon	Johns, W. Dan	Roberts, John
Davis, W. H.	Johnson, L. Hal	Robertson, Grundy
Dement, Luss	Johnson, Rev. W. H.	Robertson, Luke
Drennon, T. J.	Jones, R.F.	Rucker, S.B.
Edwards, Buck	Jones, W.H.	Rucker, Thomas W.
Edwards, J. E.	Kennedy, John L.	Sellars, Eli D.
Edwards, W. H.	King, M.F.	Simmons, Calvin J.
Foster, A. J.	Lannom, Andy J.	Sims, Geo.
Grissom, Albert	Lannom, Joe	Sullivan, Ben F.
Grissom, James	Lannom, N.P.	Sullivan, Thomas J.
Grissom, John	Lannom, P.L.	Sullivan, Wm. H.
Gwyn, J.W.	Leonard, Fred C.	Summers, James H.
Gwynne, H. Robert	McCrary, James	Vann, John
Hackney, W. W.	McCrary, John	Vaughn, R. D.
Hagar, Reuben B.	Mount, J. W.	Vaughters, Wm. G.
Hamilton, Alex.J.	Nelson, J. W.	Woodrum, Wm. F.
Harrison, H.	Nipper, John W.	Young, P. Bailey
Harrison, James	Oliver, J.T.	

---

[1] This roster of Company G was supplied by John "Bev" Spickard.

Appendix C

Memoirs of Colonel John A. Fite,
Seventh Tennessee Infantry, CSA

February 10, 1832 to August 23, 1925

John A. Fite was captain of Company B, Seventh Tennessee Infantry, as was S. G. Shepard, captain of Company G. His family talked him into putting his memoirs to paper, and this he did in 1910. The State of Tennessee asked their veterans to commit their memories to paper in 1914 to 1921. Colonel Shepard did not comply. Those who did offer history an unforgettable and incomparable opportunity to see the War Between the States through the eyes of Southern participants and to glimpse our fledgling country in its growing years. The following excerpt from Fite's memoir reveals a little-known side of Colonel Shepard, when he and Colonel Fite took some "undocumented" time away from the war.

Pages 62 through 66
Camp at Winchester, VA
February 1862

    Shepard and I were the only Captains in our regiment that had never had a furlough so we concluded we'd go to Richmond. There was an order that no soldier or officer could leave the command without a furlough signed by the Major General. Loring [Major General William Loring] had left us, and General Anderson [General George Anderson] had gone somewhere. General Manny [General George Manny] had assumed command in Loring's division. Shepard and I went to Hatton [Colonel Robert Hatton, commander of the Seventh Tennessee Infantry Regiment] and he gave us a paper, which said that Captains Fite and Shepard have permission to be absent from his command for seven days. This was signed by Colonel Hatton. We took it to Manny, or rather I did, and he refused to sign it. Shepard and I concluded we'd go anyhow so we went down to town and got into a stage for Strausberg [sic]. When the stage came around in front of the hotel, it stopped and a little Lieutenant with a big red sash around him, and a guard, came up and stopped and called for our furloughs. I handed him my paper, and he said, 'There ain't no Major General approving this, and you will have to get it countersigned by a Major General." I told him he was a hell of a fellow if he couldn't tell the difference between a furlough and a leave of absence. He said, "Let me see that paper again." I handed it back to him. He said, "I beg your pardon sir." I said, "The Army must be in a hell of a fix if it can't afford an officer of the day who couldn't tell the difference between a furlough and a leave of absence." He apologized, and we went on. When we got to Strausberg [sic], we went to a hotel, and there we met a whole lot of fellows, mad and cussing, because they were not allowed to go on the train, not having a Major General's furlough. Shepard was scared and wanted to go back. I told him no, we wouldn't go back. I went to the clerk at the hotel and told him I wanted some paper and pen and ink sent up, and I wanted a room. He assigned us a room, and we went up into it, and I wrote. The first thing I wrote was that "Captains Fite and Shepard are hereby detailed to go to Richmond and get saber bayonets for the Seventh Tennessee Regiment." I signed that "Robert Hatton— Colonel commanding." Then I wrote another one on the back of that, "approved, George Manny, Commanding division," and made Shepard sign that, and then I wrote another: "approved, T.J. Jackson by J. Shelby Williams, Adj. General." We didn't either one of us know who Jackson's Adjutant General was, but Shelby Williams had just come there to be Adjutant for old man Anderson. Shepard was scared all the time. We then went down and got on the train. Shepard said I'd have to do the talking, so I got in one end of the car, and he got in the other. Soon after the train started an officer, who had a guard with him, came through the train examining the furloughs and when he came to me he wanted to know who in the hell was J. Shelby Williams. I said I didn't know but that he was at Jackson's headquarters and had signed the paper. The fellow looked at it, and he finally said, "There's too much of this in the same handwriting." I said, "Maybe you think it's a forgery." He said, "It does look damm [sic] suspicious." I said, "You better arrest us then." He said, "You needn't talk so damm [sic] smart." I didn't talk much more, except told him if he had us stopped, old Jackson would ring his neck. He said he wasn't afraid of that. We got down to Manassas Junction. Shepard wanted to turn back. I told him "No." While we were there waiting for the train to leave for Richmond I saw two ladies standing there. One of them had a basket. I walked up to one of them and said, "Madam, you are a friend I know to an old soldier." She said, "Yes, I'd be glad to do anything I could for one." I knew if I could get in the ladies coach, I wouldn't likely be interfered with or turned back. The conductor came along and showed these ladies which couch to get in. It was the hindmost coach. I asked her to let me carry her basket in, and she handed it to me and walked on into the train. I followed right behind her. There was a soldier there with a gun who stopped me. He says, "You can't get in here." I said, "What right have you to part a man and his wife?" He said, "Was that your wife?" I said, "Certainly it was." He said, "Go on in then." Shepard had his woman's basket, and he never said a word to Shepard. If he had said a word to Shepard, he'd have caught him, but we had no further trouble from that on to Richmond.

We stayed there several days and were there on the 22nd of February, the day Jefferson Davis made his inaugural address. We learned, by some means that our Regiment had left Winchester, and we didn't know where it had gotten to. General Loring was there stopping at the Spotsville Hotel. I supposed he would know where the Regiment was, and I went down to see him. He said, "Yes, your regiment was to reach Fredericksburg Saturday."

Shepard and I went down and got on the train and went to Fredericksburg. When we got there, we couldn't hear anything of our regiment. I went to the quartermaster and to the commissary both, and they said they had not heard of our Regiment. I knew if the Regiment was to be there, they'd know it so we went back to Richmond and the next day took the train for Winchester.

When we got to Gordansville, we saw Andrew Martin [It is unknown who Martin is.]. He was on his way to Richmond and had a paper almost precisely in the language that Shepard and I had forged. He told us the regiment was still at Winchester, so we went on and when we got to Winchester, we heard of all sorts of places as to where our Regiment was. One fellow told us he was provo martial, said it was about six miles out from Winchester, said that they expected an attack from the Yankees, and didn't want the Yankees to know where the Regiment was. Shepard and I got very anxious to find where the Regiment was. I told him we'd go up to Jackson's headquarters and *could find out. Shepard said, "Old Jackson will put us in the guard house if we do." I told him I thought not.*

We knew if the Regiment got into a fight and we were not there, we'd be disgraced, so we went up to Jackson's headquarters, walked in, and walked up to a young man at a writing desk and told him that Shepard and I had been off on a short furlough and that we were anxious to join our Regiment, but didn't know where to find it. Jackson was standing back there; he spoke up and said, "Your regiment will be at Manassas Junction tonight. I've just had a courier from over there." I hadn't noticed Jackson being there before, so Shepard and I took a stage for Strausberg [sic], a train from Strausberg [sic], and just before we got into Manassas Junction, we saw the Regiment. We didn't take long to join it, and I swore then I'd never leave it again without the proper papers.

Appendix D

Private Sam

The story of Colonel Samuel George Shepard would not be complete without including more than just a mention of the Colonel's colorful grandfather—Private Sam—Revolutionary Sam. The Colonel was named after his grandfather, and that was the reason the Colonel was called George. The facts regarding the grandfather became so interesting that it became necessary to devote more than a small space to him. Actually, Private Sam's story needed a special place of its own. To be sure the whole Shepard family is wrapped in this country's red, white, and blue. One relative traced the Shepard family back to the early colonization of this country, but that is another story.

Private Sam was born on June 3, 1762 in Goochland, Virginia,[1] and died in Wilson County, Tennessee, in 1845, at the age of eighty-three.[2,3] The *Revolutionary War Soldiers of Wilson County* lists his demise as 1846.[4] In his pension deposition, he claimed he ascertained his age from his father's family record.

Private Sam entered the Revolutionary War several times—when, and as, he was needed. He was at Yorktown (Little York), Virginia, when Lord Charles Cornwallis surrendered; Private Sam helped guard those prisoners. His brothers, Thomas and William, were also in the

---

[1] *National Archives of Federal Pension for Revolutionary War, Samuel Shepherd* [sic], *S3894*. All of the information in this chapter is from the pension application unless otherwise stated.

[2] Samuel Shepard Will, December Term, 1845.

[3] Thomas Partlow (compiled by), Samuel Shepard Will, *Wilson County, Tennessee, Wills, Book 1–3, 1802–1850* (Lebanon, TN), 247; settlement 221–222.

[4] Thomas E. Partlow (compiled by), *Revolutionary War Soldiers in Wilson County*, Wilson County, Tennessee, Miscellaneous Records 1800–1875 (Lebanon, TN), 151.

Revolutionary War. William was killed. Private Sam cast his first vote in the newly-established United States of America for George Washington and his last for Henry Clay.

Years after the war, Sam married Jane Guill and migrated to Wilson County, Tennessee. He became a farmer. Wilson County records show Private Sam Shepard as one of the original two dozen families.[5] His pension declaration of 1832 says he migrated to Tennessee twenty-seven years after the peace and lived in Wilson County the following twenty years. He and Jane had five sons and two daughters.

It is also interesting to note here that the name "Shepard" has many spellings and that Private Sam could neither read nor write, which was not unusual for this country's Revolutionary War population. Private Sam's pension papers show "Shepherd" obtaining the pension for which a Samuel "Shepard" made the application declaration with his X. His brother, Thomas, corroborated the declaration with his own X. The Wilson County census of 1840 states that Private Sam could neither read nor write.[6]

Private Sam's will is indicative of the time. Sam mentions his seven children—James M., William, Robert, Samuel, John, Martha (Logan) and Mary (Guill). John was the Colonel's father. Private Sam left everything to his wife, Jane, of course. But upon Jane's death, James M. was to have the 77¾ acres, one bed and furniture, one cow and calf, one sow and pigs, and two head of sheep. Samuel was to get one bed and furniture, one cow and calf, one sow and pigs, two head of sheep. The balance of the estate—household and kitchen furniture and stock of all description—was to be sold on a twelve-month credit, and the money to be equally divided among all his children and the heirs of his late son, John, who had preceded Private Sam into death by ten years. James M., the executor, had to file for an extension in June 1846 and reported at the time that he had collected $27.90 from William Shepard, $12.75 from James Rutland, and $151.35 of pension money.

---

[5] Thomas E. Partlow, *Two Dozen Families of Wilson County, Tennessee*, (1976), 172.

[6] *Federal Census of 1840*, Wilson County, Tennessee.

He was known to be a colorful family character who frequently traveled in Europe to visit relatives, particularly Spain. The granddaughter Alice thought his wife may have had relatives in Spain. After returning from one trip to Europe, Sam tried to get the neighbors in the county interested in importing the Spanish custom of bullfighting. He set out to demonstrate this great fete with his neighbors watching. He apparently went through the motions to get the bull interested but didn't realize that a goat was watching and waiting, determined to upstage him with a head-butt to the buttocks. The result was Sam was upended, and the neighbors were entertained—though not enticed into bullfighting.

Once, when returning from England to the United States prior to the revolution, Sam was apparently not sold on the idea of a revolt. He traveled frequently to Europe and had friends and relatives there. His spoken reluctance caused a fight at the local pub when he defended England.

In September 1832, Private Sam applied for the war pension called the Act of Longevity of the Seventh of June 1832. On August 30, 1833, it was granted, and he received an initial compensation of $200— retroactive to March 4, 1831—and then $80 annually until his death, at which time his estate was given $151.35.[7]

Private Sam's application lists that he was in the battles of "Monmouth Plains" and "Little York." He enlisted in the Continental Army on January 16, 1778. He was under sixteen years old when he was one of seventy who marched to Valley Forge, Pennsylvania, to join the Main Army Command led by General George Washington. During his term of service in the "Campaign of 1778," he marched from the Goochland County courthouse in Virginia to Fredericksburg, Virginia— then to Frederick and Fredericktown, Maryland—then to Lancaster and York, Pennsylvania. From York, he marched to the headquarters at Valley Forge, where he wintered. He was at Valley Forge until the battle of Monmouth Plains, New Jersey, near the courthouse on June 28, 1778. He was attached to the First Regiment of the Virginia Militia of the Continental Line and to the Second Division during the battle.

---

[7] James Shepard, Report of Executor of Samuel Shepard's Will, supplied by Carver family, Shepard descendants.

He mentions he knew General Charles Lee, who was later "charged for cowardly conduct" at the Monmouth Plains battle. He comments that he knew Baron Friedrich Von Steuben by sight and frequently saw him. (The Baron was hired by the Continental Army to train the soldiers.)

In addition to his one-year enlistment, Private Sam was called back to the Virginia Militia five more times: four times for three months each and once for one month. Figure D-1 shows the dates and his commanders. After each service, he would return to his father's farm in Goochland County, Virginia.

One assignment was to guard Richmond, Virginia, but before his unit could get there, General Benedict Arnold "burnt the rope works and foundry and other public buildings." His unit was detailed to follow in pursuit. They returned to Richmond unsuccessful of a capture. The one-month tour was to prevent an anticipated invasion in the lower part of Virginia.

Another of his three-month enlistments was to guard Major General John Burgoyne's prisoners that had been taken in the North. And another was under the command of General Marquis de Lafayette when the general retreated from Richmond to the Rapidan River under the "superior force" of Lord Cornwallis.

His last tour of service was again with General Lafayette, starting about 1 August 1781. His unit rendezvoused at Williamsburg, Virginia. Two weeks later, General George Washington arrived and took command of the whole army.

Private Sam dictates:

> In a few days, we were marched down to Little York where siege was laid against Lord Cornwallis. [Switching from first-person to third-person:] He was there during the siege and until after the surrender of Lord Cornwallis. He was then attached to the forces which had been assigned to guard those prisoners at Winchester, Virginia. He remained there a few days and was then discharged and returned home because his three months were up.

His namesake grandson, Colonel Samuel George Shepard, would also fight to protect Richmond and follow some of the same paths taken by his grandfather some eighty years before.

Private Sam fought to defend this country's right to become a nation and to establish its own laws as a nation—to be independent of another government. His grandson would later fight to interpret these laws that were established—the individual rights of states, the issue of slavery. Private Sam was called a Revolutionary War "Rebel" or "Johnny Rebel." His grandson was to be called a "Reb" or a "Johnny Reb," referring to those who fought in what some called "the Rebellion."

REVOLUTIONARY WAR RECORDS SECTION. 3—525

DEPARTMENT OF THE INTERIOR,

BUREAU OF PENSIONS.

Washington, D. C., ..., 19__

· In reply to your request of ...., received .... for a statement of the military history of Samuel Shepherd a soldier of the REVOLUTIONARY WAR, you will find below the desired information as contained in his (or his widow's) application for pension on file in this Bureau.

Dates of enlistment or appointment.	Length of service.	Rank.	Officers under whom service was rendered. Captain.	Colonel.	State.
Jany 16. 1778	11 mos.	Pvt.	Nathaniel Morris		Va.
			Augustus Kendall	Richard Parker	
1779	3 mos.		Thomas Miller		
Fall 1780	1 mo.		John Curd		
Dec 1780	3 mos.		Stokely Towles		
Spring 1781	3 mos.		Thomas Bates		
Aug. 1. 1781	3 mos.				

Battles engaged in, Monmouth Siege of Yorktown.

Residence of soldier at enlistment, Goochland County Va.

Date of application for pension, Sept. 27 1832 His claim was al—

Residence at date of application, Wilson County Tennessee

1832 71 1762 Age at date of application, born June 3. 1762.

Remarks: It is not stated whether he had a wife or children

Respectfully,

brothers Thomas + William

Commissioner.

Figure D-1. Dates and lengths of service for Private Sam.

Bibliography

"About Capitulation at Appomattox." *Confederate Veteran.* vol. V (Aug. 1897): 405.

Boscobel College. *Annual Catalogue, 1893–1894.* Nashville, TN: Tennessee State Library and Archives.

Boscobel College. *Catalogue Announcement from September 1912 to May 1913.* Nashville, TN: Tennessee State Library and Archives.

"Boys in Gray." *Lebanon Democrat.* (14 Oct. 1897).

Burns, Frank, ed., *The History of Wilson County, Tennessee: Its Land and Its Life.* Memphis, TN: Memphis State University Press, 1983.

———. *The History of Wilson County, Tennessee: Its Land and Its Life,* 2nd Ed. Memphis, TN: Memphis State University Press, 1987.

Burns, Ken. *The Civil War: The Universe of Battle,* 1863. 1990.

Harris, Capt. F. S. "Spaniard." *Confederate Veteran* (Nov. 1895): 334.

———. "What Command Was It?" *Confederate Veteran* (Aug. 1895): 239.

Carpenter, V. K., trans., *Wilson County, Tennessee, Population Schedule of the United States Census of 1850.* Huntsville, AR: Century Enterprises, 1969.

Baldwin Brothers Directory Company. *City Directory, Lebanon, Tennessee, 1927,* vol. 1. Knoxville, TN: Baldwin Brothers Directory Company (1927). Nashville, TN: Tennessee State Library and Archives.

"Col. Shepard Dead in Lebanon," *Nashville Banner,* June 7, 1917, 14.

Confederate Military History. Atlanta, GA: Confederate Publishing Company, 1899.

Corlew, Robert E., *Tennessee: A Short History.* Knoxville, TN: University of Tennessee Press, 1989.

The Encyclopedia of Southern Baptists, 1958 ed., vols. I and II. Nashville, TN: Broadman Press, 1958.

Federal Census of 1840. Wilson County, TN. Lebanon, TN: Wilson County Archives.

Federal Census of 1860. Wilson County, TN, Civil Districts 16–25. Lebanon, TN: Wilson County Archives. (Please see references under Wilson County for more census records.)

Fellowship Baptist Church, Lebanon, Records (located outside Gladeville in Rutherford County), Lebanon, TN: Wilson County Archives.

Finney, Raymond Alfred. "A History of the Private Educational Institutions of Franklin County, Part I: Mary Sharp College." *Franklin County Historical 22 Review* (1991). Nashville, TN: Tennessee State Library and Archives.

First Baptist Church, Lebanon, Records, 1889–1935. Lebanon, TN: Wilson County Archives.

Fite, John A. *Memoirs of Colonel John A. Fite, 7th Tennessee Infantry, CSA, February 10, 1832–August 23, 1925.* Sarasota, FL: John Fite Robertson (collection) 1935.

Franklin County Historical Review, vol. XXIV, no. 2, 1993. "Catalogue of the Mary Sharp College for the Collegiate Year Closing June, 1858." (Winchester, TN). Nashville, TN: South-Western Publishing House, 1858. (Cross-referenced).

"Gathering in Lebanon, Tenn. to Dedicate Monument to Gen. Robert Hatton," *Confederate Veteran*, July 1912.

Goodspeed History of Wilson County, Tennessee (1886). Nashville: Tennessee State Library and Archives.

Green, A. Wilson, and Gary W. Gallagher. *National Geographic Guide to the Civil War: National Battlefield Parks.* Washington, D.C.: the National Geographic Society, 1992.

Grime, J. H. *History of Middle Tennessee Baptists.* Cave City, KY, c1900.

History of Tennessee. Nashville, TN: Goodspeed Publishing Co, 1886. Reprinted Columbia, TN: Woodward and Stinson Printing Co., 1972.

Jones, Maj. J., "Report 550: Twenty-Sixth North Carolina Infantry, Commanding Pettigrew's Brigade, 9 August 1863—The Gettysburg Campaign." *The War of the Rebellion: A Compilation of the Official Records of the Union and Confederate Armies*, ser. I, vol. XXVII, pt. II (1889). Washington, D.C.: Government Printing Office.

"Letters from the People." *Nashville Daily American*, January 19, 1876.

Lindsley, M.D., D.D., John Berrien. *Military Annals of Tennessee*, vol. I. Nashville, TN: J. M. Lindsley & Co. Publishers, 1886. Reprinted Wilmington, NC: Broadfoot Publishing Company, 1995.

Marriage Bond (between Fanny J. Shepherd [sic] and Jordan T. Robinson). Lebanon, TN: Wilson County Archives.

Marriage Contract (between John Shepherd [sic] and Francis G. Graves). Lebanon, TN: Wilson County Archives.

Marriage License (between Fanny J. Shepherd [sic] and Jordan T. Robinson), Lebanon, TN: Wilson County Archives.

Marriage License (between Francis G. Graves and John Shepherd [sic]. Lebanon, TN: Wilson County Archives.

Mary Sharp College. *Catalogue of the Mary Sharp College, Winchester, Tenn., for the Collegiate Year Closing 1858.* Nashville, TN: South-Western Publishing House; Graves, Marks & Co., 1858. Reprinted in

Franklin County Historical Review, vol. XXIV, no. 2 (1993). Nashville, TN: Tennessee State Library and Archives.

McBride, Robert and Dan M. Robison, eds., *Biographical Directory of the Tennessee General Assembly,* vol. II, 1861–1901. Nashville, TN: Tennessee State Library and Archives, and the Tennessee Historical Commission, 1979.

McCrady, James Waring. "Art and Music at the Mary Sharp College: I Sobriety." Collection of Mrs. T.C. Simmons, Winchester, TN. Nashville, TN: Tennessee State Library and Archives.

———. "The Mary Sharp Superlative, Winchester, Tennessee." Memphis, TN: Memphis State University Press, 1987, Nashville, TN: Tennessee State Library and Archives.

Merritt, Dixon, editor and senior contributor. *The History of Wilson County: Its Land and Its Life.* Nashville, TN: Benson Publishing Company, 1961.

Military Records, Civil War (1861–1865). "S. G. Shepard, Pension No. 14493." Nashville, TN: Tennessee State Library and Archives.

Moore, Capt. J. H., and Capt. F. S. Harris. "Heroism at the Battle of Gettysburg." *Confederate Veteran,* (Jan. 1901): 15–16.

"Mrs. S. G. Shepard Dies in Lebanon," *Nashville Banner*, June 22, 1915.

"Mrs. S. G. Shepard Passes Away," *Lebanon Democrat,* June 24, 1915.

National Archives of Federal Pension for Revolutionary War. "Samuel Shepherd [sic], S3894."

National Archives and Records Service, General Services Administration. *Compiled Records Showing Service of Military Units in Confederate Organizations, Tennessee, First through Seventh Infantry.* Washington, D.C.: The National Archives, 1971.

National Archives and Records Service, General Services Administration. *Index to Compiled Service Records of Confederate Soldiers Who Served in Organizations from the State of Tennessee.* Washington, D.C.: The National Archives, 1956.

National Park Service, Department of Interior, Washington, D.C.

"News from Across the River." Letters from Fannie John Shepard to her cousin Fannie Logan Graves, 1856, and a letter from Louisa V. Spickard to Fannie L. Graves, 1859. Contributed by Erick Montgomery to the Wilson County Archives.

Old Military and Civil Service Records, Washington D.C., National Archives of Military Service Records, Col. S. G. Shepard.

Partlow, Thomas E. *An Alphabetical List of Wilson County, Tennessee, Residents, 1820.* Lebanon, TN: Wilson County Archives, 1974.

————. *An Alphabetical List of Wilson County, Tennessee Residents, 1830,* Lebanon, TN: Wilson County Archives, 1974.

————, (compiled and edited). *Minutes, United Confederate Veterans Camp #941, Wilson County, Tennessee, 1897–1928.* Baltimore, MD: Gateway Press, Inc., 1975.

————. *Revolutionary War Soldiers in Wilson County.* Wilson County, TN.

————. *Two Dozen Families of Wilson County, Tennessee, 1976.*

————. *Wilson County, Tennessee, Miscellaneous Records 1800–1875.* Lebanon, TN: Wilson County Archives.

————. *Wilson County, Tennessee, Wills: Books 1–13, 1802–1850.* Lebanon, TN: Wilson County Archives.

Policy, J. B. "Simple Justice Asked." *Confederate Veteran,* Oct. 1895.

Reardon, Carol. *Pickett's Charge in History and Memory.* Chapel Hill and London: University of North Carolina Press, 1997.

Rutherford County Historical Society, Publication No. 11. Murfreesboro, TN, 1978.

Schlink, Ellen Taylor. *This Is the Place: A History of Lebanon, Tennessee, 1780–1972,* vol. II. Lebanon, TN: 1972.

Senior Class of 1886. *The Argo of Mary Sharp College.* Winchester, TN, 1886. Nashville, TN: Tennessee State Library and Archives.

COLONEL S. G. SHEPARD

"Spaniard" comment, *Confederate Veteran* (May 1895): 145

Shepard, Lt-Col. S. G. "Report 552: Report of Lieut. Col. S. G. Shepard, Seventh Tennessee Infantry, Of Operations of Archer's Brigade, June 3–August 1, 1863—The Gettysburg Campaign, 10 August 1865." *The War of the Rebellion: A Compilation of the Official Records of the Union and Confederate Armies,* ser. I, vol. XXVII, pt. II (1889). Washington, D.C.: Government Printing Office.

Sloan, Eugene H. "Soule College." Murfreesboro, TN: Rutherford County Archives, 1978.

Tennesseans in the Civil War: A Military History of Confederate and Union Units with Available Rosters of Personnel, pt. II. Nashville, TN: Civil War Centennial Commission, 1965.

White, Virgil D. *Genealogical Abstracts of Revolutionary War Pension Files,* vol. III, N–Z. Waynesboro, TN: The National Historical Publishing Company, 1992.

Wilson County, Tennessee, *Federal Census of 1880, Districts 21–25.* Lebanon, TN: Wilson County Archives.

Wilson County, Tennessee. *Census of 1900: Districts 11–25.* Lebanon, TN: Wilson County Archives.

Wilson County, Tennessee. *Census of 1910: Districts 1–10.* Lebanon, TN: Wilson County Archives.

Wilson County, Tennessee, Twenty-Third Civil District. *1870 Federal Census of the United States.* Lebanon, TN: Wilson County Archives.

Zepp, George. Boscobel College (Nashville, TN).